ART AND DESIGN

The Skin of the Film

The Skin of the Film

Intercultural Cinema, Embodiment,

and the Senses LAURA U. MARKS

DUKE UNIVERSITY PRESS   Durham and London   2000

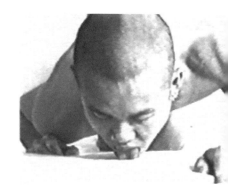

Contents

List of illustrations

Preface

Of the many cinematic images to which I return throughout this book, three are most insistent. One is the image of a woman filling a canteen with water, a memory-image that Rea Tajiri creates of her mother in the videotape *History and Memory: For Akiko and Takashige* (1991). Another is the movement of a camera caressing the surface of a still photograph of the artist dressed in her mother's sari, in Shauna Beharry's *Seeing Is Believing* (1991). Finally, there is the blurry, tactile image of the naked body of the artist's mother in Mona Hatoum's *Measures of Distance* (1988), as a voice-over speaks of her longing to press her faraway daughter close to her heart again. The similarity of these images struck me only long after I was convinced of the works' importance. In each of them the artist, a woman, attempts to recreate an image of her mother that has been erased or blocked through some movement of cultural dislocation. In each, she creates the new image from the memory of the sense of touch. These multisensory images stayed with me as I wrote *The Skin of the Film*, imparting an urgency to the hypothesis underlying this writing: that many new works in film and video call upon memories of the senses in order to represent the experiences of people living in diaspora.

The title of this book, *The Skin of the Film*, offers a metaphor to emphasize the way film signifies through its materiality, through a contact between perceiver and object represented. It also suggests the way vision itself can be tactile, as though one were touching a film with one's eyes: I term this *haptic visuality*. Finally, to think of film as a skin acknowledges the effect of a work's circulation among different audiences, all of which mark it with their presence. The title is meant to suggest polemically that film (and video) may be thought of as impressionable and conductive, like skin. I mean this both to apply to the material of film and videotape, as I argue in chapter 3, and also to the institution of cinema and cinema-going. I want to emphasize the tactile and contagious quality of cinema as something we viewers brush up against like another body. The words *contact, contingent,* and *contagion* all share the Latin root *contingere,* "to have contact with; pollute; befall." The contingent and contagious circumstances of intercultural cinema events effect a transformation in its audience. As hybrids, the works challenge the separateness of cultures and make visible the colonial and racist power relations that seek to maintain this separation. The works pollute viewers' ideas of cultural distinction, implicating each of us in them. In addition, as well as bearing meanings to the audience, these works receive impressions from the people who have seen them. Intercultural cinema builds up these impressions like a palimpsest and passes them on to other audiences. The very circulation of a film among different viewers is like a series of skin contacts that leave mutual traces.

The intercultural works to which this book is devoted share concerns with other recent movements in film and video, and thus many of the issues I discuss are relevant to other kinds of experimental work. For example, the limits of visuality are a question for many film- and videomakers. Embodiment and sense perception have become concerns for many artists, and also issues in the reception, theory, and criticism of film. Haptic visuality shows up in other cinematic genres, such as feminist film and video, experimental film and video that deals with perception, and experimental sexual representation, and indeed I would suggest that it is a growing trend among artists disaffected, for one reason or another, with optical visuality. Feminist work is closely concerned with the representation of the senses and embodiment; the key works I analyze are feminist as well as concerned with intercultural experience.

Commercial film and television share some interest in the sensuous qualities that experimental works evoke. However, given their constraints (to put it kindly), commercial media are less likely to dedicate themselves to such exploration. Experimental and independent works often develop strategies that later get taken up in, or stolen by, mainstream media. Thus the sensory exploration that is newly being taken up by experimental and noncommercial film and video is beginning to show up in mainstream and commercial media as well.

Despite these shared interests, my goal is not to develop a comprehensive theory of embodiment and sensory representation in cinema. These are areas of growing critical interest, to which this book is a contribution. All of us hold knowledge in our bodies and memory in our senses. Experimental and mainstream narrative cinema are increasingly interested in representing these kinds of knowledge and memory. But for most Western cinema, these sources are *supplements* to the many other representational resources it has at its disposal. By contrast, intercultural cinema needs to appeal to embodied knowledge and memory in the absence of other resources. Intercultural cinema has quite specific reasons for appealing to the knowledge of the senses, insofar as it aims to represent configurations of sense perception different from those of modern Euro-American societies, where optical visuality has been accorded a unique supremacy. A related difference between intercultural cinema and other kinds of experimental and mainstream cinema is that it stresses the *social* character of embodied experience: the body is a source not just of individual but of cultural memory. Consequently, my discussion of embodiment and sense perception is not wholly applicable to works in the individualistic tradition of avant-garde cinema. For the same reason, it cannot be imported wholesale to describe commercial cinema. I believe and hope that the theory of representation that emerges by the end of this book—auratic, embodied, and mimetic—will be appropriate to many kinds of cinema other than the intercultural works I describe here. It is, however, these works that have raised the stakes of such a theory of representation, and it is from them that it developed.

This book's interdisciplinary approach draws on sources within and outside film theory, including postcolonial theory, art history, anthropology, feminist theory, phenomenology, cultural geography, and cognitive science. My argument is especially informed by theories of embodied spectatorship, which have a lineage in phenomenology and feminist criticism. Anthropological research in the embodiment of culture, and the translation of cultural experience through travel, also supports my contentions. Within film theory, the work of Gilles Deleuze is an important unifying element

throughout the book, worth briefly discussing here. As cinema theorists such as Kobena Mercer (1988), Trinh T. Minh-ha (1989, 1991),
and Hamid Naficy (1993) have demonstrated, intercultural cinema
is fundamentally concerned with the production of new languages,
and the difficult task of defining intercultural cinema rests in its
emergent character. Deleuze and Guattari's contribution to theories
of "minor" literature, and Deleuze's expansion to cinema of his work
with Guattari, inform my discussion of this process of emergence in
chapter 2. As a new people comes into being, they argue, new cultural forms are produced. Deleuze's rigorous terminology allows me
to carefully examine how intercultural cinema experiments with the
representation of cultural history and memory. These works' inten-
tional obliqueness indicates their opposition to dominant, univocal
histories. I expand and critique Deleuze's theory of cinema to address specifically the postcolonial situation of intercultural cinema.

Deleuze's theory of cinema relies on the work of Henri Bergson,
and I return to Bergson in later chapters in order to begin to understand the role of the senses in cinematic representation and spectatorship. I will suggest that Deleuze's theory of time-image cinema
permits a discussion of the multisensory quality of cinema, given
its basis in Bergson's theory that memory is embodied in the senses.
This exploration branches from Bergson to phenomenology, and in
turn to neurophysiology, in order to explain how sense memory is
embodied. In addition, the theory of haptic visuality branches from
Deleuze and Guattari's distinction between the haptic and the optical, which they connect to "smooth space," or a space that enables
transformation, and "striated" or codified space. Perhaps my basic
debt to Deleuze, and to Guattari, is for their model of thinking as
an open system, always ready to make connections where they are
most productive, rather than most expected. My engagement with
the many films and videos, as well as the written works, that have
inspired me is an attempt to make such rhizomatic connections, to
let my words and my ideas be productively pulled off course.

Of course, what pulls this writing most forcefully is the films
and videos themselves. The works I examine in this book are themselves works of theory, many explicitly so. They are not waiting to
have theory "done to" them; they are not illustrations of theory but
theoretical essays in their own right. The works themselves have
developed a sophisticated argument for how cinema can represent

embodied experience, and why it should do so. Indeed one reason for writing a book about intercultural film and video is to catch up verbally with arguments that these works have developed in audio-visual (as well as verbal) form. As much as possible I engage with these films and videos as I engage with theoretical writings. I rely on them to draw out and critique the ideas with which I am working. Only rarely do I "critique" or even analyze them; instead I weave the works into my argument as much as possible on the same level as the written resources.

The reader will notice that many of the works I describe in this book are quite wordy, what with the use of voice-over, dialogue, and written text. This practice is partly drawn from the voice-over tradition in documentary, although the content of the voice-over tends to be quite poetic or speculative. It is partly a reflection of the general, often deconstructive emphasis on language in experimental films and videos of the period in question, the mid-1980s to the mid-1990s. In addition, many works of intercultural cinema rely on spoken words to present cultural countermemories, through oral histories, explanatory voice-overs, and dialogue. These works fall back on words to say what they cannot show. Words suture the work together in the absence of a stable, informative image or a linear storyline. Not only experimental works, but also dramatic narratives like Julie Dash's *Daughters of the Dust* (1992) often use dialogue pedagogically, to coax out the memories suggested in image and sound. Voices, not only informative witnessing or testimony, but also casual conversation, the texture of talk, and the simple presence of a clear or incoherent voice in counterpoint to the image, activate cultural memories. In some cases the words become more poetic, less an explanation of what cannot be imaged than an evocative layer of their own, as in works by Shani Mootoo, Roula Haj-Ismail, and Seoungho Cho. I find that many artists have been gradually shifting away from this emphasis on language, as they grow impatient with the word and begin to trust the sound and image to work on their own.

The Skin of the Film is devoted to sensory representation in intercultural cinema, but it does not undertake a detailed discussion of the role of sound, important though it is. I acknowledge that I am giving short shrift to the power of nonverbal sound to have meaning in ways that cannot be reduced to simple signification. Sound can be uncanny, moving the listener in ways that cannot be easily described or contained. Also, like the other senses, the use of hearing differs markedly from culture to culture. Characteristically, in Western societies and urban spaces, sound is primarily an information medium (Rodaway 1994, 113), and dialogue-centered narrative cinema reflects this use of sound. But sound can also be ambient and textural: as I suggest briefly in chapter 3, sound too can be haptic. Music, talk, ambient sound, and silence are important to many of these works and to the feeling of embodied experience they produce. Yet sound in intercultural cinema is such a large topic that I would not be able to discuss it effectively as a separate subject. It has been provocatively theorized by several writers (for example, Jafa 1992, Gabriel 1989, Masayesva 1995). Ultimately, the reason that I tend to exclude sound from this discussion is that I am most interested in meaning that lies outside the means of cinematic signification, namely, visual image and sound, altogether. I have chosen to focus on the intriguing question of how film and video represent the "unrepresentable" senses, such as touch, smell, and taste; and of course sound plays a large part in the answer. Sound does come into play insofar as it is experienced kinesthetically; for example, the booming in the chest caused by deep bass tones, or the complex effects of rhythm on the body. And ultimately the exile of the senses of hearing and vision in my analysis is only temporary, for I will return to argue that all the senses work together in the embodied experience of cinema.

Cinema is not fundamentally verbal and thus does not carry out lines of reasoning the way written theory does. Cinema exists on the threshold of language, and language must bring it across in order to have a conversation with it. As much as possible I attempt a kind of writing that stays close to its object rather than analyzing it from a distance, allowing the work in question to suggest the most appropriate response. This is especially the case with works such as I discuss, whose politics and poetics are inextricable, and which evoke a response that is simultaneously intellectual, emotional, and visceral. As these film- and videomakers are developing cinematic languages, so am I developing a critical and theoretical framework to meet their work: my language, like theirs, is necessarily exploratory and evocative.

In the case of emerging forms of expression such as those of intercultural cinema, it is important to be sensitive to the ways they

can convey meaning that do not find ready analysis in current film
theory. The films and videos I discuss in this book have taught me
how to understand them (or to recognize the limits of my understanding), how to be attentive to their subtleties, silences, and surprising visceral effects. Through engaging with these works, I have
found it necessary to understand how meaning occurs in the body,
and not only at the level of signs. The elements of an embodied response to cinema, the response in terms of touch, smell, rhythm,
and other bodily perceptions, have until recently been considered
"excessive" and not amenable to analysis.[1] I will argue that they can
indeed be analyzed—or, more properly, met halfway. Ultimately I
argue that our experience of cinema is mimetic, or an experience of
bodily similarity to the audiovisual images we take in. Cinema is not
merely a transmitter of signs; it bears witness to an object and trans-
fers the presence of that object to viewers. The mimetic relationship
between viewer and cinema easily describes the relationship between writing and cinema as well. Writing about these films and
videos requires imposing a form on them but also allowing them to
point beyond my words. I draw them into my arguments, but in the
end they slip beyond my use of them. They are critical works, but
the point of their criticism is to make room for something to emerge.

Acknowledgments

Over the course of the researching and writing of this book, I have been inspired, shocked, and blessed by the company of many artists, scholars, and friends. I am most grateful for the intellectual generosity of the people who have read portions of this manuscript and otherwise helped it along, including Shauna Beharry, Lisa Cartwright, Paolo Cherchi Usai, Robert Foster, Faye Ginsburg, Peter Harcourt, Dick Hebdige, Mike Hoolboom, Randi Klebanoff, Ming-Yuen S. Ma, Scott MacDonald, Charles O'Brien, Bethany Ogdon, Walid Ra'ad, Ian Rashid, David Rodowick, Jayce Salloum, Vivian Sobchack, Tran T. Kim-Trang, Diane Waldman, Janet Walker, Janet Wolff, and Patricia R. Zimmermann. I am also grateful to Ken Wissoker of Duke University Press and to Dana Polan and Catherine Russell, the readers whose thoughtful and incisive comments helped bring the manuscript through its gangly adolescence. My unbounded thanks go to Akira Mizuta Lippit, whose rigorous and creative intercessions sharpened the dull corners of the manuscript. Natalie Neill produced an exquisite index. For inspiration I credit the Robert Flaherty Seminar, where I first saw many of these works. Finally, my deepest thanks and love go to my parents, Anne Foerster, William B. Marks, and Jack Diamond, who have supported my efforts with unquestioning love and their own shining intellectual examples. I especially thank Anne Foerster for sharing her neuroscientific research with me.

I thank the Luce Foundation and American Council of Learned Scholars, the Mellon Foundation and Pew Charitable Trust, the Rush Rhees Foundation, and Carleton University for generous fellowships that allowed me to complete this work relatively quickly. Portions of this writing were also supported by the Lyn Blumenthal Fund for xx Independent Video, the Arts Council of Ontario, and the Banff Centre for the Arts.

Part of chapter 1 has been published in an earlier version as "A Deleuzian Politics of Hybrid Cinema," *Screen* 34:3 (Autumn 1994). Parts of chapter 2 have been published in earlier versions as "Transnational Objects: Commodities in Postcolonial Displacement," *Parachute* 81 (Spring 1996), and "Fetishes and Fossils," in *Feminism and Documentary,* ed. Diane Waldman and Janet Walker (Minneapolis: Minnesota University Press, 1999). Part of chapter 3 has been published in an earlier version as "Video Haptics and Erotics," *Screen* 39:3 (Autumn 1998).

Introduction

In this book I trace, with a great deal of optimism, an elusive and exciting body of work, which I call intercultural cinema. Most of this work comes from the new cultural formations of Western metropolitan centers, which in turn have resulted from global flows of immigration, exile, and diaspora. Most of the artists whose work is central to this movement are cultural minorities living in the West, often recent immigrants from Asia, the Caribbean, the Middle East, Latin America, and Africa, as well as First Nations makers. I focus on work produced in the United States, Canada, and to a lesser extent Great Britain, but this movement is an international phenomenon, produced wherever people of different cultural backgrounds live together in the power-inflected spaces of diaspora, (post- or neo-) colonialism, and cultural apartheid.

Intercultural cinema is characterized by experimental styles that attempt to represent the experience of living between two or more cultural regimes of knowledge, or living as a minority in the still majority white, Euro-American West. The violent disjunctions in space and time that characterize diasporan experience—the physical effects of exile, immigration, and displacement—also, I will argue, cause a disjunction in notions of truth. Intercultural films and videos offer a variety of ways of knowing and representing the world. To do this they must suspend the representational conventions that have held in narrative cinema for decades, especially the ideological presumption that cinema *can* represent reality (Mercer 1994b, Deleuze 1986). Formal experimentation is thus not incidental but integral to these works. Intercultural cinema draws from many cultural traditions, many ways of representing memory and experience, and synthesizes them with contemporary Western cinematic practices. I will argue that many of these works evoke memories both individual and cultural, through an appeal to nonvisual knowledge, embodied knowledge, and experiences of the senses, such as touch, smell, and taste. In particular, I explore in the third chapter how certain images appeal to a haptic, or tactile, visuality. Haptic images, I suggest, invite the viewer to respond to the image in an intimate, embodied way, and thus facilitate the experience of other sensory impressions as well. These sense experiences are not separate, of course. They combine to form culturally defined "sensuous geographies" (Rodaway 1994), or our sensory experiences of place. More fundamentally, they inform each person's sensorium, the bodily organization of sense experience. My challenge is to suggest how film and video, which are audiovisual media, can represent nonaudiovisual sense experiences.

Intercultural cinema is a movement insofar as it is the emerging expression of a group of people who share the political issues of displacement and hybridity, though their individual circumstances vary widely. On the one hand I see this movement eventually leading to significant changes in the politics and poetics of representation at a broad cultural level. On the other, I recognize that many of these works are quite ephemeral, and I wish to celebrate them at the moment of their brief flowering.

Though in some ways intercultural cinema is as old as the movies themselves, the movement in its new and most powerful incarnation emerged roughly between the years 1985 and 1995. This emergence reflects the conjunction of several factors: the rise of multiculturalism as an intellectual and policy issue; major changes in the availability of funding for noncommercial cinema in the United States, Canada, and the United Kingdom; and an intellectual climate characterized by the disintegration of master narratives and a growing conceptualization of knowledge as partial and contested.

The periodization that I propose is also in part determined by the fact that intercultural cinema is ceasing to be a movement and becoming a genre, that is, a body of works with shared concerns about style and content. Some commercial feature films have also been produced during this period that deal in sophisticated ways with intercultural representation; in addition, some of the makers whose work I explore here have "graduated" to quasi-commercial feature film production. Many of the characteristics of intercultural cinema that I describe in the following chapters have become more mainstream, in theatrically released films that deal explicitly with the contemporary mixing of cultures in metropolitan centers, sometimes in formally experimental ways. These include, for example, Stephen Frears/Hanif Kureishi's *My Beautiful Laundrette* (1985) and *Sammy and Rosie Get Laid* (1986), Mira Nair's *Mississippi Masala* (1992), Srinivas Krishna's *Masala* (1991) and *Lulu* (1995), Julie Dash's *Daughters of the Dust* (1992), Haile Gerima's *Sankofa* (1993), Trinh T. Minh-ha's *A Tale of Love* (1995), and some other films that fall into the gray area between noncommercial and commercial production. I hope that this genre will become more common, fed by the experiments in intercultural cinema of the 1980s and early 1990s. Indeed, I would hope that the category of intercultural cinema will cease to be conceptually useful, as the intercultural and transnational status of all cinema becomes harder to ignore.

However, this periodization also has to do with the dwindling opportunities for people to make this work. Institutionalized racism prevents many artists from ever gaining the recognition and funding to continue to produce their short films and videos, let alone feature-length work. Multicultural public funding policies, for all their many problems, have meant that artists of color had some access to financial support, but as public funding vanishes it is exceptionally difficult for them to gain support from private or commercial sources, harder than it is for a white independent or experimental filmmaker (see, for example, Givanni 1995). Also, most of the works that inform my argument are short (under one hour) and in some way formally experimental, qualities that are easiest to accommodate in noncommercial contexts. I worry that the proliferation of such work over the last ten years or so will diminish to a trickle, given the demise of public funding. This would mean that there will be less opportunity for the sort of formal experimentation and work on the politics of representation that have been crucial to the development of intercultural cinema. Even more important, and integral to the "formal" characteristics of this work, are the alternative production, distribution, and exhibition structures that support it: these too are threatened by the combination of mainstreaming and defunding of intercultural cinema. Both political and experimental cinema movements have always been suspicious of mass circulation, and making commercial cinema still involves significant compromises. The rise of director Mira Nair to panderer of cultural exoticism for white audiences, in her recent films *The Perez Family* (1995) and *Kama Sutra* (1996), is but one example of how the commercialization of multiculturalism tends to evacuate its critical effects. And so I fear that the period I describe may conclude in *both* the popularization of intercultural cinema and the crippling of its most critical potentials. I will be delighted if events in the coming years prove this fear to be unfounded.

The history of intercultural cinema parallels, and in some cases prefigures, a broader history of Western intellectual interests of the past fifteen or so years. Many individual works of intercultural cinema reflect all this history in themselves, intellectual ontogeny recapitulating phylogeny, as it were. Many of these artists (those who were making work fifteen years ago) were making explorations of language and representation at a time when academia was seized by semiotic theory; many have done work of a psychoanalytic bent; many have made primarily feminist films and tapes; many began making primarily queer work. Such young veterans include Mona Hatoum, Jayce Salloum, Rea Tajiri, Janice Tanaka, and Paul Wong. When broader cultural interest (or, narrower academic interest) turned to questions of racial and ethnic identity, many artists shifted their work to address these concerns. Indeed, some have argued that the intellectual fashion for multiculturalism has forced them in the direction of "representing the race" because that is where funding has been available (Fusco 1988b; Bray 1996). Yet identity politics have been productive for many artists, who often conclude that identity must be viewed as a process rather than a position. This process is a painful one, leading to a feeling of cultural homelessness that is the subject of many films and tapes. At the same time, the frustrated search for identity has compelled a turn to history, in order to produce and record individual and communal histories. At this point much of the work is clearly activist, tracing the effects of racist, colonial, and imperial mis- (or non-)representation on the lives of now-diasporic peoples. Yet often the work of historical excavation is done in the full knowledge that these stories are willful constructions of irretrievable histories, based on collective fantasies and dreams (Hall 1988a).

It is at this point that my work in *The Skin of the Film* begins. Many works continue to be produced that reflect the agendas described above. It is more recent that intercultural artists are in a position to interrogate the historical archive, both Western and traditional, in order to read their own histories in its gaps, or to force a gap in the archive so that they have a space in which to speak. Yet to undertake all this work, which requires the sometimes traumatic interrogation of personal and family memories, only to create an empty space where no history is certain, can be a psychically draining experience. The story suspends in order to contemplate this emptiness, which is narratively thin but emotionally full: it is the product of a process of mourning, a search for loved ones who have vanished and cannot be recalled with any of the means at the artist's disposal. These lost loved ones may be people, places, or even ways of inhabiting the world. The grief may be individual or widely shared, but in these films and tapes it becomes a collective experience.

What I wish to examine in this book is the tentative process of creation that begins at the time of grieving: in effect, the scent that rises from the funeral garlands. This process describes the movement from excavation to fabulation, or from deconstructing dominant histories to creating new conditions for new stories. It is the holding on to artifacts of culture, including photographic and filmic images, in order to coax the memories from them. It is the attempt to translate to an audiovisual medium the knowledges of the body, including the unrecordable memories of the senses. When verbal and visual representation is saturated, meanings seep into bodily and other dense, seemingly silent registers. The films I explore here coax these silent registers, not to make signs (which is the work of semiosis), not to tell stories (the work of narrative), at least not initially, but to have meaning by virtue of their very implacable difference from the visual and the audible. From the traumatic dislocations of culture and efforts at remembering, "newness enters the world" (to borrow Bhabha's phrase, 1994a).

Why "Intercultural Cinema"?

Before examining the term "intercultural" and its alternatives, let me here note why I refer to this body of work as "cinema." Many of the works I examine are videotapes, which are often excluded from the category of motion pictures. While for many of these artists, working in video is an aesthetic choice, it is clearly also an economic one.

Many artists refer to themselves as filmmakers despite the fact that they work in video; many begin in video and move to 35mm film production, often bypassing 16mm as they venture into the feature film market: for example, Shu Lea Cheang and Elia Suleiman each moved from experimental video to 35mm film. Thus it is important to establish a continuity between the media even while noting their formal, institutional, and perhaps ontological differences. Whether they are short experimental works or feature-length narratives, I choose to refer to all these works as cinema, because not only are they all time-based, audiovisual media, but also the word refers to the experience of an audience gathered in a theater. That these theaters are often drafty screening rooms in nonprofit galleries, and not the well-upholstered halls the term usually connotes, makes it a perverse pleasure to include these marginal viewing situations squarely inside the institution of cinema.

It is with some hesitation that I have chosen the rather mild term "intercultural" to describe these works. I do not intend this term to bear a great deal of conceptual weight: we have plenty of words that do that, which I will continue to use. Many terms have been proposed and later rejected to describe this kind of cultural production and its sociopolitical context: these include "Third World," "minority," "marginal," "antiracist," "multicultural," "hybrid," "mestizo," "postcolonial," "transnational," "Third Cinema," "imperfect cinema," "hybrid cinema," "interstitial cinema," and so on.[1] In some cases it is more useful to return to a term we are supposed to have "got over," as Stam and Shohat (1995) do when they reassert the usefulness of thinking in terms of "multiculturalism," as well as of other unfashionable terms such as "Third World" and "Fourth World," in order to indicate the continuing urgency of issues that the coining of a new term seems to resolve.[2] By surveying some of these terms, I would like to begin to suggest the issues at stake in intercultural cinema. At the same time I would caution that, while many terms are strategically useful, none should be able to contain this work and thus to dictate what it ought to be.

"Intercultural" indicates a context that cannot be confined to a single culture. It also suggests movement between one culture and another, thus implying diachrony and the possibility of transformation. "Intercultural" means that a work is not the property of any single culture, but mediates in at least two directions. It accounts

for the encounter between different cultural organizations of knowledge, which is one of the sources of intercultural cinema's synthesis
of new forms of expression and new kinds of knowledge. A problem
with this term is that it could suggest a politically neutral exchange
between cultures, and this is never the case in any of the works I discuss. However, the term avoids the problem of positing dominant
culture as the invisible ground against which cultural minorities appear in relief. Instead it implies a dynamic relationship between a
dominant "host" culture and a minority culture. Certainly the dominant in the cases I discuss is almost always the hegemonic, white,
Euro-American culture. But the site of power is always sliding and
its agents regrouping, and to discuss cinema as a relation between
cultures makes room for a variety of "hosts," destinations, and sites
of power. Also, the term "intercultural" can describe exchanges between nondominant cultures.

Hamid Naficy's "independent transnational genre" reclaims filmmakers like Michel Khleifi and Trinh T. Minh-ha from the marginal
genres of "ethnic" and "avant-garde" respectively (1996, 120). By acknowledging the transnational position of exile, émigré, and refu-
gee filmmakers, the genre allows films to be read both as authorial
texts and "as sites for intertextual, cross-cultural, and translational
struggles over meanings and identities" (121), which are also concerns of the works I discuss here. The difference is that many intercultural filmmakers, though they identify with more than one cultural background, live in the country in which they were born.

"Multiculturalism" has been and sometimes still is a useful term
to remind us that we live in a society composed of many groups—
but it implies the perspective of white or other dominant people who
have been able to assume that their society continues to constitute
the overarching culture. Because of its use in official policy, such as
arts funding quotas, the term "multiculturalism" has come to mean
the naming and slotting of difference (Bailey 1991) and often ends
up homogenizing the struggles of the diverse groups it intended to
empower (Marchessault 1995b). A later term to arrive into general
use, "hybridity," provides a provocative contrast with the notion of
multiculturalism. Cultural hybridity, like the metaphor of genetic
mutation from which it draws, is necessarily unpredictable and un-
categorizable. The hybrid reveals the process of exclusion by which
nations and fixed cultural identities are formed, forcing the domi-

nant culture to explain itself (Bhabha 1994b). Hybridity does not simply turn the tables on the colonizing culture: it also puts into question the norms and knowledges of any culture presented as discrete, whole, and separate.

The term "hybrid cinema" also implies a hybrid form, mixing documentary, fiction, personal, and experimental genres, as well as different media. By pushing the limits of any genre, hybrid cinema forces each genre to explain itself, to forgo any transparent relationship to the reality it represents, and to make evident the knowledge claims on which it is based. Hybrid cinema is in a position to do archaeology, to dig up the traces that the dominant culture, and for that matter any fixed cultural identity, would just as soon forget. One cannot simply contemplate a hybrid (or a work of hybrid cinema): one cannot help but be implicated in the power relations upon which it reflects. This power of contamination and implication is something I will return to in the discussion of fetishes and fossils in chapter 2.

"Postcolonial" and other terms that describe relationships among nations are only somewhat useful to describe the movement of cinema I discuss here. Despite its theorists' intentions, "postcolonialism" has become a conceptually omnivorous term that swallows distinctions of nation, location, period, and agency. Aijaz Ahmad (1995) points out that "postcolonial" ignores political relationships other than, and sometimes predating, colonial ones and maintains the binary relation between former colonizer and colonized. An advantage of the term "postcolonial" is that it emphasizes the history of power relations between the entities it designates, even if the identity of these entities is uncertain and the "postness" of those power relations a matter of debate. In this it has an advantage over a term like "multicultural," or, for that matter, "intercultural." Yet the relations between cultures that animate the film and video works I describe here can only be termed colonial, or postcolonial, or neocolonial in the broadest sense. Certainly the long-term effects of European colonization in Africa, the Middle East, Asia, and Latin America, and the colonization of Mexico, Puerto Rico, and the Pacific Islands by the United States, prompted a great deal of the international flow of immigration that brought people from these nations to Western metropolitan centers. Slavery is a particularly violent instance of colonization, so violent that the experience of African Americans and Canadians and British Blacks[3] from the Caribbean is better described as exile or diaspora. And the case of aboriginal or First Nations people[4] cannot be subsumed under the term "colonization": "apartheid" is more appropriate to describe the appropriation of land, confinement to reservations, and forced education.

Ideologies of cultural nationalism conflate the dominant, usually white culture with a national culture, both of which intercultural cinema works to denaturalize. Yet intercultural cinema tends neither to seek inclusion for another cultural group in the national mosaic (multiculturalism) nor to posit an alternative nationalism (separatism). Hence part of the slipperiness of the term "intercultural": often the relationship is not between two cultures but between a racial minority group (Black, Asian, Latino, First Nations, and so on) and a Eurocentric nationalist discourse. Issues of nation, nationalism, and national borders will recur throughout these chapters. However, "culture" is something that travelers bring with them more consistently than "nation"; it is the stuff that passes through national borders and transforms nations from within.

Nationalist discourse prevents the understanding of diasporan experience in quite practical ways as well. Works by minorities who continue to claim a nonassimilated cultural heritage are often rejected as "not really" American, Canadian, British. Many of these works are produced in more than one nation: Lebanon-Canada, Jamaica-England, Hong Kong-United States. Films and videos about issues that cross national borders often cannot secure funding from national sources alone, and often must combine international funding sources. National funding policies that give priority to exclusively national artists constrain production, distribution, exhibition, and criticism of intercultural cinema, realigning this work with the very nationalist discourses that it critiques.

Finally, the powers at work in global movements of people are increasingly less those of nations than of corporations, whose transnational power has begun to exceed that of governments. Intercultural cinema takes part in a global current that flows against the wave of economic neocolonialism, by making explicit the cultural and economic links between peoples that capital erases (see Zimmermann and Hess 1997). In chapter 2 I examine how intercultural films retrace the paths of global capital, as well as more idiosyncratic flows of people and things, rematerializing and re-embodying the global movements that transnational capital seeks to render virtual.

Formal and Political Precedents

The formal experimentation of most intercultural cinema has an aesthetic and political legacy that is worth briefly exploring. Questions of form cannot be separated from the political conditions in which these works were produced. Cultural diaspora is a productive as well as a destructive movement. When experience takes place in the conjunction of two or more cultural regimes of knowledge, filmmakers must find ways to express this experience that cannot be in terms of either: experimental form helps to express the emergent knowledge conditions of intercultural experience. The synthetic qualities of intercultural cinema draw on histories of formal cinematic experimentation. Thus its genealogy includes Euro-American experimental cinema, especially its uneasy but productive intersection with political work. Experimental documentary, or what Nichols (1991) calls "reflexive documentary," such as the work of Chris Marker, Jean Rouch, and Trinh T. Minh-ha, provides a generous legacy to intercultural cinema.

Certainly, much of intercultural cinema qualifies as what Julio García Espinosa (1970) calls "imperfect cinema" because the makers' resources are limited. More importantly, these works share García Espinosa's ideal that the films of an emerging political movement are necessarily partial and incomplete. They manifest "imperfection" in quite different ways, however. Much of the intercultural work descended from the activist Third World Newsreel tradition values a by-any-means-necessary look: different film stocks mixed with video, hand-held camera, in-camera editing, and so forth. British film/videomakers, in contrast, have developed a convention of elegant, polished-looking images made economically by filming in the studio. The stylized tableaus in works by John Akomfrah, Pratibha Parmar, Isaac Julien, Ngozi Onwurah, and other British artists, which derive in part from their resources in television, have influenced the style of a number of Canadian and U.S. artists, particularly, it seems, those whose work has been produced in the well-equipped studios of the Banff Centre for the Arts.

Intercultural cinema has been implicitly and explicitly theorized by a number of writers and artists, including Black Audio Film Collective, Julio García Espinosa, Coco Fusco, Fernando Solanas and Octavio Getino, Teshome Gabriel, Kobena Mercer, Hamid Naficy, and Trinh T. Minh-ha, who describe the ways that cinematic form cultivates a politics and poetics by which to represent the experience of racial minorities and diasporic peoples. Their writings often emphasize this work's double movement of tearing away old, oppressive representations and making room for new ones to emerge.

From its earliest formulations, intercultural cinema obviates the distinction between "Western" and "non-Western" practices. Many of the Latin American makers and theorists of the Third Cinema movement took up critical and activist traditions of European and North American cinema. Similarly, Teshome Gabriel's (1988) theory of nomad aesthetics is Afrocentric but intercultural in its synthesis of European, African, Latin American, and Asian sources. In short, the works of intercultural cinema cannot be attributed a single cultural origin; they are wholly products of cultural synthesis.

The relationship between politics and form is most clearly articulated, thus worth a closer look, in the development of one of the most important sites of intercultural cinema production. The new Black British cinema emerged in the context of a new class of Black intellectuals in Britain. In British polytechnics, or public universities, numerous Black artists and scholars took up the dialogue between theory and activism that had come to define British cultural studies (see Hall 1986). This intellectual context is inextricable from the context of the Black uprisings in the borough of Lambeth in early 1981 (the "Brixton riots") and in Handsworth and Tottenham in 1985, in response to police brutalization and murder of Black people. The racist national response to these uprisings and the lack of media representation of Black stories precipitated organized responses by British Blacks, including the urgent demand for self-representation.[5] The body of work produced by Black Audio between 1986 and 1993 was concerned with the historical archive—what gets included in it, and who has access to it—in terms from the rigorously theoretical to the literal. The structural, as well as visible, racism of the mainstream documentary media of film, television, and the print press is a subject that recurs throughout Black Audio's works. Their first, controversial feature, *Handsworth Songs* (1986), responded to the racist media coverage of the "riots" in Handsworth following the death of Mrs. Cynthia Jarrett after a bungled police raid. Attempting to trace the story from within the Black neighborhoods, the film found only, in an often-quoted line, "ghosts of stories." This film, and Sankofa's *Passion of Remembrance* (1986), can be seen as precedents for much of intercultural cinema's interest in questioning the political and cultural limits of what can be represented (see Fusco 1988a).

The energetic debate over the political and aesthetic concerns of the new Black British cinema culminated in several events and documents in 1988, including *Screen* 29:4, "The Last 'Special Issue' on Race?" edited by Isaac Julien and Kobena Mercer, and *ICA Documents 7: Black Film, British Cinema* (1988), the expanded document of a conference held at London's Institute of Contemporary Art. These essays and interviews by filmmakers and scholars return repeatedly to the "new language" these works were creating and the enthusiastic, puzzled, and hostile responses they engendered among critics and audiences.[6] Noting the varied reactions to *Handsworth Songs* and *The Passion of Remembrance*, Kobena Mercer undertook to describe the "difficult," self-reflexive aesthetics of this work. Mercer's essay "Diaspora Culture and the Dialogic Imagination" (1994), first published in "The Last 'Special Issue,'" amounts to a manifesto of intercultural cinema. Black British filmmaking of the 1960s enjoyed a brief creative period (Pines 1988, 29–30), but these films relied upon the "reality effect" of dominant cinema in order to communicate clear statements of protest and political mobilization (Mercer 1988a, 57). By contrast, Mercer argues, the new modes of Black film discourse critique naturalistic representation and liberate the filmic signifier "as a material reality in its own right." This strategy describes other modernist cinematic practices as well, but what distinguishes the new Black British cinema is that the signifiers are "liberated" in order to represent collective memory. The goal is, in Mercer's words, to "reclaim and excavate a creole countermemory of black struggle in Britain, itself always repressed, erased and made invisible in the 'popular memory' of dominant film and media discourse" (58). In other words, there is an alternative archive of Black knowledge that resides in some different order from the framing discourses. Paul Gilroy (1988) similarly argues that the emerging cinematic language will be a redemptive modernism specifically in-

formed by African diaspora aesthetic and philosophical traditions.
Black cultural politics, he writes, is "not about the waning of affect
but about its preservation and reproduction" (46). Like the creole
countermemory Mercer describes, the affective memory Gilroy recognizes at the foundation of African diasporic narratives is a memory that cannot be expressed in Eurocentric terms: a memory stored
in safekeeping until a means of translation can be found. This search
for the means to represent memory, clearly visible in the intellectual
and political history of Black British cinema, is paralleled in more
diffuse ways in other nodes of intercultural cinema production.

Infrastructure

The infrastructure of intercultural cinema is a delicate but nevertheless material web connecting artists, sources of funding, production
sites, and venues for distribution and exhibition.

Many intercultural artists are young, "emerging" (an optimistic
term which assumes that resources will continue to be available to
them), or even first-time makers. Some have master's degrees in art
or film production, while others are self-taught or picked up their
skills in workshops and apprenticeships. Most of these film- and
videomakers are familiar with contemporary critical theory, indeed
steeped in it. Many of them are poor, given the typical downward
mobility of artists in the Western countries in question. Understandably, many communities of recent immigrants ascribe a stigma to the
choice to work in the arts instead of some useful, income-generating
profession, and this underscores the feeling among intercultural
film/videomakers of existing between two (or more) worlds. They
earn their living like other independent artists: they work for commercial film and television production, they teach, they occasionally have grants that cover subsistence, and they cobble together
part-time jobs.

Much of this work relies on outside funding. The ludicrously tiny
and yet still embattled amounts of state funding for independent
media can be seen in proper perspective when Fernando Solanas
and Octavio Getino advocate "producing and distributing guerrilla
films with funds obtained from expropriations of the bourgeoisie—
that is, *the bourgeoisie would be financing guerrilla cinema with a
bit of the surplus value that it gets from the people*" ([1969] 1983,

60; italics in original). Arts funders could do worse than to take this as their mandate. In the three countries under consideration, alternative filmmakers and artists of color rely on government funding. In Canada, the Canada Council, the National Film Board of Canada, Telefilm Canada, the provincial arts councils, the Ontario Film Development Corporation, and other state-run agencies are encouraged (though not mandated) to support a high percentage of work by so-called visible minorities. This climate of support is partly a result of quasi-protectionist Canadian cultural policies in response to the barrage of U.S. popular and "high" culture. These resources began to crumble in recent years as a result of the Canadian recession and new funding policies that replicate the slashing of public funding in the United States. In 1997 Parliament legislated a $25 million *increase* in the budget of the Canada Council for the following five years, but this still does not return funding to previous levels. Private foundations are virtually nonexistent in Canada, which means that most not-for-profit cultural production is subject to government guidelines; hence, perhaps, the atmosphere of cultural responsibility that some Canadian artists find slightly suffocating. Nevertheless, the relatively high rate of funding has meant that in Canada, as in Britain, more artists have been able to produce outside academic settings than is the case in the United States.

Nothing like the high levels of Canadian public funding for artists of color exists in the United States. However, beginning in the mid-1980s, public funding initiatives by the National Endowment for the Arts (such as its Expansion Arts category), the state arts councils, the Independent Television Service (a subsidiary of the Corporation for Public Broadcasting founded in 1988, in response to pressure from independent makers for more representation on PBS), and others were launched to allocate funds to cultural minorities. Yet the rise of public funds targeted to minority artists in the 1980s has been more than offset by overall cuts in state arts funding. Part of these cuts have taken the form of regional redistribution, at the levels of grants both to organizations and to individual artists. While the purpose of this funding shift was ostensibly to limit bureaucracy at the federal level, it reflects the general "new federalist" shift of responsibilities to state and nongovernmental sources, relieving the federal government of its mandate to set policy for the allocation of money for the arts. Private foundations have taken up multicultural policies as well, especially in the United States. State policymakers there expected private foundations to rush into the breach of government funding cuts to the arts. Foundations can afford to be more daring than government agencies in their funding policies, one of the most progressive being the Rockefeller Foundation's Intercultural Film/Video Fellowships. But these foundations' resources, as well as being finite, are also capriciously and interestedly disbursed; the Ford Foundation, Philip Morris, and other foundations understandably invest in projects that will reflect well upon their sponsors. Notwithstanding all our criticisms of multiculturalist slotting, the loss of a government mandate to fund innovative art and art by people of color increases the likelihood that what does get funded will be politically and aesthetically conservative, and dominated by white makers.

Independent feature funding is a somewhat different issue, since most feature-length works need seed money from distribution or broadcast sources while the work is still in its early stages. Again, while in Britain and Canada there has been a greater degree of support specifically for makers of color, in both these countries and in the United States it is extremely difficult for independent features by people of color to get off the ground. Despite demographic evidence to the contrary (such as the 25 percent of U.S. cinema ticket sales to African Americans), commercial distributors and broadcasters tend to doubt the profit-making potential of these projects. Long traditions of independent feature filmmaking by people of color exist in all three countries, but in general the ability to experiment with the means of representation has been seen as a "luxury" that makers could not afford. Films and videos that experiment with the means of representation are thus doubly difficult to fund (Davis 1995, 452). Years of devotion are required for makers of color (and, to a smaller degree, all independent producers) who work in experimental styles to produce feature films. Those who have done so include Julie Dash (*Daughters of the Dust*, 1992), Haile Gerima (*Sankofa*, 1993), Shu Lea Cheang (*Fresh Kill*, 1994), Srinivas Krishna (*Lulu*, 1995), Dee Dee Halleck (*The Gringo in Mañanaland*, 1994), Lourdes Portillo (*El Diablo Nunca Duerme* [The Devil Never Sleeps], 1994), Thomas Allan Harris (*Vintage: Families of Value*, 1995), Midi Onodera (*Skin Deep*, 1995), Elia Suleiman (*Chronicle of a Disappearance*, 1996), and Rea Tajiri (*Strawberry Fields*, 1997). The title of Chris Eyre's "calling card" short for *Smoke Signals* (1998), *He Who Crawls Silently Through the Grass with a Small Bow and One Bad Arrow Hunting for Enough Deer to Feed the Whole Tribe,* illustrates the headstrong resourcefulness of the intercultural feature filmmaker.

The films and videos I discuss in this book were produced within a large network of sites, including media access centers, colleges and universities, public television stations, cable access programs, and of course garage and bedroom studios. Some were produced as student works. Individual makers often shepherd their work through every tortuous stage of production, from applying for production grants to submitting the finished work to festivals. But a number of these works benefit from umbrella organizations that integrate the fundraising, production, and exhibition processes. These organizations have the resources to support intercultural production over a long term, rather than the debilitating step-by-step process undergone by film/videomakers working alone. For example, Third World Newsreel trains and supports productions by young makers of color, often distributing their final products. The now disbanded British workshops, including Black Audio Film Collective and Sankofa, and television production companies such as Igloolik Isuma Productions, have been able to follow multiple projects through the development, production, and broadcast stages. The Inuit Broadcasting Corporation supports all stages of the production process, allowing some individuals to train up from novices to professional producers (see Roth and Valaskakis 1989; Brisebois 1991; Valaskakis 1992; Marks 1994a). Examples of IBC programming include *Igliniit* (1989–91), a live hunting show produced by Philip Joamie; *Super Shamou* (1990–94), a children's show by Barney Pattunguyak, featuring the hybrid superhero of the title; *Kippinguijautiit* (1986–) a magazine-style teen program produced by Mosesie Kipanik; and *Takuginai* (1987–) a children's show featuring Muppet-like puppets, produced initially by Blandina Makkik and later by Leetia Ineak. Some of these producers have left IBC, including Pattunguyak, Makkik, and producer Paul Apak; the latter now works with the independent Igloolik Isuma Productions. The corporation has been bitterly criticized by members of Igloolik Isuma Productions for constraining and exploiting its Inuit staff producers (see Bourgeois 1997, Cohn 1999). Nevertheless, such production centers are remarkable for their ability to support ongoing production and, in the case of IBC and the British workshops, to have direct access to broadcast. They mark exceptions to the general pattern of individual production for intercultural film and video.

Once the work is made, intercultural film/videomakers have a great challenge to distribute and exhibit it. Since many of these works are short, they struggle in a market oriented toward features or, at the shortest, half-hour television programs. Many short independent films are produced as "calling cards" to entice industry to invest in the filmmaker's feature script, but this is rarely the case in intercultural cinema, for several reasons. Some of these films and videos are ephemeral, one-time works by artists who, like Mona Hatoum and Shauna Beharry, usually work in other media. Many of these short, experimental works are self-sufficient, making a point perfectly in 11 or 27 minutes that would be lost in a feature-length production. Since so many of these works are not considered commercially viable because of their subject matter and style, their makers are, ironically, freed from the pressures to court commercial production sites. The pressure to produce a feature, regardless of whether it is appropriate at this stage in an artist's development, has created costly and time-consuming disasters. Nevertheless, some of the artists whose work I discuss in this book, including Shu Lea Cheang, Cheryl Dunyé, Helen Lee, Alanis Obomsawin, Elia Suleiman, and Rea Tajiri, "graduated" more or less successfully to feature film production. Screening slots on Channel Four in England, PBS in the United States, the CBC in Canada, a tentatively increasing number of cable channels such as the Independent Film Channel, BET (Black Independent Television), and the Sundance Channel, satellite ventures such as Deep Dish TV, and local public television stations, have made it viable for some of these makers to produce for or market to television. However, much of this work cannot be screened on television, given that medium's requirements of high production values and minimally unconventional form. Some videomakers have shifted to video installation, which has a higher profile in the gallery scene than single-channel video does; others have moved from video to interactive media.

For these short films and videos and short-run theatrical features, independent distributors, such as those listed in this book's film/videography, are crucial. These distributors deal with festivals, galleries and museums, and academic bookers, with management styles ranging from actively marketing film/video packages to complete laissez-faire. Often subsidized by government grants—and dependent on rentals and sales to museums, universities, and other institutions that are themselves lately in crisis—even the longest established distributors have a precarious existence. The choice of distributor is an important decision for artists, who may feel a political alliance with one distributor and an aesthetic affinity to the work of another; many ultimately choose distributors who have the most efficient bureaucracies and guarantee the makers their percentage of rentals and sales, even if this means some sacrifice of political or aesthetic integrity. Some film/videomakers choose to distribute their work themselves.

Like other experimental cinema, intercultural cinema rarely makes it into commercial theaters. Instead it circulates to nonprofit and artist-run centers, galleries, museums, festivals, colleges and universities, public and satellite television, community centers, and activist organizations. Feature films do receive runs at art-house theaters. For short works, thematic programming is crucial. It is at the level of programming that the decision whether to organize around identity politics or around more intercultural themes often rests. For example, programs at LA Freewaves and Toronto's Images festival tend to organize works from very racially diverse video artists, teenaged makers, and activist groups around idiosyncratic themes. This allows the festivals to showcase the complexity of each work and the unexpected connections among them. Similarly, in 1991 and 1993 Third World Newsreel's Lorna Johnson organized two packages, "D'Ghetto Eyes" and "D'Ghetto Eyes II," featuring films and videos made through Newsreel's production workshop. Director Ada Gay Griffin describes the movement from production to exhibition as

an organic process. We're interested in young artists at the early stage of their careers, and in building audiences for people who have difficulty trying to find audiences. Participants in our workshops have been getting more and more sophisticated and clear about how they wanted to use the media, new artists like Michael Cho or Thomas Harris that could be marginalized [in other contexts]. Short works alone are interesting, but how do you get African Americans to see Asian American works that they might like? We deal with a number of audiences that have issues in common—issues of

humor, of style, of hybridity, especially in an urban setting. Younger audiences get into it. (Griffin 1993)

The discourse around intercultural cinema that these events support is, of course, extended into print, but considerably less often
than that for more established bodies of work. Often festival and distribution catalogues and slim screening brochures contain the only
written information about these works (for example, Fusco and Colo
1991, Rashid 1993, and Salloum 1996); others leave no traces at all in
writing, only in the word of mouth of people who have seen them.

Audiences: The Skin of the Film

Intercultural cinema assumes the interestedness, engagement, and
intelligence of its audience. As Toni Cade Bambara remarks, the re-
ward of a demanding film such as *Daughters of the Dust* is participatory spectatorship and an "empowered eye" (1993, 133). Similarly,
Victor Masayesva Jr. (1995) argues that Native audiences are impatient for works that will push the expressive boundaries of film and
video in order to tell their stories.

Is there an intercultural audience? In the preceding pages I have
paid more attention to the "live" audiences at festivals and the like
than the presumably larger, but diffuse and perhaps disinterested,
television audiences. It is at the live events that one can see the
audience that has been constituted around this work, and this is
a thrilling event that the circumstances of virtual audiences just
don't permit. Screenings of intercultural cinema witness the building of an audience, often from surprisingly disparate individuals. As
Douglas Crimp points out, coalitions based on shared identity are
"productive of collective political struggle, but only if they result
in a broadening of alliances rather than an exacerbation of antago-
nisms" (1993, 12). Such cross-identification means that identities are
never static but always relational, capable of creating links among
different groups that transform those groups. Coalitions must result in mutual transformation if groups are not to simply come together around a joint purpose and then go their separate ways when
their goal is accomplished. Intercultural cinema itself, as one of the
visible traces of cosmopolitanism, carries out the process of transforming a coalition into a new cultural formation.

In a more subtle but no less important process, transformative coalitions are also built over time as well as in shared space. When a small, independent film or tape circulates among different audiences, each context adds to the meaning of the work. Most of these works are rare and hard to get hold of. Few copies are in circulation, and anyone who undertakes the complicated arrangements to screen them cannot help but be aware of their farflung itineraries, shipping from, say, Rotterdam to Vancouver to New York. They carry whatever physical damage they may incur from one engagement to the next. In their rarity, such works are like bodies that must be assiduously protected (Marks 1997a).

Because the audiences for intercultural cinema are small and disparate, they have a more proprietary relationship with the works than do audiences for commercial cinema. Intercultural cinema moves in specific, traceable paths, from local broadcast to college lecture room, from community hall to art museum, from a screening for the maker's family and friends to a artist-run center. Each viewing expands the meaning of a work; as reception theorists say, it completes it. Each new discursive context becomes part of the material of the film or video, and subsequent viewers often take these contexts into account as part of their experience of the work. For example, *Daughters of the Dust* came to art-house audiences already claimed by enthusiastic audiences of African American women. A work like Richard Fung's *Chinese Characters* (1986) or Nguyen Tan Hoang's *Forever Jimmy!* (1996) brings traces of its queer audience to its screening at an Asian American festival, and carries the marks of its Asian viewers to the queer festival circuit. Igloolik Isuma Productions' *Qaggig* (1989), first screened on Inuit television, was already marked by Inuit viewers when it screened at the Museum of Modern Art; anthropology students viewing *Qaggig* in a classroom should be aware of traces of both the work's art-museum and Inuit audiences. What word of mouth has already established, journalism and criticism solidify in tracing the links between audiences.

Reproducible though they are, the media arts cannot be conceived of separately from the sets of viewers that give them meaning. Traces of other viewings, of differently seeing audiences, adhere to the skin of these works. I am arguing that mechanical reproduction does not necessarily turn a work into a simulacrum, endlessly available for reinterpretation—at least not works like these, whose production

and distribution is community bound. Instead of being wrenched
from one context into another, intercultural films multiply their
contexts. Their very circulation is a kind of coalition building, reinforced by networks both ephemeral and concrete, from gossip and
e-mail to community organizations, university classes, and funding
agencies.

Toni Cade Bambara describes the audience of African American
women as *Daughters of the Dust*'s "authenticating audience." But
most audiences cannot authenticate: intercultural works are tailor-
made only for a very few people. A viewer of intercultural cinema
may be aware that her understanding of it is imperfect, but that other
viewers' knowledges complement her own. She knows that meaning
inheres in the image, whether or not it can be deciphered. Obviously,
the appeal of intercultural cinema to a politics of identity is limited,
since the identities it presents are almost always shifting and emerging. Intercultural cinema appeals to the limits of naming and the
limits of understanding, and this is where it is most transformative.

In the first chapter of this book I discuss the intellectual and aesthetic grounds of many works of intercultural cinema in terms of
a search for the language with which to express cultural memory.
This search leads initially to a confrontation with silence and absence. I suggest that intercultural cinema performs an excavation of
the available sources of recorded history and memory, only to find
that cultural memory is located in the gaps between these recorded
images. Consequently, I argue, many works of intercultural cinema
begin from the inability to speak, to represent objectively one's own
culture, history, and memory; they are marked by silence, absence,
and hesitation. All these works are marked by a suspicion of visuality, a lack of faith in the visual archive's ability to represent cultural
memory. The use of silence and absence of visual image in these
works may make them appear insubstantial, but I consider it to be
an opening toward the exploration of new languages, new forms of
expression.

Chapter 2 establishes a basis for these new languages that involves
a radical reconsideration of how cinema signifies, one less visual
than material. I propose a concrete, "fetishistic," and auratic theory
of representation. Amplifying the rather wistful fetishism of Walter
Benjamin and André Bazin, I argue that film or video may be con-

sidered to have aura, because it is a material artifact of the object it has witnessed. Thus cinema functions like a fetish, in the anthropological sense described by William Pietz: an object whose power to represent something comes by virtue of a prior contact with it. Gilles Deleuze's term for certain kinds of images with the power to revive memories, the "fossil," is also powerfully descriptive of cinema's disturbing ability to recreate its object in the present. I examine a number of films and videos that deal with traveling objects, objects that materially embody the culture they represent. The rest of the chapter centers on the work of Shauna Beharry, whose video *Seeing Is Believing* uses the medium's ability to make tactile contact with, not simply visual record of, an object: her own mother's body, and the sari she wore.

As chapter 2 suggests, one of the important ways that cinema can embody cultural memory is by awakening memories of touch. Chapter 3 explores how the sense of touch may embody memories that are unavailable to vision. I posit an epistemology that uses touch, rather than vision, as its model for knowledge, namely, mimesis. I go on to suggest that if vision can be understood to be embodied, touch and other senses necessarily play a part in vision. I argue that, since memory functions multisensorially, a work of cinema, though it only directly engages two senses, activates a memory that necessarily involves all the senses. I suggest that an understanding of the embodied experience of cinema is especially important for representing cultural experiences that are unavailable to vision. Finally, I offer a theory of haptic visuality, or a visuality that functions like the sense of touch. A number of works of intercultural cinema use haptic images to engage the viewer tactilely and to define a kind of knowledge based in touch.

Chapter 3 begins to suggest how cinema represents different cultural organizations of the senses, but it is in the final chapter that I discuss at length how the importance assigned to different kinds of sense experience varies from culture to culture. In chapter 4 I look at a number of works that appeal to touch, smell, taste, and indeed entire environments of sense experiences. Anthropologists describe how the organization of the sensorium reflects these cultural priorities. Neurophysiology and cognitive science suggest how all the senses are capable of learning and of encoding memory, and thus how they can be vehicles for cultural knowledge. Although cinema is an audiovisual medium, synesthesia, as well as haptic visuality, enables the viewer to experience cinema as multisensory. These sensory experiences are, of course, differentially available to viewers depending on their own sensoria, but I argue that sense experience can be learned and cultivated. I suggest that the meeting of cultures in the metropoli is generating new forms of sense experience and new ways of embodying our relation to the world. These emerging configurations of sense experience contribute a countercurrent to global culture's increasing simulation of sensory experience.

1

The memory of images

Intercultural cinema by definition operates at the intersections of two or more cultural regimes of knowledge. These films and videos must deal with the issue of where meaningful knowledge is located, in the awareness that it is between cultures and so can never be fully verified in the terms of one regime or the other. Yet the relationships between cultures are also mediated by power, so that the dominant regime—in the following examples, some configuration of the historical Euro-American hegemony—sets the terms of what counts as knowledge. Other knowledges cannot be expressed in its terms. They may evade expression because of censorship; because memory is inaccessible; or because to give expression to those memories is to invite madness. They may become subsumed to the dominant regime and forced to speak its language: this is the tokenism of multicultural cinema. In the face of these erasures, intercultural cinema turns to a variety of sources to come up with new conditions of knowledge: written history, sometimes; the audiovisual archive; collective and personal memory; fiction; and the very lack of images or memories, itself a meaningful record of what can be expressed. Cultural knowledges are lost, found, and created anew in the temporal movement of history and in the spatial movement between places. In this chapter I dwell on archaeological models of cultural memory, while in the next chapter spatial acts of travel and physical contact will predominate.

Intercultural cinema moves backward and forward in time, inventing histories and memories in order to posit an alternative to the overwhelming erasures, silences, and lies of official histories. There are many examples of film/videomakers who have begun by confronting the lack of histories of their own communities that result from public and personal amnesia. These artists must first dismantle the official record of their communities, and then search for ways to reconstitute their history, often through fiction, myth, or ritual. I can mention only a few of the best-known of this large body of archaeological works: it includes much of the work of Black Audio Film Collective, such as John Akomfrah's *Handsworth Songs* (1986), *Testament* (1988), and *Seven Songs for Malcolm X* (1993), and Reece Auguiste's *Mysteries of July* (1991) and *Twilight City* (1989); Maureen Blackwood and Isaac Julien's *The Passion of Remembrance* (1986), Julien's *Looking for Langston* (1989), and other works by Sankofa; Julie Dash's *Daughters of the Dust* (1992); Janice Tanaka's *Memories from the Department of Amnesia* (1990) and *Who's Gonna Pay for These Donuts Anyway?* (1992); Cheryl Dunyé's *The Watermelon Woman* (1996); Elia Suleiman's *Homage by Assassination* (1992) and *Chronicle of a Disappearance* (1996); Elia Suleiman and Jayce Salloum's *Muqaddimah Li-Nihayat Jidal (Introduction to the end of an argument) Speaking for oneself . . . speaking for others* (1990); Jayce Salloum and Walid Ra'ad's *Talaeen a Junuub (Up From the South)* (1993); Richard Fung's *The Way to My Father's Village* (1988) and *My Mother's Place* (1990); Yun-ah Hong's *Memory/all echo* (1990) and *Through the Milky Way* (1992); Alanis Obomsawin's *Kanehsatake: 270 Years of Resistance* (1993), and Victor Masayesva's *Ritual Clowns* (1988), *Siskyavi: The Place of Chasms* (1991), and *Imagining Indians* (1994). This chapter focuses on a number of archaeological works, paying special attention to Rea Tajiri's *History and Memory: For Akiko and Takashige* (1991), Raoul Peck's *Lumumba: The Death of a Prophet* (1992), Marlon Fuentes's *Bontoc Eulogy* (1995), Atom Egoyan's *Calendar* (1993), and John Akomfrah/Black Audio's *Who Needs a Heart?* (1992).

As in many intercultural films and videos, the acts of excavation performed by these works is primarily deconstructive, for it is necessary to dismantle the colonial histories that frame minority stories before those stories can be told in their own terms. Yet once this deconstruction has been accomplished, no simple truth is uncovered. There is a moment of suspension that occurs in these works after the official discourse has been (if only momentarily) dismantled and before the emerging discourse finds its voice. This is a moment of silence, an act of mourning for the terrible fact that the histories that are lost are lost for good. Yet this moment is also enormously suggestive and productive. It is where these works begin to call upon other forms of cultural knowledge: it is where the knowledges embedded in fetish-like objects, bodily memory, and the memory of the senses, which this book explores, are found. This process of discovery is like scavenging in a tide pool for the small, speaking objects that are briefly revealed there before the water rushes in again. In what follows I will note how the works in question point to these moments where new kinds of knowledge may emerge, knowledges to which I return in the following chapters.

I find the cinematographic philosophy of Gilles Deleuze most useful to explore how intercultural cinema performs a multiphased activity of excavation, falsification, and fabulation, or the making up of myths. I shall dwell on Deleuze's use of concepts from Bergson and Foucault; however, the ideas of Peirce, Nietzsche, Leibniz, and others are as thickly woven through Deleuze's cinema books. One of the most appealing aspects of Deleuze's two books on cinema is their open-ended quality. At first glance at these texts' astonishingly broad range of cinematic material and plethora of new terms, one could almost imagine Deleuze saying, like Walt Whitman, "You say I contradict myself; Very well, I contradict myself—I contain multitudes." In fact (like Whitman's), their open-endedness is part of the internal coherence of Deleuze's philosophy. These writings on cinema may be brought productively to works of which he was not aware or that did not exist at the time of his writing. His cinematographic philosophy is always open to transformation, to producing new concepts. As Dudley Andrew has written, "Deleuze does not read images; he sees with images, using them as a source for what can yet be thought, not as a record of what has already been thought" (1997, xi). I intend to make his theories think by bringing them into contact with new images. Intercultural cinema draws out the political implications of Deleuze's theory of cinema. To demonstrate this I want to emphasize the alliance between dominant narrative form and official history, to draw out the political potential of mythmaking and of ritual, and to stress the collective nature of memory and perception. If we trace Deleuze's understanding of perception back to its origin in Bergson, the disjunctions within the kinds of information offered by a film can evoke other sorts of memory that slip from both official history and the audiovisual record: namely, memories encoded in senses other than the auditory and the visual. My discussion is drawn from Walter Benjamin's critique of Bergson, theorists of hybrid and minority cinema such as Teshome Gabriel and Hamid Naficy, and most importantly, the films and videos themselves.

One of Deleuze's important basic distinctions is that between *movement-image cinema,* in which frame follows frame causally, according to the necessities of action, and *time-image cinema,* which frees time from causality. Simply, in the movement-image, Arnold grabbing the gun is followed by Arnold shooting the bad guy; in the time-image, Arnold grabbing the gun might be followed by Arnold going into a reverie, or perhaps a step-printed reprise of the gun-grabbing shot. Deleuze attributes the rise of time-image cinema to postwar European directors such as Rossellini, Antonioni, and Godard. His very derivation of the categories of movement-image and time-image implies that the new cinema became possible in an intercultural space. In order to emphasize the revolutionary potential of the new time-image cinema, Deleuze places great importance upon the "any-spaces-whatever" that came to proliferate after the Second World War:

The fact is that, in Europe, the post-war period has greatly increased the situations which we no longer know how to react to, in spaces which we no longer knew how to describe. These were "any-spaces-whatever", deserted but inhabited, disused warehouses, waste ground, cities in the course of demolition or reconstruction. And in these any-spaces-whatever a new race of characters was stirring, kind of mutant: they saw rather than acted, they were seers. (Deleuze 1989, xi)

I would argue that these any-spaces-whatever are not simply the disjunctive spaces of postmodernism, but also the disruptive spaces of postcolonialism, where non-Western cultures erupt into Western metropolises, and repressed cultural memories return to destabilize national histories. In this case the "new race . . . kind of mutant" to which Deleuze refers (in terms that suddenly take on a rather xenophobic cast) describes the very real conditions of migration, diaspora, and hybridity that characterize the new populations of Europe and North America, especially in the periods following wars. The end of the modern period is characterized not only by industrial ruins but also by the dismantling of colonial power, whose ruins are perpetuated in the lives of the people it displaced. These people are "seers" in the metropolitan West, aware of violent histories to which its dominant population is blind. They possess what Fatimah Tobing Rony (1996) calls a third eye, which allows them to perceive the dominant culture from both inside and outside.

Let me note here that Deleuze considered any-spaces-whatever to constitute images that arouse an emotional or visceral response, that is, *affection-images.* Yet, whereas it is conventional for these emotional responses to be immediately followed by action (Arnold feels anger and reaches for his gun), in any-spaces-whatever no action is possible. Instead, emotion or feeling opens us to the experience of time (Arnold slips into a reverie). This disengagement of affective response from action will become important later in this chapter, and in this book as a whole, as I examine how the body may be involved in the inauguration of time-image cinema.

Cinema as Archaeology

Intercultural cinema is in a position to sort through the rubble created by cultural dislocation and read significance in what official history overlooks. In what follows I use a geological/archaeological metaphor for these historical searchings, so it is useful to carry a mental diagram, a cross section of sedimented layers that, at their deepest, harden into granite, but whose surface is volatile and vulnerable to wind, water, and other, more violent, forces.

Deleuze's cinema theory draws from the simple principle, which he elaborated with Félix Guattari, that discourses are not only restrictive but enabling. While they limit what can be said, they also provide the only language in which to say it. In order to find expression, emerging thoughts and things must speak in the terms of the discourses that are established, though at the same time they break away from them. Political (indeed any) change must be effected in a sort of dance between sedimented, historical discourses and lines of flight, between containment and breaking free. This is the act of archaeology: combining elements from different strata in order to resist the order that would be imposed by working on one stratum alone (Deleuze and Guattari 1987, 503), knowing that the result will be contradictory and partial. For intercultural cinema, this translates to the need to work critically within dominant discourses, both cinematic and more broadly cultural, while simultaneously developing the powerful emergent lines of flight that will open them to the outside.

In Foucauldian terms, intercultural cinema works at the edge of an unthought, slowly building a language in which to think it. What can already be thought and said threatens to stifle the potential emerging new thoughts. The already sayable against which intercultural cinema struggles is not only official history but often also identity politics, with their tendency toward categorization. Some of the works I will discuss confront the limits of thought, for example by showing what stories cannot be told through either official histories or individual remembrance. Others begin to work at the limits of what can be thought, by referring to the memories of objects, the body, and the senses. Many do both these things.[1]

In intercultural cinema, the choice is usually to hold the image open to those possibilities of expression that are both threatening and enabling. The moments of thinness, suspension, and waiting in these films are not encounters with a dreadful void but with a full and fertile emptiness. The sorts of new thoughts enabled by "the *unsummonable* of Welles, the *inexplicable* of Robbe-Grillet, the *undecidable* of Resnais" (Deleuze 1989, 182) are generated as well by the unevocable images of Peck, the undecidable images of Suleiman, the inexplicable images of Tajiri. Deleuze compares the "powerlessness at the heart of thought" to a mummy (166): the thought that cannot yet be expressed appears paralyzed, petrified. Hence the quality of stillness that characterizes many of these works. The petrified object regains life only in the process of developing a thought that can think it, a language in which it can be spoken.

Intercultural cinema is not sanguine about finding the truth of a historical event so much as making history reveal what it was not able to say. Any truth is lost in the event's discursive representation, in the layers of words and things that build up over it. In the famous line from *Handsworth Songs,* "There are no stories in the riots, only ghosts of stories." Yet it is only by being inscribed in this way that an event can be said to occur at all. A film can recreate, not the true historical event, but at least another version of it, by searching into the discursive layers in which it was found. "If we want to grasp an event we must not show it," Deleuze writes, "we must not pass along the event, but plunge into it, go through all the geological layers that are its internal history (and not simply a more or less distant past)"

(1989, 254–55). Many intercultural works rely on idiosyncratic, personal narratives, because these provide a slim thread back into the strata of history.

Following Foucault, Deleuze argues that experience cannot be represented directly and in its entirety, but only approached partially by the orders of the discursive and the visible, or the sayable and the seeable. These orders cannot be reduced one to the other. They are two incommensurable forms of truth that confront each other at a given historical moment. " 'What we see never lies in what we say', and vice versa" (Deleuze 1988b, 64; quoting Foucault). A given discourse must be broken open to find its implicit statements, which cannot be conceived of in the terms of the discourse. Similarly, things must be broken open to find the visibilities implicit in them: "Visibilities are not forms of objects, nor even forms that would show up under light, but rather forms of luminosity which are created by the light itself and allow a thing to exist only as a flash, sparkle, or shimmer" (Deleuze 1988b, 52).[2] Discourse and the visible, then, do not embrace the world, but only encapsulate what can be known at a given time. The seeable and the sayable approach each other asymptotically, showing each other to be false even as they require each other to be true. Cinema, because it is an audiovisual medium, is the privileged record of the disjunctive quality of "truth" in a given historical formation. Reading Foucault literally, Deleuze understands the cinematic image to correspond to the notion of the visible, the layer of things in which one can read about a particular stratum or historical formation. Cinema is able to hear (though it rarely does) what is just beyond discourse and see the flash at the edge of known things. Image and sound tracks usually corroborate each other, but they can also be used to undermine each other, to show the limit of what each is able to represent. In the image is revealed "the deserted layers of our time which bury our own phantoms" (Deleuze 1989, 244). What Deleuze's optical image does is "finally SEE" what has not been encoded in discourse, and finally hear it as well. Deleuze calls the visual and sound images that butt into each other but cannot be reconciled in a single discourse "incompossible" images (a term from Leibniz), and such images abound in intercultural film and video.

By the sayable, Deleuze seems to mean the dialogue in a film. This is limiting, because the sound track contains far more than words and symbolic sound. For that matter, some elements of the image track exceed the seeable, in that they are *not* acknowledged in the dominant discourse or regime of signs. All these extradiscursive sounds and images appear as noise. This points to the uneven fit between a theory of "words and things" and the merely audiovisual object of cinema. In addition to Foucault's two categories, I believe it is also possible to talk of an order of the *sensible,* which, like the seeable and the sayable, is the sum of what is accessible to sense perception at a given historical and cultural moment. Just as we can only speak in the language that surrounds us, so we can only feel in the ways we have learned it is possible to feel. These matters will be addressed in due course, especially in chapters 3 and 4.

This theory of an archaeology of the image helps show how intercultural cinema expresses the disjunction between orders of knowledge, such as official history and private memory, by juxtaposing different orders of image, or image and sound tracks that do not correspond to each other. Intercultural cinema reveals new history as it is being formed, the new combination of words and things that cannot be read in terms of the existing languages of sound and image but calls for new, as yet unformulated languages. To read/hear the image, then, is to look/listen not for what's there but for the gaps— "mind the gap!," as notices read in the Toronto subways—to look for what might be in the face of what is not. Hence the importance of absent images (often, video black or black leader), barely legible images, and indistinguishable sound in so many of these works.

History and Memory: For Akiko and Takashige, by Rea Tajiri, winds back through the images of Japanese Americans in fiction films and government newsreels during and after World War II, with a slim thread of imaginative narrative. *Lumumba: The Death of a Prophet,* by Haitian filmmaker Raoul Peck, attempts to reconstruct the life of Patrice Lumumba, the first postindependence leader of Congo, from the very events that prevent him from making a "proper" documentary: he mines political history from home movies, shots taken in an airport and a museum, and long, empty stretches of black film leader. *Calendar,* a film by Atom Egoyan, confronts a tourist's commodified images of his ancestral Armenia with incoherent memory-images of that country, from which a profoundly repressed grief erupts. John Akomfrah/Black Audio's *Who Needs a Heart?* uses a mocking, irreverent, and ultimately mournful fictional narrative to retrace the foundered history of the Black Power movement in Britain, weaving stories around the inaccessible historical facts of the career of Michael DeFreitas, or Michael X. Finally, Marlon Fuentes's *Bontoc Eulogy* retraces the filmmaker's Filipino colonial history through the journey of his grandfather Marcot from tribal life in the Philippines to the 1904 Saint Louis World's Fair. A viewer gradually realizes that Fuentes' tale is a fabulation.

History and Memory attempts to reconstruct Tajiri's Japanese American family's memory of their internment during the Second World War. The tape is both the record and the active process of her struggle to reactivate the past from the fragments of available image. Images exist to corroborate official accounts of the internments of Japanese Americans and Canadians during the war. But the unofficial histories of Tajiri's family's experiences cannot be documented, and the few artifacts they retain from the experience are silent. Furthermore, inexplicably for Tajiri, those who were in the camps seem willfully amnesiac—her mother barely remembers a thing about her imprisonment. It is by bringing together visual and audio images that are inadequate alone and contradictory together that Tajiri is able to evoke scenes and events that can't be reconstructed.

The tape begins with a black screen, and a scrolling text describing a scene viewed from overhead:

. . . Slowly, very, very slowly the ground comes closer as the tops of trees disappear. The tops of the heads of a man and woman become visible as they move them back and forth in an animated fashion. The black hair on their heads catch and reflect light from the street lamps. The light from the street lamps has created a path for them to walk and argue. *(The spirit of my grandfather witnesses my father and mother as they have an argument about the unexplained nightmares of their daughter on the 20th anniversary of the bombing of Pearl Harbor . . .)*

The bombing would lead to the forcible detainment of 110,000 Japanese Americans. This written description of an image (with no image) is followed by another, this time spoken. Tajiri's voice-over says:

I don't know where this came from, but I just have this fragment, this picture that's always in my mind. My mother, she's standing at a faucet, and it's

1. Still from *History and Memory: For Akiko and Takashige*

really hot outside, and she's filling this canteen, and the water's really cold, and it feels really good. And the sun's just so hot, it's just beating down, and there's this dust that gets everywhere, and they're always sweeping the floors.

This second description is accompanied by a brief flash of a visual image, a dark-haired woman filling a canteen. These two sequences, detailed descriptions of events for which there are no images, attempt to replace the images that have "happened in the world while there were cameras watching," or that "we restage in front of cameras, to have images of." Such pictures must suffice, for none of the contemporary images—Office of War Information films of the camps, American and Japanese newsreels, and Hollywood war movies like *From Here to Eternity*—can serve as memory vehicles for Tajiri's family. Tajiri calls upon the spirit of the dead, namely her grandfather, to supply an image, drawing upon communal memory as a source of images when no others exist. When no image is available, in short, archaeology must be done in order to create images.

The confrontation with official versions of history may be a violent one, or it may be a gentle drawing out of those histories' internal contradictions, as in the work of Anishnabek filmmaker Alanis Obomsawin. Her film *Kanehsatake: 270 Years of Resistance* (1993), which deals with the Mohawk uprising at Oka, Quebec, in 1990, gently insists that the truth lies neither in legalistic government positions, mouthed by the callow young Canadian soldiers on one side of the barricades, nor in the authenticity of testimonies by Mohawk fighters on the other. She does not put one Mohawk in the position of spokesperson, for that would merely mimic the authoritarianism of government officials. Rather, she lets the many voices of the First Nations community suggest that the truth of their claim to the land cannot be expressed in the terms of legalistic, territorial discourse. Like many intercultural filmmakers, Obomsawin maintains a skeptical distance from seemingly authoritative visible evidence. Oral histories and evocative drawings provide the Mohawk counterhistory to the seemingly more substantial archival documents of the European and Canadian colonizers.

Trinh T. Minh-ha is another filmmaker who refuses the reassuring mutual reinforcement of sound and image that gives a sense of authenticity to conventional documentary. In Trinh's *Surname Viet Given Name Nam* (1989) the audio/visual disjunction consists in the discovery, as several women talk on camera about their sufferings in Vietnam, that they are performing themselves. Their hesitation on camera is not "Asian" shyness but the uncertainty of underrehearsed actors. As slightly different versions of their words simultaneously scroll down the screen, one begins to doubt the women's halting statements. The women are there, but they are in a sense performing their own absence, or their replacement by images. Rather than supply the clichéd images of testimonial documentary, the visual and sound images of the women (who are actually Vietnamese women living in the States) refuse to be authenticated. They underscore the limitations of a film language that insists on examination and truthful revelation. Such a language would individualize and render digestible the women's stories of suffering.

Lumumba: The Death of a Prophet similarly plays image and sound tracks off each other in order to tell a story that cannot be communicated in either one alone. The film documents, or attempts to document, the career of Patrice Lumumba, who held a two hundred-day tenure in 1960 as the first postindependence leader of the Belgian Congo, later Zaire. Lumumba inherited a brutal colonial regime, and its power was still entrenched when he took office. He was assassinated a year into his term, and little information is available about the conditions of his murder. Lumumba was believed by many to be the only politician who could establish a real democracy in Congo: the film assembles shadowy pictures of a passion-

2. Archival photograph from
*Lumumba: The Death of a
Prophet.* Courtesy of California
Newsreel.

ate, visionary, and perhaps naive man. Peck has an oblique angle
on this history as a Haitian who was raised in the newly independent Zaire. Narrated by the filmmaker, *Lumumba* interweaves a
fractured history of Lumumba's short career with reminiscences of
the filmmaker's childhood, each supplementing the other at crucial
points. Peck includes among his influences Jean-Luc Godard and
Chris Marker (Peck 1992), and the film consists of a violent confrontation between different orders of truth, as in Godard's work, and a
gentle, caressing rumination on the impossibility of recovering history from its representations, as in Marker's.

Like Tajiri, Peck was stymied in his research. The little archival information he found about Lumumba came from the European
news media, which were already clouded by Europeans' paternalis-
tic imaginings of African politics. He also found that this official history cost money. Peck complains that Movietone charged him $3000
for the rights to the footage of a British newsreel of Lumumba's ar-
rest on 27 November 1960. "Memories of a murder are expensive," he
says. Turning away from these sources, he draws history from home-
movie footage of his childhood in Haiti and Zaire, accompanied by
tales of political intrigue told by his mother. The filmmaker's inser-
tion of himself into the history of the country is especially appro-

priate because his circumstances for being in Zaire have everything to do with the postindependence changes: the Peck family was part of a Haitian black elite that emigrated to Zaire during the transition from colonial rule in order to fill government positions vacated by the Belgians. His mother held a government post in the country for a time and knew a lot of information that did not make it into official records.

Given the blackout on official information in Zaire and the corruption of European sources, Peck draws heavily on his mother's memory as an alternative historical authority. The voiced-over tales that he begins with "Ma mère raconte . . ." are not cosy private memories. His mother recounts, for example, that she quit her job one morning after she was asked to order rope, wood, and cloth for shrouds, to be used in the assassination of Lumumba's allies. The visual image is of young Raoul and his little friends dancing for the benefit of his father's home movie camera; but on the sound track his mother's stories of the simultaneous political events react caustically with the images. For the viewer, this sequence's eeriness reflects a fall through the gap between seeable and sayable, the gap that movement-image cinema attempts to keep closed.

Black Audio Film Collective uses a similar strategy of divorcing the visual from the verbal. As I noted in the Introduction, the collective's representations of Black diasporan experience were always formed in struggle with hegemonic media images. By the time of *Who Needs a Heart?* it seemed that Black Audio had decided to devote an entire film to "the ghosts of stories." The film proceeds entirely without dialogue, and this is part of what prevents the viewer from easily connecting its visual images with official representations of the Black Power movement that contain and dismiss it. The film crystallizes around the rise of the movement in Britain and the figure of Michael X, variously considered a charismatic leader, opportunist, or petty criminal. It follows the lives of a fictionalized group of people in Michael X's circle from 1963 to 1975.

In their struggle to recreate the history of British Black Power and Michael X, Black Audio found that the archives of personal memory and recorded history around Michael X were closed. Most of the television archival footage had been destroyed. Co-producer Avril Johnson says that the footage was destroyed after Black Audio first contacted the television networks, apparently in a measure to pre-

3. Frame enlargement from *Who Needs a Heart?*
Courtesy of Black Audio Film Collective.

vent it from being reexamined (Johnson and Gopaul 1994). Also, like Raoul Peck, the filmmakers discovered that what footage they could find was prohibitively expensive (Johnson and Gopaul 1994). In addition, former Black radicals and rich whites who had slummed with the movement refused to go on record. So, as Akomfrah says, "What's the best way of quoting people who don't want to be acknowledged? Make them mute" (Akomfrah and Givanni 1993). For this reason, *Who Needs a Heart?* had to rework documentary as docudrama, weaving a fictional story around a thread of questionable history. The blocking of access to historical images often produces what Deleuze calls *recollection-images,* those floating, dreamlike images that cannot be assigned a connection to history. But the film's powerful affect shows that the infinite deferral of historical truth is painful and maddening.

Another strategy filmmakers use to divorce the visual from the verbal record is to eschew full translation into English (or the language of the dominant culture). Partial translation is an important strategy for many intercultural film/videomakers, including Trinh, Salloum and Ra'ad, Guillermo Gomez-Peña, and Igloolik Isuma Productions. Hopi videomaker Victor Masayesva Jr. exhibits many of his works in Hopi with either no translation or a clearly incomplete one. In *Siskyavi: The Place of Chasms* (1991), an old woman explains to her granddaughter, in alternating Hopi and English, the

4. Frame enlargement from *Calendar.*
Photo: Atom Egoyan. Courtesy of Alliance
Atlantis Communications.

5. Frame enlargement from *Calendar*

6. Frame enlargement from *Calendar*

significance of the ceremonial patterns she is painting on a pot. A non-Hopi (or a Hopi who does not speak the language) will comprehend that what she is describing is sacred; but the sacred elements of her speech are not translated. This not only protects the culture from prying eyes, but defies a viewer's conventional ethnographic expectation that the image is a window onto the culture.

Atom Egoyan's *Calendar* is also structured around the losses that take place in acts of translation. The protagonist (played by Egoyan) is a Canadian photographer of Armenian descent (as is Egoyan) whose living and very mode of existence are to replace experience with images. His reason for being in Armenia is to produce photographs of country churches, turning the rustling, fragrant landscape into cheesecake images to be marketed in the West, perhaps for nostalgic exiles. The photographer's ignorance of and disinterest in the country of his heritage reflect the general Western disinterest and ignorance of Armenia's ancient culture, almost destroyed by genocide. His wife (played by Egoyan's real-life spouse, Arsinée Khanjian), also a Canadian of Armenian heritage, becomes attracted to their native Armenian guide, Ashot. Watching through the viewfinder of his camera, the photographer is in thrall to images of his wife talking and wandering with the guide, and knows that he is losing her.

These scenes, shown as flashbacks, alternate with scenes in which the photographer, back in his Toronto apartment, hires a series of women who vaguely resemble his wife to do the following: come to his apartment for dinner, excuse themselves on a prearranged cue, and make an erotic telephone call in their first language, be it, say, Macedonian or Turkish. As the woman-of-the-moment stands next to a picture of the church-of-the-month, talking on the phone, they function as two virtual images (a concept I explain below), of the woman and the country the photographer refused to see.

Categories of Image and Processes of Memory

Among Deleuze's many categories of images, the actual image, virtual image, cliché, optical image, and recollection-image are especially important for my discussion of intercultural cinema, so it is necessary to devote some discussion to these terms.

Drawing on Bergson's philosophy of duration, Deleuze proffers an image of time as always splitting into two parts: the time that moves smoothly forward, or the "present that passes"; and the time that is seized and represented (if only mentally), or the "past that is preserved." What Deleuze, following Bergson, refers to as the *actual image* and the *virtual image* are the two aspects of time as it splits, the actual image corresponding to the present that passes, the virtual image to the past that is preserved. Thus we see that at the very moment that they diverge, the two types of image create two disjunctive representations of the same moment. ("Image" in Bergson signifies not simply the visual image, but the complex of all sense impressions that a perceived object conveys to a perceiver at a given moment. See Bergson [1911] 1988, 36–38.) An example may be found in home videos of family gatherings. At the moment that the video is shot, the two aspects of time look the same; but the present-that-passes can never be recalled (I feel ill; I am angry at my mother), while the past-that-is-preserved (we were gathered around the table, smiling) becomes the institutionalized representation of the moment. Virtual images tend to compete with recollection-images—the memory I have of the gathering that is not captured in the video—and, as we know, their power is such that they often come to stand in for our memories.

In effect, the past-that-is-preserved has hegemony over the representation of the event, be it home movies of Thanksgiving 1998 or the televised Los Angeles rebellion of 1992. If instead of home movies we think of television news, for example, the political implications of these divergent sorts of image become apparent. Clearly this is not a question of which image is "true," but of which has a more tenacious representation, and which representation has more continuity with the layer of images that preceded it. Television, movies, and other "public" images compose a sort of official history, while the unpreserved present-that-passes is more like unofficial history or private memory. To confront one with the other is to dig between discursive strata—in the process, perhaps finding trace images of unofficial or private memories.

The photographer in *Calendar* rigorously controls the process of image construction, as though to hurry actual images into their suspension in virtual images. He spends the entirety of the trip to Armenia fixed behind the viewfinder of his video camera, while his wife and her guide and apparent lover wander in and out of the frame. When she translates the guide's information to the photographer, she conveys his disapproval as well: "He doesn't like to tell about this place—he thinks you should let your eyes discover it." She tries to convince him to leave his camera and join them for a walk, but the photographer is adamant, adding in a retrospective voice-over, "What I really feel like doing is standing here and watching while the two of you leave me and disappear into a landscape that I am about to photograph." His substitutions are highly fetishistic, both in psychoanalytic terms and in the sense that he is seeking to establish a uniform commodity value for all his experiences. He obsessively reviews the footage he shot of his wife, rewinding and fast-forwarding, in the attempt to manage her image and her memory. The women who come to him from the escort service barely resemble his wife, but they are meant to be equivalents, in the way that one dollar equals another. He adopts a foster child in Armenia and watches a videotape of her. "She costs me $28 a month," he tells one of his paid dinner companions. "Do you have children? How much do they cost a month?" The photographer's life is built of such uniform, interchangeable images.

As I have noted, a certain quietism of the image characterizes many works of intercultural cinema, a reluctance to swing easily into narrative. This reluctance results from the fact that images are not neutral reflections, but representations made from an interested point of view. Perception, according to Bergson, is always partial and interested, since it is located in a specific perceiver; it is necessarily embodied, located, and contingent (Bergson [1911] 1988, chapter 1). Perception is, then, *subtractive* insofar as it means a thing is not perceived in its fullness but only in those aspects that interest the perceiver (Deleuze 1986, 63–64). The movement-image re[...] t the subjectivity implied in the image, to [...] form of perception. "It could be said," D[...] .jective-image is the thing seen by some- or[...] t as it is seen by someone who forms part of that set" (1986, 7[...]) movement-image films, the viewer is supposed to share the subjectivity implied in causality. The "qualified" viewer of action movies accepts the connection between Arnold shooting and the bad guy dying; the qualified viewer of dramas accepts the connection between a facial close-up and an interior monologue. (Though of course a viewer could, either through perversity or cultural unfamiliarity, refuse to make these connections and watch movement-image films in a state of wonderment.) By contrast, the time-image—which evokes a stranded eyeball, powerless to draw upon resources of common sense—questions everything about how *this* particular image got to be constructed from a given perception. It thus compels the viewer to start the act of perceiving all over again, choosing which part of the available image is relevant. In fact, Deleuze argues, cinema necessarily pulls the viewer between objective and subjective poles, between accepting and reflecting upon a given image. In general, Deleuze's characterization of time-image cinema describes avant-garde works that, in their suspicion of representation, force the viewer to draw upon his or her subjective resources in order to complete the image. In intercultural cinema there is an additional, more overtly political suspicion of the image, given that its clichés bear the weight of dominant history. For many works of intercultural cinema, then, the image is barely a beginning, and any extension into narrative must be hesitant, or suspicious. In these works still or thin-looking images are ultimately the richest.

Deleuze writes that the absence of image, such as with a black or white screen, underexposed or snowy image, has the "genetic" power to restore our belief in the world (1989, 200–201), to bring something new out of the ruins of the image. These thin images call on the viewer to search for their hidden history. In *History and Memory*, grainy old Super-8 footage smuggled from the prison

7. Still from *History and Memory: For Akiko and Takashige*

8. Still from *Measures of Distance.* Courtesy of Video Out.

camp shows a woman skating on a tiny frozen pond in the desert. In Seoungho Cho's *I Blinked Three Times* (1993), a roadside bar dissolves in a blur of colors before the eyes of a weary traveler. In Mona Hatoum's *Measures of Distance* (1988), the grainy, flesh-toned images, accompanied by a longing voice-over, are gradually revealed to be still photos of the artist's faraway mother. All these images are quite slight and "meaningless" in themselves, but they call up volumes of images that are not or cannot be represented.

Lumumba depends upon the mutual relation between the thinness of the image and the viewer's rigorous engagement, with the double purpose of emphasizing the fleeting and conditional nature of recorded images and forcing the viewer to recreate for herself the unrepresentable events. Peck planned to shoot the film in Zaire. He recounts that he was first denied a visa, then granted one. Upon his arrival at the Brussels airport to make the flight, he spoke on the telephone with the Zairian officials who would be meeting him. Finding that they were unusually knowledgeable about him and his project, Peck realized that he would certainly be arrested as soon as his plane landed. He canceled his trip and, marooned, decided to make the Brussels airport the setting for his excavation of Zairian political history (adapting the strategy of Godard's *Far From Vietnam,* 1967). Brussels, then, becomes a blank screen on which Peck constructs his own alternative history of post-independence Zaire. In between he trains his camera on harried travelers, making up stories about them: "He wanted to be a classical guitarist. . . . She is in love with him, but he does not know." Peck's voyeuristic compassion for these children of the Belgian colonizers of the Congo is quite moving, and a wry reversal of the patronizing attitude of the Belgians toward their African subjects.

Unable to represent Africa "live," Peck films the African exhibits in the Brussels natural history museum. He uses British newsreels from the 1950s to represent early events in the transition from colonial rule. Both sources perpetuate many of the representations of Zaire that he intends to critique, but by showing only these images he reinforces the difficulty of representing a "view from the people's eyes." Like Tajiri, he inserts long segments of black leader, so that we see only darkness while his gentle spoken commentary sustains the film. This strategy is sometimes an acknowledgment that there is no other image for the events Peck is attempting to describe, sometimes a refusal to represent a horrific event. Referring to these sections of leader, he asks, "Are these black holes more corrosive than the images they hide?"

Of course no records exist of Lumumba's assassination. When the voice-over finally comes to discussing the grisly murders of Lumumba and his two associates, Peck's camera is moving among the elegantly dressed and well-padded bodies at a state reception in Brussels. This strategy takes advantage of the lack of corroborating images—which would be red herrings in any case—to situate

9 and 10. Frame enlargements from *Lumumba: The Death of a Prophet*

the responsibility for the assassination back in the colonial capital. While Peck relates details of the disposal of the bodies—the hanging, the burning, the teeth found embedded in the bark of a tree—he shows us a single still image, a pen-and-ink drawing of the location in the forest where the murders took place. Between the delicate colors in which the site is captured and the sound of Peck's reticent, gentle voice, the horror and ugliness of the betrayal of Lumumba and his nation emerge with consuming power. The slightest of virtual images suffices to signify, through omission, the overwhelming power of the historical event.

11. Frame enlargement from *Lumumba: The Death of a Prophet*

Such apparently thin images, which Deleuze calls *optical images,* are characteristic of time-image cinema. The optical image is contrasted with the sensory-motor image of movement-image cinema, in particular the *cliché,* a commonsense, hegemonic image that extends unproblematically into action. Arnold with his gun, the American newsreels of the Japanese internment camps, and the European news stories of the postcolonial transition in Zaire are clichés, calling on a habitual recognition without reflection. The optical image defamiliarizes the cliché by severing it from its context. The resulting image *looks* rarefied and abstract compared to the thickness of clichéd images. But it is really the cliché that is abstract. It perceives from the image only what is useful in the terms of causal connections. As Deleuze puts it, "It is grass in general that interests the herbivore" (1989, 45) — cows see in sensory-motor images, rather than perceive each tuft of grass in its completeness and particularity. By contrast, the restraint and thinness of the optical image "bring the thing each time to an essential singularity, and describe the inexhaustible, endlessly referring to other descriptions. It is, then, the optical image which is really rich, or 'typical'" (Deleuze 1989, 45). While clichés hide the object in the image, the optical image makes the object visible, in Foucault's sense of revealing what knowledge it constitutes.

The optical image, because it cannot be explained and mobilized

12. Frame enlargement from *Who Needs a Heart?* Courtesy of Black Audio Film Collective.

into action, requires the viewer to puzzle over it. The inability to rec-ognize an image encourages us to confront the limits of our knowl-edge, while the film's refusal to extend into action constitutes a refusal to "explain" and neutralize the virtual image. Because the viewer cannot confidently link the optical image with other images through causal relationships, she is forced to search her memory for other virtual images that might make sense of it.

This frustrating effect of the optical image seems to account for the anxiety that I noticed in many viewers at screenings of *Who Needs a Heart?:* an anxiety for solid biographical details about Michael X, for a clear plot line, for history, for causality. What the film gave were indeterminate circuits of virtual images. The reason for this is that no actual images of the events in question could be estab-lished: not even personal memories that could be drawn out into histories; not even obvious lies that the filmmakers could refute. *Who Needs a Heart?* is structured like a certain mode of remem-bering that excavates events that occurred in nonverbal, perhaps unconscious registers. It is a lush, stylized film. But its lushness comes not from the density of actual images and information but the opposite: it is the thinness of the optical image, emptying the image of information and filling it back up with color and sound. Trevor Mathison's palimpsestic sound track is as important as the images for creating a sense of meanings that are evoked and then withheld. As Sean Cubitt describes it, "Built up from overlapping musics (gospel, blues, free jazz, Buddhist chants), electronic effects and samples, sound effects subtly unanchored from the image, direct, pre-recorded and re-recorded dialogue, the audio track operates as well alongside the image, marking the diasporan scattering of meanings and peoples in repetition and polyrhythms" (1998, 116).

Returning to Bergson's terminology, we do not "perceive" an optical image purely in the cognitive sense, but rather our "attentive recognition" comes into play. Attentive recognition is the way a perceiver oscillates between seeing the object, recalling virtual images that it brings to memory, and comparing the virtual object thus created with the one before us. In so doing we create anew "not only the object perceived, but also the ever-widening systems with which it may be bound up" (Bergson [1911] 1988, 105). Engaging with the freshly perceived object, we recreate it in higher expansions of memory and on deeper strata of reality. Thus the optical image provokes evocative contemplations whose temporality takes a spiral path through the circuits of memory rather than the forward motion of action (Deleuze 1986, 46). Attentive recognition is a *participatory* notion of spectatorship, whose political potential shouldn't be ignored. If a viewer is free to draw upon her own reserves of memory as she participates in the creation of the object on screen, her private and unofficial histories and memories will be granted as much legitimation as the official histories that make up the regime of the cliché—if not more.

The act of attentive recognition, although it sounds dry in Bergson, is often a traumatic process. For example, for the photographer in *Calendar,* his effort to freeze the events in Armenia in photographs backfires as the thin optical images call upon his memory to supply what really happened. In the pivotal scene in the film, the grainy, bluish Super-8 footage he shot of a flock of sheep running alongside the car is paired with another virtual image, his wife's voice on the answering machine. "As you were taping, he placed his hand on mine. I remember because I gripped his hand so hard, watching you grip your camera as if you knew all the time. Did you know? Were you there? Are you there?" Her voice echoes metallically over the

13 and 14. Frame enlargements from *Handsworth Songs*

long-distance connection. Though the photographer attempted to manage memories by manufacturing virtual images, the inadequate visual and sound images of the video and answering machine force him to fill their gaps, with the painful memory of losing the woman he loved. Similarly, in *Handsworth Songs,* footage from the 1950s shows Caribbean families arriving by ship in England, the women in pretty dresses and their children disembarking full of anticipation. Haunting music diverts this scene from the cheery multicultural rhetoric that might ordinarily accompany it. The music renders the footage a series of optical images, ghosts of the hopes of two generations of Black British people. Watching it, a viewer who experienced the emigration, or whose parents did, would be able to reconstitute these virtual images through memory, perhaps recalling how the high spirits of the newly arrived women sank to despair as they confronted walls of British institutional and everyday racism.

Deleuze remarks that many films made by minorities invoke memory—not a psychological memory, but "the strange faculty that puts into immediate contact the inside and the outside, the people's business and private business" (1989, 221). Because official histories, with their official image repertoires, are often at odds with the private histories of disenfranchised people, it is *recollection-images*— such as the memories of Tajiri's family members and the unsettling *racontes* of Peck's mother—that must confront the public and the private with each other. A recollection-image embodies a past event that has no match in the present image repertoire. It is one sort of virtual image called up by the process of attentive recognition.

A recollection-image is not the direct image of a memory, however. "No doubt a recollection, as it becomes actual, tends to live in an image, but the converse is not true, and the image pure and simple will not be referred to the past unless, indeed, it was in the past that I sought it" (Deleuze 1989, 54; quoting Bergson). A recollection-image embodies the traces of an event whose representation has been buried, but it cannot represent the event itself. Through attentive recognition it may provoke an imaginative reconstruction, such as a flashback, that pulls it back into understandable causal relationships.

What is more disturbing is when the optical image cannot be connected to any living memory. When I find a high school yearbook at a flea market, or when I contemplate Christian Boltanski's wartime photographs of anonymous Jewish schoolchildren, I confront a virtual image that does not correspond to my experience, nor perhaps to anybody's memory, yet it cries out to have a memory assigned to it. When attentive recognition fails—when we do not recognize or cannot remember—it creates. Rather than hooking up with sensory-motor extension, the optical image connects with virtual images that are dreams, fantasies, the sense of a general past (Deleuze 1989, 55). When remembrance fails, the story must be creatively falsified in order to reach the truth. Jalal Toufic (1996, 46) expresses this beautifully: "What I dread when I am asked to bear witness is not only or primarily the pain of accessing extremely painful memories; and/or the pain of discovering all or part of what I thought unforgettable; but that I am asked also to definitively forget in order to release, this side of the event horizon, the created voice that can tell about a created but true event."

The recollection-image, an image that confronts what cannot be represented and attempts to bring it into dialogue with memory, is very similar to Walter Benjamin's definition of the dialectical image. Benjamin's unfinished *Passagen-Werk* was intended to be a montage of visual images and verbal signs, true to Foucault's dictum that "what we see never lies in what we say." He was especially fascinated by the detritus of nineteenth-century popular culture, in whose passé fashions and obsolete commodities he read the failure of the modernist ideology of progress (Buck-Morss 1989, chapter 3). As Bergson's recollection-image breaks loose from memory, so Benjamin's dialectical image drifts in the flotsam of history. The recollection-image has the power to falsify history, and the dialectical image demonstrates the wreck of modernity. The difference between them is that while in the dialectical image one can read the quasi-metaphysical essence of capitalism (Buck-Morss 1989, 73), in a sort of Marxist divination, the recollection-image is more partial, a road back to particular memories and partial histories.

It is these inexplicable images that testify most profoundly to the forgettings of both official history and private memory, and that prevent intercultural works from confidently recreating a community history from scraps of footage and passed-down stories. When images cannot be made to represent, when they refuse to connect to memory, they float loose from history. Unearthed in the excavation of discursive history, these images stare up at us, like "strangely active fossils, radioactive, inexplicable in the present where they surface, and all the more harmful and autonomous. Not recollections but hallucinations" (Deleuze 1989, 113). Such images are "harmful" because they cannot be reconciled with either official history or private memory—but they are more harmful to official history, because they falsify it or reveal it to be incomplete. They are volatile treasures for intercultural cinema, because if they can be made to speak they can activate the process of memory.

Virtual images of people (and things) are sometimes so volatile that they consume the film that contains them. One strikingly "radioactive" encounter with a virtual image occurs in Marlon Fuentes's

15. Archival photograph from *Bontoc Eulogy*.
Courtesy of Marlon Fuentes.

Bontoc Eulogy (1996). The filmmaker has been telling the fiction-alized story of the Filipino tribespeople who were exhibited at the Saint Louis World's Fair in 1904, "illustrated" by ethnographic film and archival footage from the fair. When a member of the Bontoc tribe disappeared and was later found dead, Fuentes says, the dead man's captive relatives mourned him in the traditional way. What accompanies this story is footage of three (presumably) Bontoc women passionately (and silently) wailing. Successive close-ups re-veal their repeated gestures of despair, their faces twisted with grief. Yet this indexical record of three anonymous women, at some un-specified date, probably filmed by ethnographers in the Philippines, far exceeds the narrative use Fuentes makes of it. We long to know the real circumstances of these long-dead women, to assign a mem-ory to their image, but their image cries out to be recognized in vain.[3] "There are many instances in documentary," David MacDougall writes, "of the physical and spiritual being of a person seeming to

16. Frame enlargement from *Bontoc Eulogy*

overflow the film that sets out to contain it. The film 'transmits' the presence, but it is as though the film is then consumed by it" (1994, 32). The three anonymous women consume the film. Their grief becomes the "sense of a general past" that haunts Fuentes' film. By using these archival images, Fuentes partially redeems them—not by filling in their stories, but by mourning the eternal loss of those stories. They are mediums of distant events that infect the present.

Deleuze's theory does not account for the ardent desire with which intercultural filmmakers apply themselves to the rediscovery of memory and history in these strange and silent, "harmful and autonomous" images. Like those dry paper flowers that expand in water, a recollection-image, moistened with memory, springs to life.[4] Intercultural works redeem these stranded images by bringing them into the very present, even into the body of the viewer. In the following chapter I will return to these cinematic fossils and the imaginative, and ultimately bodily, processes by which they are brought back to life.

Whose dreams are engaged in this process? Not the rare viewer who immediately "recognizes" an optical image, for she will be able to bring it into contact with actual images. Not someone who prefers the luxury of clichéd images and can't be bothered to investigate optical images, unless perhaps as a perceptual exercise. Whether these thin images merely annoy or engage the viewer depends on what stakes the viewer has in the image. Similarly, it seems that recollection-images would prompt deeper reflection on the part of viewers who feel acutely the disturbance they create. Someone who is curious, who aches to know about the stories hinted at in these grainy images, scraps of archival footage, and maddeningly silent protagonists will be more likely to search the optical image and attempt to bring it to life. Personal (and collective) history informs the liveliness of the engagement with the optical image. So, for example, when Raoul Peck ponders in the chill corridors of the Brussels airport, the blanks will be filled differently depending on whether one has never heard of Lumumba, believes or doubts the newsreel reports about him, or has heard rumors of the actual conditions of his murder. The suspension of action and lack of explanation will prompt many different reflections and circuits of recollection (or lack thereof) among *Lumumba*'s audience.

Claude Lanzmann's *Shoah* (1985) is discussed both by D. N. Rodowick (1997, 145–49) and by Jalal Toufic (1996, 40–49) as a deeply moving example of how memories might be willfully recreated in the absence of sound and image, and in the face of a blinding historical forgetting, in this case the obliteration of all traces of the Nazi death camp at Chelmno, Poland. Yet every remembering comes at the cost of another forgetting. In a footnote, Toufic remarks that the Polish survivors whom Lanzmann interviews compare the forests in Israel with those of Lithuania, but that the filmmaker neglects to ask them about the exiled Palestinians who can no longer experience the forests of their homeland (258). Certainly Lanzmann could not have been expected to ask this question. But another filmmaker has. The displaced Palestinians' return to the forests of their homeland is memorialized in a bittersweet short film by Michel Khleifi, *Ma'loul fête sa destruction* (Ma'loul celebrates its destruction, 1991). The film follows the Palestinians who once lived in the town of Ma'loul, razed by Israeli soldiers in 1948. A forest is all that remains of the town, to which the villagers travel to make an annual picnic. Ironically, they can only make the trip on Israeli Independence Day, which celebrates the Palestinians' eviction from the land, because that is the only day the state allows them to travel to the site in what is now Lebanon. *Ma'loul* is composed from "incompossible" images: 8mm footage of the old village; the official narration of the establishment of Israel on the same territory, which a schoolteacher half-heartedly explains to his students in Arabic; and a fresco, painted by one of the former residents of Ma'loul, that lovingly recreates every building in the former village. People find their former homes on the fresco, then on the day of the picnic attempt to locate them by the placement of olive trees and cacti. Official history would deny that the village existed at all, and even enlists nature in its support: at the edge of the overgrown territory that once was Ma'loul, a plaque declares it to be "Balfour Forest" (after the 1917 Balfour Declaration, which initiated the establishment of a Jewish homeland in Palestine). Khleifi's film allows all these different orders of history and memory to approach each other asymptotically, to give sound and image to memories that cannot be witnessed by the historical site.

Cinema as Expression of Collective Emergence

Deleuze's formulation of a notion of political cinema, repeated often throughout his writings, is this: "If there were a modern political cinema, it would be on this basis: the people no longer exist, or not yet" (1989, 216). According to Deleuze, while the prewar Soviet and American cinema had a certain confidence that the "masses" they represent did in fact exist, postwar political cinema reached an impasse in the discovery that there is no revolutionary proletariat or other collective entity for it to represent. If such an organized force exists in the postwar period, it is already inscribed in modern political institutions, already in discourse. As I have suggested, identity politics depends strategically on the recognition of ethnic, national, gender, and other affiliations in order for these groups to take part in established political debates. Yet it tends to be the people who slip between the cracks of identity politics' categorizations that stir up political ferment. A contemporary political cinema must be sought in the temporary nodes of struggle where people are just beginning to find their voices.

We can pinpoint these struggles to the very sites where a people's existence is denied: "The moment the master, or the colonizer, proclaims 'There have never been people here,'" Deleuze writes, "the missing people are a becoming, they invent themselves, in shanty towns or in camps, or in ghettos, in new conditions of struggle to which a necessarily political art must contribute" (1989, 217; also see Rodowick 1996, chapter 6). Indeed, keeping Foucault's criterion of visibility in mind, we may expect people to be "inventing themselves" best when official discourse has explained them squarely away: as extinct, picturesque, rioters, terrorists, shopkeepers, model minorities. Such discourses include the World War II patriotic musicals that emblematize who is "American enough" (in *History and Memory*); the French newspapers' reduction of Zaire's struggle for political autonomy to intertribal disputes (in *Lumumba*); the ethnographic footage that renders the Bontoc people picturesque savages (in *Bontoc Eulogy*). A political cinema is characterized by gaps and silences, the sites of emergence from these smug, sedimented discourses.

Not only is the historical archive available primarily to the victors, but also it is often those in the land of the victors who have access to a culture lost by the vanquished. Hence the paradoxical ability of Western (or dominant cultures') activists to document atrocities that cannot be visualized, that are unavailable, to the people who suffered them. For example, when Jon Alpert travels to Iraq to document *Saddam Speaks* (1993), he has access, with his protected passage and camera crew, to sites and spectacles that no Middle Eastern filmmaker could capture. The images of the destruction of Iraq, suppressed during the war by both Iraqi and mainstream Western press and only hinted at by the left-wing Western press, are finally recorded by Alpert: the razed homes, the unequipped hospitals, the starving infants that are the civilian casualties of the Allied embargo. Yet images of the exile's country are less available to the exile than to anyone else because he or she knows them to be myths of an unattainable past (Toufic 1996, 68–72). Monuments carried off to Western museums can only be painful reminders of the expropriation of an exile's culture. Literary works like *The Thousand and One Nights* (Pasolini's *Arabian Nights*, 1974) and traditional myths like the Korean *Tale of Kieu* (Trinh's *A Tale of Love*, 1995) may signify a rich cultural heritage to outsiders, but to those to whom this heritage belongs they signify the irrevocable loss of the past. Thus it is important for many postcolonial and exile filmmakers not to attempt to represent their culture in a (mythical) former state of wholeness, for that would be speaking in the language of the colonizers who have untroubled access to these artifacts. Postcolonial stories must be told both by sympathetic people from the colonizing country, who have access to rich image archives (for example, Alpert's *Saddam Speaks;* Tom Hayes's *People and the Land,* 1996, about the Pales-

17. Still from *Credits Included: A Video in Green and Red*

tinians; Dee Dee Halleck's *The Gringo in Mañanaland,* 1995, about the Latin American countries colonized by the United States) and by the colonized, whose archives are much slimmer.

When postcolonial filmmakers make difficult, hard-to-read works, they are not simply trying to frustrate the viewer, but to acknowledge the fact that the most important things that happened are invisible and unvisualizable. Toufic's *Credits Included: A Video in Green and Red* (1995) is a maddening work, because throughout it presents the destruction, homelessness, and insanity that the Lebanese "civil" war produced, without suggesting any possibility of a return to normal life or normal speech. The tape is filled with recollection-images that are forever stranded, refusing to be redeemed by the memory of one who would make sense of them. The videomaker draws a parallel between the destroyed buildings of Beirut and the men who lost their minds living in a southern Lebanon village that was constantly shelled by the Israelis. Madness, *Credits Included* suggests, is not only the most logical way to respond to war: madness is also an image of ruin, an image that cannot be connected to memory.

The refusal to connect images to memory is especially marked in a number of works by diasporan Lebanese and Palestinian filmmakers. This would seem to be a response to the lack of sympathy for their struggles in the West, and the knowledge that the official histories of Lebanon and Palestine are especially intractable. *Muqaddimah Li-Nihayat Jidal (Introduction to the End of an Argu-*

18 and 19. Stills from *Muqaddimah Li-Nihayat Jidal
(Introduction to the End of an Argument) Speaking
for oneself . . . Speaking for others.* Courtesy of V Tape.

ment) Speaking for oneself . . . Speaking for others (1990), by Jayce
Salloum and Elia Suleiman, laments the impossibility of speaking
as an Arab, particularly a Palestinian, when one is already so utterly
spoken for in Western contexts (see Marks 1992). The tape is a jarring pastiche of images of Arabs borrowed from American movies,
cartoons, and television news. In Salloum's tape *This Is Not Beirut*
(1994), most of the images are public and street scenes of Beirut, but
the videomaker uses a battery of techniques to prevent them from
signifying the city, or signifying much at all. Many shots are taken
from a speeding car; jump cuts obliterate objects just coming into
view and abort dialogue in midsentence. The effect is jarring and
frustrating, and it effectively blocks the stereotype that automati-

20. Still from *This Is Not Beirut*

cally links the adjective "war-torn" with the noun "Lebanon." More than an antiportrait of Beirut, the tape is a meditation on political representation. The desire to describe a political situation, and the tendency to founder in the act, are captured in a shot of the hands of Walid Ra'ad (Salloum's collaborator on *Talaeen a Junuub*) sketching an immensely complicated chart of the political relations among the various people they are interviewing.

Paralysis, the literal inability to translate affection into action, is expressed in the bodies of both film and actor in two works by Elia Suleiman. In *Homage by Assassination* (1992), the Palestinian character ES (played by the filmmaker) is waiting out the Gulf War in his New York apartment, while reports of the war clamor from the television. ES is a person whose actions have no consequences. He does not or cannot speak, though he uses the communicative prostheses of computer, photocopier, and fax: his body itself is incapable of expression. The film begins with a radio announcer's repeated attempts to reach the "young Palestinian filmmaker" on the phone for an interview: each time ES picks up the receiver, the connection fails. ES begins to doubt his own physical existence; he steps repeatedly onto a scale, trying to register his weight. He doesn't even have the strength to piss standing up. When one's existence is as inconsequential in the world as that of a Palestinian in New York during the Gulf War, one's perceptions cease to extend into action. ES becomes a character of pure affect. In one scene that lasts an eternity, he stands at the stove watching a pot of milk boil over.

Suleiman as actor intercedes for Suleiman the director again in his feature film, *Chronicle of a Disappearance* (1996). The film is set largely in Nazareth, where his parents live. As the title suggests, it measures the gradual disappearance, following the Oslo Agreement, of Palestinian identity and agency in Israel. It has a relatively (for Suleiman) lively plot, involving a Palestinian woman who finds a walkie-talkie of the Israeli police and uses it to issue confounding directions to the cops (there's even a gun, though it turns out to be a cigarette lighter); but the main sense of the film is of passivity, in-fighting (reflecting the corruption of the newly established Palestinian Authority), and paralysis. Suleiman again plays the unnamed protagonist, who again is both mute and utterly ineffectual throughout the film. He keeps a friend company in a souvenir shop that remains unvisited all day long, its postcard rack squeaking in the slight breeze. In another recurring scene, a car screeches to a halt in front of a gas station, two Arab men get out and start to beat each other up, and the service station attendants must break up the fight before they kill each other. It is as though time is in a rut: going forward is impossible, so actions are repeated, like music on a scratched vinyl record. At one point Israeli commandoes burst into his apartment and muscle around with guns, apparently searching for a suspect. Our protagonist pads around after them in his bathrobe, but they do not seem to notice him. Later, on the stolen walkie-talkie, he hears their exhaustive inventory of the apartment's contents, which concludes, "And a guy in a bathrobe." As in *Homage by Assassination,* his presence is incapable of extending into action. Yet this prohibition from participating in events allows the character, and us the viewers, to perceive events in their absurdity and tenderness, as well as their injustice. The film's last shot fondly records the filmmaker's aging parents, fast asleep in front of the television as programming signs off for the night, the Israeli national anthem playing over a fluttering flag. There is a sense of exhaustion and failure, a terrible disillusionment in the brief hopes for Palestinian autonomy. Are "the people" of Palestine still emerging, or has the foundering of the nationalist struggle left them with less than before?

Intercultural cinema is constituted around a particular crisis: the directly political discrepancy between official history and "private" memory. Deleuze describes such a crisis in European and North American cinema as well. Here, however, the terms of the crisis

21 and 22. Frame enlargements from *Chronicle of a Disappearance*. Courtesy of Aska Films.

are more existential—the helplessness of Antonioni's and Godard's characters confronting strange industrial and commercial landscapes, for example; or the free-floating perception that characterizes the films of North American structuralist filmmakers, such as Michael Snow and Ken Jacobs. These latter films, Deleuze argues, formulate a sort of *gaseous* perception, comparable to the experience of being on drugs (Deleuze 1986, 84) in that they free perception from subjectivity. Gaseous perception, as individualistic as a drug-induced hallucination, floats free from interested, subjective perception. Much experimental cinema affords this sort of individual temporal exploration, including some of the films and videos I discuss in this book (such as the formally experimental work of

Seoungho Cho and Gariné Torossian). But what generally characterizes intercultural cinema (and also, for example, some feminist
experimental film and video) is that it uses experimental means to
arouse *collective* memories. Perception in such works is not just an
individual exploration but socially and historically specific: it embodies a collective expression even as it is highly personal.

Since it is participatory and culturally informed, Deleuze's theory
of cinematic perception could be extended into a theory of collective
reception. Deleuze does acknowledge that some forms of knowledge
are collective, notably that of the storyteller. "Story-telling is not an
impersonal myth, but neither is it a personal fiction: it is a word in
act, a speech-act through which the character continually crosses
the boundary which would separate his private business from politics, and *which itself produces collective utterances*" (1989, 222).
However, when discussing perception itself, Deleuze tends to suggest that individual perception is possible without recourse to collective memory. In contrast, I argue that the element of communal
experience that is implicit in Bergson's theory of perception necessarily informs the process of cinematic spectatorship as well. Perception is never a purely individual act but also an engagement with
the social and with cultural memory. "Where there is experience
in the strict sense of the word, certain contents of the individual
past combine with material of the collective past" (Benjamin 1968a,
157). As Teshome Gabriel points out, the process of viewing a film,
especially a minority film, underscores the collective character of
its form of expression: "There is a significant continuity between
forms of oral tradition and ceremonial story-telling and the structures of reception of Third Cinema. This continuity consists of a
sharing of responsibility in the construction of the text, where both
the filmmaker and the spectators play a double role as performers
and creators" (1989, 62). This collective process, I argue, takes place
in all film viewing and is simply more explicit, and more motivated,
in intercultural cinema, which is motivated to use individual stories
to represent collective histories. Minority cinema makes it clear,
by virtue of its critical relationship to dominant languages, that *no*
utterance is individual.

Let me draw upon critiques of Bergson in order to refashion some
of Deleuze's ideas about film, memory, and the social. Bergson's
notion of *durée,* or duration, which is central to Deleuze's theory of

time-image cinema, depends upon a person experiencing the passage of time. As both Benjamin and Emmanuel Levinas pointed out, however, Bergson elides the fact that this experience ends in the individual's death. "Bergson in his conception of the *durée* has become . . . estranged from history," Benjamin writes. "The *durée* from which death has been eliminated has the miserable endlessness of a scroll. Tradition has been excluded from it" (1968a, 185). Levinas too notes that, in its focus on individual perception, Bergson's was a "deathless philosophy," for time is not merely duration as experienced by the individual, but an endless opening onto mystery. "The very relationship with the other is the relationship with the future. It seems to me impossible to speak of time in a subject alone, or to speak of a purely personal duration" (1989, 46, 44). The sense of endlessness and estrangement these writers attribute to Bergson's theory of duration seems distinctly to describe the sort of modernist films that Deleuze tends to privilege. Their sense of alienation is expressed in individual terms and afforded individual, existential solutions (though a vague political movement is often on the horizon). Such works actualize the experience of the *durée* by not permitting images to extend into action, by cutting off all causal relationships. The wandering character of an Antonioni film "has gained in an ability to see what he has lost in action or reaction: he SEES so that the viewer's problem becomes 'What is there to see in the image?' (and not now 'What are we going to see in the next image?')" (Deleuze 1989, 272). Characters in intercultural cinema wander and contemplate, too, as we have seen. But their individual uncharted journeys are more likely, ultimately, to evoke some kind of common struggle. To raise the stakes of the optical image, we might ask what's the point of "finally SEEING" if there's nothing to see? What's the point of having our clichés and preconceptions blown by the intensity of the time-image experience if we have no subsequent course of action? Might there be a more pressing purpose to this act of suspension—such as the claiming of collective experience?

To answer this, I want to return to an exploration of the idea of memory, in a critique more of the Bergsonian roots of Deleuze's philosophy than of Deleuze's philosophy itself. Memory is more like a minefield (or bed of fossils) than like the limpid reflecting pool that Bergson describes. Bergson is too sanguine about an individual's ability to partake in the fullness of experience, moving back and forth between the circuits of perception and recollection with ever-increasing satisfaction, as though at some great phenomenological buffet table. He cannot acknowledge the traumatic effect of memory. Bergson's *pure memory* is unconscious, not in the psychoanalytic sense but in the sense that it is latent until called upon in action. Proust, however, changed the term to *voluntary memory* (*mémoire volontaire*), or remembrance, and added a notion of *involuntary memory* (*mémoire involontaire*), which Benjamin, in turn, called simply memory (1968a, 157–58). Involuntary memory cannot be called up at will but must be brought on by a "shock"— whether this be the fragrance of the madeleine Proust dunked in his cup of tea or, for Deleuze, the assault of the optical image upon the immobilized viewer. Unlike remembrance, Benjamin wrote, (involuntary) memory aims not to protect impressions but to disintegrate them (1968a, 159–60). Remembrance actually shields consciousness from experience. Remembrance is thus very much like the built-up layers of virtual images that compose official history. In contrast, memory, one might say, deterritorializes remembrance. It takes a shock to unroot a memory, to revive a flow of experience. Such a shock is what Deleuze looks for in time-image cinema. What you "SEE," then, in the suspension of motor extension, is a little closer to the repressed *collective* contents of memory than simply a phenomenological Thereness. Experience, as Benjamin (1968b) argued, necessarily involves a connection with the social character of memory, and this connection is increasingly difficult to make where the social character of public life has been undermined. In such circumstances collective memory comes as a shock. Intercultural cinema shows that this process of reconnecting experience with the social is often traumatic.

When the recollection-image is connected to memory, when the stories can finally be told, a film shifts from time-image to movement-image. Such are the moments when Tajiri is finally able to create an image that captures her mother's memory of imprisonment, or when Peck tentatively assigns an image to Lumumba's mysterious death. At these moments there is a great feeling of relief—a relief that is often audible in the audience. The moments when memory returns and stories can finally be told are moments when a collective begins to find its voice. Later, perhaps, these newfound stories cause for celebration.

Powers of the False

People whose lives are built in the movement between two or more cultures are necessarily in the process of transformation. The expression of this experience is impossible not only within hegemonic discourse, but also within any single cultural regime of knowledge. What Deleuze calls "powers of the false" in the cinema are at work when there is no single point that can be referred to as real or true. Recall that in the forking model of time, of present-that-passes and past-preserved, there can be no objective record of the past. The past is preserved among various discursive strata that confront each other with incommensurable truths. Actual and virtual images are constituted around the splitting of time, and their indiscernibility, the inability to designate either as the true image, constitutes the powers of the false. Such a complex of indiscernible images he calls a "crystal-image": the original point at which actual and virtual image reflect each other produces, in turn, a widening circuit of actual and virtual images like a hall of mirrors. When a film reflects upon its own production process, its obstacles, and the very cost of its making, it acts as this sort of catalytic crystal, reflecting the film-that-could-have-been in the complex of its virtual images (Deleuze 1989, 76). Many of the films I have discussed, including *Calendar, Lumumba, History and Memory, Bontoc Eulogy, Talaeen a Junuub, The Watermelon Woman,* and numerous works by Black Audio, are constructed around the setbacks that block their production—the canceled interviews, the amnesiac interviewees, the censored images, the destruction of real archives. All the events that prevent the production of images stimulate circuits of memory. These points across which virtual and actual regard each other function as fossils, preserving the "radioactive" quality of the original contact rather than explain and resolve it.

Cinematic archaeology is not a question of exhuming the "authentic voice" of a minority people—for that would be a unitary voice. And, in fact, it would simply replicate the transparent domination by which a minority is forced to speak in a minority voice. The intercultural artist must undo a double colonization, since the community is colonized both by the master's stories and by its own. It is tempting for exiles to fetishize images of homeland in the melancholic longing for an irrecoverable past. Hamid Naficy suggests that the pain of exile, as well as the fact of censorship, moves political expression into other registers in what is a basically fetishistic process. The question is whether this shift merely freezes a lost cultural experience in fetishized form, or facilitates the ultimately defetishizing process of cultural transformation (Naficy 1993, 130–47). To fetishize the authenticity of one's traditional culture plays into notions that minority cultures can be packaged in easily consumable signs. It reduces the volatile process of memory to the sedimenting process of remembrance. The photographer in *Calendar,* for example, begins as a packager of culture: he buys into the fetishized notion of what is Armenian, slotting the photographs of churches into the known quantity of calendarishness, while valiantly repressing the efforts of his images to speak. Many documentaries, as well as fiction works, about minority history assume that there is an intact oral history out there waiting to be tapped, recorded, and proffered to a community. While such work is important, it assumes that a history can be unproblematically reconstructed. The makers of intercultural cinema, by contrast, destroy myths from the inside. They do this not by extracting a truth from their traditional culture but by evoking the myth of culture as a necessary fiction. Watching *Bontoc Eulogy*, one gradually realizes that Fuentes's ancestral tale could not be true: the history is too far lost ever to be reconstructed. As the end credits reveal, even "his" adorable children are impostors (they are performing magic tricks in the film, which should tip us off). These are powers of the false at work: the painful effect of recovering a lost history is still there, but it becomes all the more powerful because it cannot be reduced to Marlon Fuentes's private story.

The powers of the false only undermine the hegemonic character of official images, clichés, and other totalizing regimes of knowledge. They do not privilege some other experience as truth. John Akomfrah advocates such a refusal to adopt a discourse of truth when he criticizes the imperative that Black artists submit to particular political ends:

People assume that there are certain transcendental duties that Black filmmaking has to perform. . . . Because it is in a state of emergence its means

23. Frame enlargement from *Bontoc Eulogy*

always have to be guerrilla means, war means, signposts of urgency. When that begins to inhibit questions of reflection—doubt, skepticism, intimacy and so on—then the categorical imperative does exactly what it is supposed to do—it imprisons. (in Fusco 1988b, 51)

These words describe the relationship that Tajiri, Fuentes, Peck, and other intercultural filmmakers have with their communities: rather than furnish anthems to solidarity or cheering fictions, they are fundamentally falsifiers, enabling political transformation only by refusing to adhere to a given political agenda. As Robert Reid-Pfarr (1993) has pointed out, a Black community leader like Malcolm X, safely dead, can be elevated to sainthood. Spike Lee's *Malcolm X* (1992) showed that canonization is only a step from commodification, by creating a teleological Malcolm whose life is validated in the context of official history. Black Audio, in contrast, uses the figures of Malcolm X (in *Seven Songs for Malcolm X*, 1993) and Michael X to falsify history.

Rather than appeal to a pre-existing community, Black Audio's films invent a place where African diasporic people come into being. Thus they appeal not to an identity but to the conditions of political transformation. A precise form of political struggle is involved in recognizing that "the primal encounters that are our fantasies of a national history will never be validated by official British history" (in Fusco 1988b, 51). To call these moments "primal encounters" suggests that Black Audio knows them to be fictions, enabling fictions at the foundation of identity. As such, *Who Needs a Heart?*, like many of their other works, is a fabulation, a necessary fiction produced when recorded history is unavailable or useless.

The agents of intercultural cinema are what Deleuze calls "intercessors," real characters who make up fiction. These are not the docile informants of documentary, but resistant characters who dispute the filmmaker's construction of truth at every turn: Jean Rouch's characters with their own stories to tell, Trinh's evasive interlocutors. As David MacDougall points out, the subjects who are most likely to collaborate with documentary filmmakers are those who have agendas of their own. They may be unusually "enquiring of mind," marginal to the community, or already in an intermediary position between community and explorers from outside, but in any case their agendas exceed and transform those of the filmmaker (1994, 32). The intercultural filmmaker mobilizes the stories of these opinionated tellers against official versions of history in absurd or poignant pairings, crystal images that falsify the official story while respecting the partial views of the intercessors. The political stakes of intercession are especially clear in Salloum and Ra'ad's *Talaeen a Junuub* (1993). This video deals with the near-impossibility of representing the Lebanese political situation to outsiders, particularly to North Americans, given the way "Lebanon" is circumscribed by North American political interests and cultural expectations. It is composed almost entirely of interviews with numerous Lebanese political and cultural figures, who are not identified, in a refusal of talking-head authority. One woman in particular refuses outright to discuss her opinions on tape. "I know you will only use my words to make your own point," she says (in Arabic, translated in subtitles). "Even my refusal to speak you will use as part of your argument." By frustrating the videomakers' attempts to mobilize their opinions (with, one suspects, the videomakers' willing consent), the intercessors of *Talaeen a Junuub* delaminate the notion of balanced reportage that is a trope of official history.

Fuentes creates an intercessor in his fictional ancestor Marcot in *Bontoc Eulogy,* using his tale to splinter the history of benign colonial annexation of the Philippines by the United States. Many intercultural works, given their uncertain position between documentary and fiction, position the artist him/herself as intercessor. In *The Perfumed Nightmare* (1978), Kidlat Tahimik creates a nimble

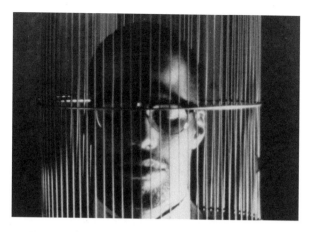

24. Frame enlargement from *Seven Songs for Malcolm X.*
Courtesy of Black Audio Film Collective.

25. Still from *Talaeen a Junuub.* Courtesy of V Tape.

intercessor in his fictional counterpart: Kidlat, the President of the
Werner von Braun Fan Club of his Filipino village of Balián. He
writes to NASA to ask what were Neil Armstrong's first words on the
moon, and duly receives a reply. He opens it excitedly before the
assembled young members of the club and reads the English words
with difficulty. "That's one — small — step for man, one — gee-ant
— leap for . . . man-kind [rhymes with *banking*]." In his role as intercessor, the uncomprehending Kidlat brings down the lofty global
imperialism of NASA with one inspired mispronunciation.

26. Production still from *The Perfumed Nightmare.*
Courtesy of Flower Films.

Storytelling crosses and recrosses between private life and politics, making the boundary between them impossible to locate. As Benjamin suggests, storytellers' knowledge is of a different order from that which passes as official information. As "the communicability of experience decreases," as official knowledge diverges from community experience (or vice versa), the storyteller's practical information becomes increasingly rare and precious (Benjamin 1968b, 84–87). Old people are thus repositories of virtual images; their death is like the loss of a past-that-is-preserved. Their stories, again, are like those "radioactive fossils" that cannot be explained in terms of the geological layer on which they are found.

In *History and Memory,* the intercessor is Tajiri's amnesiac mother, whose memory consists only somatically, in the pain caused by denial and in the memory of water. Her forgetting forces her daughter, the videomaker, to go digging herself, make up stories, indeed become a surrogate rememberer. From a few virtual images Tajiri is able to fabulate a story through the telling of which the family regains their memory and the filmmaker herself achieves an identity. Tajiri reconstitutes herself, as well as the community of Japanese Americans whose story of imprisonment was historically erased, in the process of looking for her mother's memories and the collective memories they metonymize. A double becoming takes place in all works of intercultural cinema, where individual memories are falsified in order to represent the unrepresentable history of the community.

Radioactive Recollection Images

As I have suggested, some of the most powerful images these works create are recollection-images, images that, while they do not correspond to any person's memory, cry out to tell the forgotten histories of which they are the index. Tajiri's investigation of the silent objects that witnessed the internment—a little carved bird, a scrap of tar paper—is one example of reconstituting memories from recollection-images. The ethnographic footage of the mourning women in *Bontoc Eulogy,* and the newsreel footage of the Caribbean women disembarking in *Handsworth Songs,* are material artifacts of these women's presence that call to have the memory coaxed from them. In Julie Dash's *Daughters of the Dust,* a modest piece of okra is a recollection image of the Gullah people's African history. It is brought into a slim connection with the present by the grandmother who remembers its African name, but it is the filmmaker's task to make the connection explicit. Not only visual images, but many things can be recollection-images: a song, a time-traveling object, an evocative but unnameable smell, a texture—as in *Calendar,* when Ashot's question, "Don't you want to touch and feel the churches?" suggests that by calling upon a sense knowledge that cannot be reproduced, namely touch, he can make the churches communicate their history. And *Who Needs a Heart?* draws upon memories inspired by music, by color, by the smell of incense and the feel of fabric.

Like memories, images are multisensory, and cinema uses its audiovisual means to build images around memories. In the following chapters I will examine other ways that intercultural cinema works to reassign histories to these mute objects and unrepresentable senses: to pair the song with a picture, the smell with a sound, the texture with a memory. The knowledges to which these sense memories appeal are not simply instrumental, ready to be translated into verbal information. That translation may take place, but the residual nonverbal knowledges remain a bodily repository that can only be understood in its own terms.

Many of the films and videos I discuss in this chapter appear to deflect overt political issues into matters of personal reminiscence,

27. Frame enlargement from *Calendar.* Photo: Atom Egoyan. Courtesy of Alliance Atlantis Communications.

poetic audiovisual images, and style. Moments of crisis seem to occur when the image is the thinnest, when there is the least available to represent. These works tend to be most powerfully moving—often bringing viewers to tears—at these points where the image reaches exhaustion: where there is only voice-over without picture, as in *History and Memory;* or image with the dialogue muffled, as in *Who Needs a Heart?,* or low-resolution audio- and videotape of a lost loved one played over and over, in *Calendar,* or a delicate drawing standing in for an atrocity, in *Lumumba.* I believe this response is partly caused by the intensity of a contradictory emotional response to the erasure of the dominant cultural imaginary's stock images. This response might be relief that the pressure of these images has been lifted—a pressure of which one might not have been aware, like wearing shoes that are too small. It may be dread of what new images and histories might flow in. Or it may be exhilaration, for the same reason. Of course, responses will vary according to the relationship the viewer has with the dominant stock images. Yet in any case the awareness that an empty space has been cleared into which new cultural imaginings may flow carries a powerful emotional charge.

The emotional response is also in part a reaction to the way these works shift knowledge to different registers. Deleuze's film theory points to the incommensurability between the visual and the verbal: but these films and videos suggest that there exist still other, less easily recorded and coded, orders that nevertheless leave their traces in the audiovisual media of film and video. These might be termed the sensible, or even the spiritual.

Recall that for Bergson "image" is not simply the visual image, but the complex of all sense impressions that a perceived object conveys to a perceiver at a given moment ([1911] 1988, 36–38). Thus images are always both multisensory and embodied. Pure memory does not exist in the body, but it is in the body that memory is activated, calling up sensations associated with the remembered event ([1911] 1988, 179). Bergson's insistence on the carnality of memory is crucial. Yet, as I will argue in chapter 3, he still assigns only a circumscribed role to the body in memory. Bergson undervalues bodily memory because he assumes that memory can be easily actualized when necessary, not acknowledging the individual and social prohibitions on the actualization of memory. In contrast, I argue that memory involves not simply the activation of "pure memory," nor only the bucking up of the individual unconscious, but the traces of collective life that inform the structure of perception. In later chapters I will examine in detail how cultural life informs the memory of the body, in ways that Bergson anticipated but undervalued.

For Deleuze, however, the time-image cinema does not abandon the body. Indeed, it is in the moments that the body is freed to its own gestures that perception is freed from the usual round of action, enabling us to think anew. "Not that the body thinks, but, obstinate and stubborn, it forces us to think, and forces us to think what is concealed from thought, life" (1989, 189). A certain kind of time-image, then, is both experienced in the body and invites a direct experience of time. Deleuze writes that experimental cinema rediscovers the body: both the everyday and the ceremonial body (1989, 191–92). As we have seen, the everyday body, exhausted to the point where it cannot go on, opens cinema to the time-image in the work of Tajiri, Suleiman, Egoyan, and others. As Deleuze noted with regard to French impressionist cinema (1986, 40–45), those affection images that occur in any-spaces-whatever lead to sublimation; to contemplation, rather than the reaction of movement. It is a bodily contemplation, however, not a purely intellectual response. The affection-images of these works invite a bodily response—a shudder, perhaps, as Raoul Peck quietly describes the murder; grief at the sight of the silent mourning women of *Bontoc Eulogy;* agitation as Mathison's sax drowns out the dialogue in *Who Needs a Heart?*—but they do not extend into movement as usual. Rather they are located among irrational cuts, black screens, divergent image and sound, and other time-image devices that invite continued, embodied contemplation. The affection-image, then, is the domain of what Deleuze calls the ceremonial cinema.

The ceremonial body in intercultural films and videos is intro-duced at the moment when all other action has become impossible. Ritual connects individual experience with collective experience, activating collective memory in the body. In an overwhelming num-ber of these works, the search for memory images turns out to be a process of collective mourning: of ritual. Some of these rituals are overtly staged as such: Reece Auguiste's *Mysteries of July* (1991), for example, is structured around a vigil for young Black men who died in police custody. Tania Cypriano's *Ex-Voto* (1990) is a video performed as a ritual of thanks to Nossa Senhora da Aparecida, the patron saint of Brazil, for sparing her life in a terrible fire: she offers flowers and lights candles to the video camera as though at a shrine. Paul Wong's *Chinaman's Peak: Walking the Mountain* (1995) is a mourning ritual, performed for the camera, for his lover who died. Zachery Longboy's *water into fire* (1993) is also a ritual to acknowl-edge the destruction that AIDS has wrought in his community: but, as rituals do, it draws strength from loss and from his faith in the life springing from the earth. The three women of *Who Needs a Heart?* perform rituals twice, once in jest and once in earnest. In an early scene, the three stage a scene in Millie's film: "After the I-Ching Naomi, Faith and I discover Africa." Naomi holds up a string of cowrie shells for Faith to kiss, like a rosary; Faith kisses it and then laughingly pulls it into her mouth; Millie, angry, bursts into tears. Later, after the news of Michael X's execution, Faith's lover Louis kills himself. The two black women support the body of Louis's white lover as she sobs; they burn incense around her head; and Naomi bends Faith's head down to kiss the coffin. These moments of intimacy between the women are memorable both for their unholy mingling of sacred and sensual acts and for the sense that through ritual they are founding a body at least as powerful as, and perhaps subversive of, the armed strength of the film's male radicals.[5]

28. Still from *Chinaman's Peak: Walking the Mountain.*
Courtesy of Video Out.

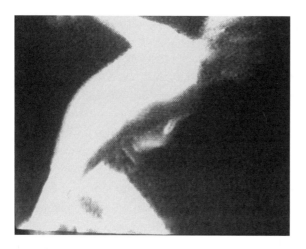

29. Still from *water into fire.* Courtesy of Video Out.

Shauna Beharry's *Seeing Is Believing* (1991), as I discuss in the next chapter, was made as an act of grieving for the artist's mother, who died once physically and once again in the inability of photographs to represent her. Similarly, works like *Lumumba: The Death of a Prophet, History and Memory: For Akiko and Takashige, Bontoc Eulogy, The Way to My Father's Village,* and *Looking for Langston* honor and mourn the filmmakers' wandering ghosts, as their titles suggest. *Calendar, Siskyavi, Homage by Assassination,* and many other works wring a collective grief from individual stories. The

30. Frame enlargement from *Who Needs a Heart?*

optical images that represent lost lives and vanished histories engender a cry to the heavens, a hymn to the ancestors, a memorial to
all that was destroyed in the histories of colonial subjugation and
official forgetting. And let us remember that rituals, including rituals of mourning, are not final acts but beginnings.

In *Lumumba*, Raoul Peck's wanderings through endless airport
corridors seem to displace the deep grief about the murder of a great
leader and the deferral of African democracy onto a bodily sensation of repetition and numbness. In *Bontoc Eulogy*, the grief of an
anonymous mourner in an antique ethnographic film elicits a similar emotion in the body of the viewer. In *Calendar*, the protagonist's
willful loss of contact with his beloved and his culture of origin are
expressed in the tactile opacity of low-grade video. In *Who Needs
a Heart?*, information about Black struggles in Britain is withheld
only to re-emerge, like secrets whispered into ears of corn, in a
susurration of music and color. In *History and Memory: For Akiko
and Takashige*, the vivid sensory image of filling a canteen with cool
water is all that remains of four years of imprisonment. These are
not simple acts of displacement: they also reveal knowledge that has
been stored only in the memory of the body. When the verbal and
visual archives are silent, information is revealed that was never
verbal or visual to begin with.

2

The memory of things

[The past is] somewhere beyond the reach of the intellect,
and unmistakably present in some material object (or in the
sensation which such an object arouses in us), though we have
no idea which one it is. As for that object, it depends entirely on
chance whether we come upon it before we die or whether we
never encounter it.

—Marcel Proust, *Swann's Way*

This chapter examines films and videos that excavate memories
from objects. Movements through space and time can be read in the
image; movement among cultures, like the passage of time, creates
disjunctive, illegible images. These images are all a particular kind
of recollection-image, which I term the *recollection-object:* an irreducibly material object that encodes collective memory. They can
in addition be variously considered fetishes, fossils, and transnational objects. What is important about all these object-images is that
they condense time within themselves, and that in excavating them
we expand outward in time. To continue to use Deleuzian terminology, when an image surfaces from another place, another culture,
it disrupts the coherence of the plane of the present culture. When
Deleuze writes, "The present itself exists only as an infinitely contracted past which is constituted at the extreme point of the already-
there" (1989, 98), the words "infinitely contracted past" seem to
describe the souvenir object, that stubborn survivor from another
place-time that brings its volatile contents to the present. An object
in a film or tape is a particular sort of recollection-image that calls up

different pasts for different people. Where Citizen Kane had Rose-bud, Rea Tajiri has a wooden bird, Shauna Beharry a silk sari, Victor Masayesva a stolen kachina mask: objects whose incommensurable pasts are the product not only of personal history but of intercultural displacement. The heirloom, the souvenir, the mass-manufactured object contain different and incommensurable stories of ownership, fantasy, and labor depending on who looks at these objects. Intercultural cinema often takes things for its images, presents them in all their fossil-like strangeness, and sometimes, by reconnecting them with their past, neutralizes their disturbing power.

Objects that travel along paths of human diaspora and inter-national trade encode cultural displacement. Even commodities, though they are subject to the deracinating flow of the transnational economy and the censoring process of official history, retain the power to tell the stories of where they have been. Intercultural cin-ema moves through space, gathering up histories and memories that are lost or covered over in the movement of displacement, and pro-ducing new knowledges out of the condition of being between cul-tures. To coin another term, by adapting D. W. Winnicott's theory of the transitional object, they can be considered *transnational objects.* The transitional object is any external object that a person partially incorporates in the process of reorganizing its subjectivity (Winni-cott [1951] 1958). So it seems useful to suggest that "transnational object" might describe the objects that are created in cultural trans-lation and transcultural movement. Many important films focus on the traffic in people. Some of these people may also be classified as "transnational objects," in that they are traded like commodities between nations as refugees, guest workers, "comfort women" and other sex workers, or the vast undocumented workforce that under-pins international commerce.[1] Needless to say, films and tapes about traveling workers are themselves only a fraction of the vast num-bers of works that trace the movement of immigrants and exiles, resulting in transformations at least as fundamental for the nation to which these people travel as for the people themselves. What I focus on in this chapter is a subgenre of what has been called trans-national independent cinema (Naficy 1994; Zimmermann and Hess 1997). If that genre focuses primarily on the diasporic movements of immigrants and exiles, these works excavate the traces left by things that "emigrate" due to similar global flows of capital, power, and desire. If the high-speed torrent of information and capital is a relentless tide, then most of the movements to which this chapter is devoted are undercurrents, carried with the tide but moving against it, or eddies created around idiosyncratic points in the flow.

As in the previous chapter, most of my examples in this chapter are documentary films and videos. Documentaries claim the privileged position of representing reality. Consequently, it is especially pressing for them to explain the transformations and disarticulations of reality under the pressures of intercultural movements. But more importantly for my purposes in this chapter, documentary's privileged relation to the real extends to the material connection to the profilmic event itself—a basically fetishistic relationship, in the anthropological sense. This material and fetishistic quality of documentary will be the focus of the second part of this chapter, in which I discuss the work of Shauna Beharry, an artist who uses video but whose encompassing medium is ritual and performance. Beharry is a third-generation Canadian of Indian descent whose work focuses on the loss of language and of cultural reference that happens with displacement, the paradox that she still carries cultural references in her body, and the sensuous or spiritual experiences that challenge translation. The stake of this exploration is to recognize the complexity of the fetishized objects that move between cultures, how they are created, how they serve memory, and how they may self-destruct when their usefulness is ended.

Postcolonial cinema responds to colonial fetishism, or the seizing upon aspects of the colonized culture in order to maintain a controlling distance from it, not only at the level of narrative content. These works also redeem fetishized objects by finding values in them that are unrecognized in the colonial context. They may show how the meaning of an object changes as it circulates in new contexts. They may restore the "radioactivity" of an object that has been sanitized or rendered inert through international trade. They may depict the object in such a way that it is protected from the fetishizing or commodifying gaze. Or they may propose a nonfetishizing form of looking, one that invites the "viewer" to experience the object not so much visually as through a bodily contact.

As well as the transnational object, I use models of the fetish and the fossil to describe how objects encode both the discursive shifts and the material conditions of displacement. Meaning, I will argue, is encoded in objects not metaphorically but through physical contact. Following historians and theorists of gifts and commodities, I suggest that objects are not inert and mute but that they tell stories and describe trajectories. Cinema is capable not only of following this process chronologically but also of discovering the value that inheres in objects: the discursive layers that take material form in them, the unresolved traumas that become embedded in them, and the history of material interactions that they encode. I go on to argue that cinema may be considered not a simulacrum but a material artifact of transnational migration. This argument involves a reconsideration of the notion of *aura* as a way to talk about how objects encode social processes.

Of the many theories of the fetish that operate in anthropology, Marxist analysis, and psychoanalysis, I focus on those that explicitly attend to it in terms of a series of historical, intercultural displacements. All fetishes are translations into a material object of some sort of affect; the fetish described by psychoanalysis in only one of these. Some objects embody memory as well as labor: theories of fetishism describe how a value comes to inhere in objects that is not reducible to commodification. I will argue that intercultural relations are necessarily fetishistic, although clearly fetishes are not necessarily intercultural.

What I wish to gain by using both the terms *fetish* and *fossil* is to forge a meeting place between Deleuze's and Benjamin's particular recollection-objects, both of which trace part of their meaning to Bergson. In this chapter I will often use only the term *fetish.* But in fact I wish to argue that the two terms are functionally similiar: or, at least, that the fetish works in the same way as the "radioactive fossil," in Deleuze's casual term for a certain kind of cinematic image (1989, 113). To explain this, let me define that crucial Benjaminian term, *aura.*

Benjamin wrote that aura is the quality in an object that makes our relationship to it like a relationship with another human being. It seems to look back at us (1968a, 188). Marx, and following him reluctantly, Benjamin, attempted to demystify the fetishistic character of auratic objects by showing that they gained their power from the human presences and material practices that constructed them. I say "reluctantly" because Benjamin was unwilling to relinquish the power of the auratic object as an object. It cannot be reduced to a narrative, as I will insist throughout this chapter. Aura is the sense an object gives that it can speak to us of the past, without ever letting us completely decipher it. It is a brush with involuntary memory, memory that can only be arrived at through a shock. We return again and again to the auratic object, still thirsty (187, referring to Paul Valéry), because it can never completely satisfy our desire to recover that memory. Hence the sense that an auratic object maintains its distance no matter how closely we embrace it: it is distant from us in time even as it is present in space. Benjamin remained a Marxist in his insistence that the auratic character of things was not simply their ability to awaken memories in an individual; not a "premature, merely private reconciliation with a fallen world" (Hansen 1987, 190), but the resonance of the reified social world in a fragment. Auratic objects, then, are fragments of the social world that cannot be read from on high but only in the witness of the object.

Benjamin's fetish and Deleuze's fossil have in common a disturbing light, an eerily beckoning luminosity. In the fetish it is called aura, in the fossil it is called radioactivity. Aura is what makes the fetish volatile, because it incites us to memory without ever bringing memory back completely. Similarly, when a fossil is "radioactive" that is because it hints that the past it represents is not over, it beckons the viewer to excavate the past, even at his or her peril.

Recollection-objects

Cinema treats the recollection-object as an especially "hard," opaque recollection-image. It confronts such initially inscrutable objects and attempts to read them by connecting them to memory. The works I discuss in this chapter document the process of translation by decoding the displacements, and the social relations, that objects carry within them. Many more or less narrative intercultural films use recollection-objects as part of the mise-en-scène, where they appear as mute witnesses to a character's history. In Martine Attile's *Dreaming Rivers* (1988), for example, the British children of a Caribbean woman stand at her deathbed, reflecting upon their memories of her. Whispered voice-over gossip suggests that she emigrated for love, only to be abandoned to "England—it's *so cold*." They comment on the objects in her room, framed photographs, dried flowers, lace, shell necklaces. The son says, "I was ashamed of the things in this house, this junk." The trendy, light-skinned daughter says disparagingly, "It's become quite fashionable: nouveau Negro." Their dark-skinned sister, who was obviously closer to her mother, defends her: "She cherished these things, she felt proud." In flashbacks we see their mother slowly combing and arranging her hair, bathing her feet with oil and rose petals, and emotionally looking over the photographs. But the whispered voice-over gossip in Creole and English does not allow her peace. In a bright, flowered dress recalling the warm country of her birth, the woman desperately lugs down a suitcase. Then, haunted by the whispering voices, she writhes in a dance of agony, crying, "Englaaand!" Yet finally she rests, bowing to the ground, palms facing up as though in renunciation. The film suggests that the intensified presence of ritualized objects could salve the woman's double heartbreak of exile and abandonment, but also they could become unbearable reminders in this cold country.

At other times a recollection-object is severed from the narrative in order to emphasize its witnessing quality. Such an object appears in Rea Tajiri's *History and Memory: For Akiko and Takashige* (1991). Having succeeded in locating the barracks at Poston where her family was quartered during the internment—in fact, having been led there by instinct—Tajiri brings back a piece of tar paper from the roof of the building. The worn, grayish object is displayed against a black background, like a jewel, even though it is not much at all to look at. A title reads "Tarpaper, Poston barrack." The tar paper's value is that it was on the scene of the events of the internment that Tajiri's mother cannot remember.[2] One could say the piece of tar paper, having been exposed to those events, "photographed" them and just needs to be developed: rectangular and gray, it even looks a bit like an old photograph. Tajiri's task, with this as with other mute objects in the tape, is to develop images from them.

A film may fail to connect a recollection-object to memory, so that the object remains illegible, a fossil trace of forgotten or inexplicable histories. These failures are just as informative as successful connections are, for by maintaining the "incompossibility" of different cultural discourses they demonstrate the unending struggle over meaning that characterizes intercultural life. Such a film is Gary Kibbins's *Finagnon* (1995), which begins its historical search with an odd artifact of postcolonial relations, a French-language reader for schoolchildren in the Republic of Benin. Kibbins approaches the

31. Still from *History and Memory: For Akiko and Takashige*

32. Frame enlargement from *Finagnon.* Courtesy of V Tape.

textbook from a number of angles to try to elicit its history, but the book remains mute. It hints at the colonial relations that engendered it, but it is unable to call up the experience of the African schoolchildren who read it.

Recollection-objects need not have a primarily visual relation to the originary event they represent. Consider Proust's *tisane* with dunked madeleine: a smell fetish, whose perfume unlocked volumes of memories. As in the previous chapter, in examining the histories contained in these images, I find that the meanings that are lost and found in the course of (space or time) travel are often expressed in terms of nonaudiovisual sense knowledges. In chapters 3 and 4 I will develop the significance of these sense knowledges in cinema and their implications in an intercultural context.

Fossils

Fossils acquire their meaning by virtue of an originary contact. A fossil is the indexical trace of an object that once existed, its animal or vegetable tissue now become stone. Consider how similar this is to the photographic process. Fossils are created when an object makes contact with the witnessing material of earth. Photographs are created when light reflected by an object makes contact with the witnessing material of film. In both cases, this contact transforms the material's surface so that it becomes a witness to the life of the object, even after the latter has decayed. Created in one layer of history, the fossil witness is gradually covered with more sedimental layers. But instead of disintegrating it solidifies and becomes transformed. So when some earthquake happens years later or continents away, these objects surface, bearing witness to forgotten histories. As C. Nadia Seremetakis writes, objects invested with sensory memory "are expressions of non-synchronicity which become material encounters with cultural absence and possibility" (1994, 12). These objects are that special kind of recollection images, fossil images, discussed in the previous chapter. To summarize briefly, the metaphor of the "radioactive fossil" describes the unsettling quality of certain inexplicable but powerful cinematic images. This is how Deleuze describes a cinematic image that seems to embody a past that is incommensurable with the present the image depicts. By virtue of its indexical character, cinema allows unresolved pasts to surface in the present of the image. To Deleuze, fossils are not cold stone objects but rather live, dangerous things. Images are fossil beds, where the fossils are those strange and stubborn images that seem to arise from a reality that is at odds with its surroundings—"memory fragments that surface repeatedly to consciousness but are mysterious in their meaning" (Sternburg 1994, 178). These images refer to the power of recollection-images to embody different pasts. When an image is all that remains of a memory, when it cannot be "assigned a present" by an act of remembering but simply stares up at one where it has been unearthed, then that image is a fossil of what has been forgotten. It is possible, though as Deleuze warned, dangerous, to examine these images and learn the histories they have witnessed.

Deleuze uses the term *fossil* only casually in the cinema books, but I have seized upon it because it indicates the material quality of the recollection-image. For Benjamin, *fossil* is much more complex. His unfinished *Passagen-Werk* reads the entire history of post-industrial Europe in the fragmentary and forgotten objects of the nineteenth-century shopping arcades of Paris, which he compares to "caves containing fossils of an animal presumed extinct," namely consumers in the early era of capitalism (quoted in Buck-Morss 1989, 64). Small, forgotten, or seemingly frivolous objects capture Benjamin's fascination throughout his writings, as when he wanders Moscow, ignoring its heroic Communist monuments in favor of toy stores and sweet shops (Benjamin 1986). Yet beyond idiosyncrasy, the power of Benjamin's attention to objects is that he sees in them a power to witness history that narratives lack.[3] In the debris of industrial culture he reads the culture's own fragility (Buck-Morss 1989, 170). Thus fossils in Benjamin's usage bear forth the history of capitalism as a natural history.

Fetishes

I would like to build a recuperative notion of fetishism for a discussion of intercultural cinema. Certainly an oppressive kind of fetishism is at work in postcolonial relations. Fetishism aptly describes the violent colonialist impulse to freeze living cultures and suspend them outside of time. Critics such as Edward Said (1979), Johannes Fabian (1983), Trinh T. Minh-ha (1989, 1993), and Homi Bhabha (1994b) have skewered this fetishistic quality of colonialism decisively. Without forgetting these critiques, I want to claim other meanings of fetishism in order to describe the transformations that occur in postcolonial and transnational movement.

In fetishism, power does not inhere in beings but flows among them. Fetish objects can encode knowledges that become buried in the process of temporal or geographic displacement but are volatile when reactivated by memory. Fetishes get their power not by *representing* that which is powerful but through *contact* with it, a contact whose materiality has been repressed. As such, fetishes, like fossils, have an indexical relation to an original scene like that of a photograph. Photographs, of course, are fetishistic in that they hypostatize an instantaneous visual aspect of a scene before the camera, forgetting all its other aspects.

Benjamin's genealogy of the term *fetish* is shared with other neo-Marxist uses of the term. It functions similarly to his usage of *fossil,* but it brings in other connotations. In the essay "On Some Motifs in Baudelaire" he continues the argument, developed throughout the *Passagen-Werk,* that collective life can be manifest in objects. In addition, following Freud, he stresses the most powerful memory fragments are those that encode an incident that remains inaccessible to conscious memory (1968a, 160), that is, fetishes. Here Benjamin demonstrates the meeting between Marxist and psychoanalytic understandings of the fetish: the fetish object encodes truths of collective life, and these truths can be discovered only through a shock that reaches the unconscious. Although this meeting is important, psychoanalytic understandings of the fetish remain less useful for my purposes than neo-Marxist and anthropological approaches.

The fetish is a product specific to intercultural encounters, as William Pietz (1987) argues in his impressive archaeology of the term. The etymology of the word *fetish* describes a long and complex history of colonization, appropriation, and translation. Briefly, Pietz traces the transformation of the Portuguese word *feitiço* from its use in Christian witchcraft law to the word *Fetisso* (also Portuguese, from the pidginization of *feitiço*) used by explorers in the part of West Africa that they called Guinea. Rather than transliterate an African term, Portuguese traders applied a Portuguese word to African cultural practices. In the later construction, "fetishism" was the sort of practice that invested lifelike powers in objects themselves, powers attained through physical contact. It came to be distinguished from idolatry because the objects concerned did not *represent* deities but in their very materiality held godlike powers. For example, the feather of a sacrificial chicken is a sacred fetish because the chicken is sacred; the relics of saints, preserved fingers or scraps of cloth, gain their value as a fetish through contact with the saint. The fetishistic relationship is between two sacred objects, not a deity and an object. Thus fetishes, to European intellectuals' way of thinking, were stubbornly nontranscendental.

The notion of the fetish was mobilized during a period of imperial expansion. Pietz argues that this notion played a significant role in establishing European preconceptions about human consciousness and the material world, preconceptions on which the disciplinary human sciences that arose in the nineteenth century were founded. For example, as he describes, the travelogues of Dutch merchants such as Willem Bosman portrayed African fetish worship as the perversion of the sort of rational self-interest that they saw as "the natural organizing principle of good social order" (Pietz 1988, 107). These writers' particular narratives were seized upon for general illustrative purposes by Enlightenment intellectuals, and also by Marx (Pietz 1993). Marx's choice to compare the abstracting process of capitalism with what was seen as the irrational practice of fetishism was a brilliantly perverse way to align materialism with rationality. However, this tactic elided the intercultural roots of the "primitive" practice Marx appropriated to bolster his critique of capitalism.

The term *fetishism* was first used by a particular stratum of Europeans to describe peasant superstitions, as well as Catholic ritual (Pietz 1987). Only later did it come to describe the practices of Africans. *Fetishism,* then, originated as a term used to separate the ruling Protestant, protocapitalist groups from others both outside *and* within the culture. The early use of "fetishism" to describe the practices of both European peasants and West Africans reaffirmed the emerging European powers' belief that, unlike themselves, these groups were irrational, incapable of abstraction, and mired in the body. Peter Stallybrass and Allon White (1986) argue in a similar vein that the rise of the European bourgeoisie necessitated a process of distantiation both inter- and intraculturally. In order to consolidate an identity that was capable of "rising above" the merely bodily, the bourgeoisie projected its own unacceptable excesses elsewhere, separating itself from the carnivalesque practices of the peasants. Colonial expansion exacerbated this process, as an even more primitive other became available for the disgusted/desiring projections of the European middle classes. Thus in some ways the forbidden object of desire is already an intercultural one, for the desire that the bourgeoisie had forbidden itself became embodied in primitivist fantasies.

It is important to note that intercultural fetishism is initiated both by the fetishizers and the fetishized: in this case, between the Portuguese traders and African middlemen who "explained" African spiritual practices to them. Pietz suggests that West African informants themselves used the term *Fetisso* to describe their practices to the Portuguese, thus pre-emptively translating an aspect of their cultural practice to the Europeans. This pre-emptive fetishism had the effect of shielding actual ceremonial practices from scrutiny.[4] It is in this sense that the discourse of the fetish "has always been a critical discourse about the false objective values of a culture from which the speaker is personally distanced" (1985, 14), always an intercultural discourse. Such an understanding of the process of fetishism avoids thinking of the fetishized person, object, or culture as simply the victim of cultural appropriation. Instead it acknowledges that fetishism is a mutual act that reveals information about both participants in the exchange.

The archaeological process of discovering the meaning of such historical fetish objects recognizes that they cannot be deciphered with finality, but must be treated as keys to a particular historical moment. Fetishes are material microcosms; as Adorno wrote, they are "objective constellations in which the social represents itself" (quoted in Mitchell 1986, 204). Pietz similarly describes the fetish in neo-Marxist terms as the nexus of a specific intercultural encounter. "The fetish must be viewed as proper to no historical field other than that of the history of the word itself, and to no discrete society or culture, but to a cross-cultural situation formed by the ongoing encounter of the value codes of radically different social orders. In Marxist terms, one might say that the fetish is situated in the space of cultural revolution" (1987, 10).

Fetishes and Fossils of Transnational Life

Fossils, fetishes, and recollection-objects should again remind us of the dialectical images Benjamin found in the nineteenth-century shopping arcades, the cracks in material reality in which one can read repressed histories. Susan Buck-Morss suggests that "fetish" and "fossil" both describe the commodity (1989, 211), in its concretization of history and concentration of affect. Such objects are rubble in the ruin of recent history. They are not only the wish images of past histories, but also the material of which "a new order can be constructed" (212). Bricoleurs—people who take the rubble of another time or place, invest it with new significance, and put it to new purposes—create the possibilities of new history. The displaced person is the preeminent bricoleur, asserts *The Last Angel of History* (1995), John Akomfrah's film about Black science fiction. The film surveys African diaspora futurist artists from the late (and mourned) jazzman Sun Ra to the novelist Octavia Butler, interspersing them with a Black flâneur figure who wanders in a sort of industrial wasteland. He says in passing, "African people have always done science fiction, because we've always been able to see the holes in the present." The bricoleur is able to find creative potential in the ruins of another culture because these objects, surrounded by a forcefield of imperfect translation, acquire a transformational quality in their travels.

Fetishes and fossils, then, are two kinds of objects that condense cryptic histories within themselves and that gather their peculiar power by virtue of a prior contact with some originary object. Fetishes and fossils are nodes, or knots, in which historical, cultural, and spiritual forces gather with a particular intensity. They translate experience through space and time in a material medium, encoding the histories produced in intercultural traffic. This view of the fetish as an object produced in the encounter between cultures strongly underscores Homi Bhabha's characterization of colonial stereotypes as fetishes: sites where cultural difference is fixed, but in their very fixity belie the instability of the encounter (1994b, 70–75). The intercultural space in which fetishes and fossils are produced is always charged with power; it is not a neutral ground where meanings can be remade with impunity.

If we understand fetishes as properly the product not of a single culture, but of the encounter between two, then we see how fetishes are produced not only in the course of built-up time, but also in the disjunctive movement through space. Colonial power relations in particular, with their propensity for crossbreeding indigenous and imported meanings, are prime sites for the production of these objects. Where two or more material discourses crash together are formed any number of peculiar artifacts: consider the Korean peasant ceramics that were taken up as aesthetic objects by their sixteenth-century Japanese colonizers (and the aestheticized copies that ensued). The famous tulip boom and bust in seventeenth-century Holland was the result of a national obsession with a flower of Persian origin, which Dutch importers crossbred again and again to achieve rarefied, arcane variations—tulips of strange colors, tulips exposed to viruses to produce tattered, variegated petals. National dishes such as mulligatawny stew (Britain) or *rijstaffel* (Holland) translate the cuisine of the colonies for local palates. These are some examples of fetishlike objects that are the product of two- (or more) directional, power-inflected appropriation and retranslation.

Postcolonial life is producing fetishes at record speed as people become displaced, especially as they emigrate to their former colonizers' lands. Cultural transformation in diaspora is usually neither a full-blown assimilation nor an utterly random "hybrid," though of course both those patterns occur. More often, cultural practices pass through a selection process that, like the baggage scales at international airports, determines what is jettisoned and what is kept in the passage. What travels best is usually high class and patriarchy-friendly. It is the peasant practices, the women's practices, and often the sensory practices, that go first; the bags of spice that spill from the overpacked luggage onto the waiting room floor. Diaspora intellectuals have usually already met the requirements for fitting into Western academic and cultural establishments, such as a cash base, a Western education, fluency in Romance languages, and membership in their indigenous elite.[5]

The interstitial space of the fetish produces meaning, lots of meanings, but they are built on incomprehension. For example, the *bindi* that Shauna Beharry's mother, like all Hindi married women, wore on her forehead signifies exotic Oriental desirability in popular erotica in the West. As she describes it in *Seeing Is Believing* (1991), Beharry's own skin takes on meanings over which she has no control. White people ask this brown-skinned Canadian woman where she comes from. If the response "Moosejaw" doesn't satisfy them, then, in order to answer, Beharry must undertake an excavation of the Indian heritage that sets her apart. Her body is inscribed with a language she must laboriously learn to read. That is, she must learn to read for the purpose of translating back to people who assume the right to know things in their own language. When she finds, for example, that she is not "typical Indian," that her skin and eyes are different because her grandfather was Chinese—well, not exactly Chinese, he was from Hong Kong—and no, she doesn't speak Urdu

or Hindi, she grew up in Ireland—the weight of explanation becomes overwhelming.

This burden of explanation is why people who are moving between cultures find that their luggage gets heavier and heavier. Their
familiar objects are fossilizing. What was taken for granted in one
culture becomes incomprehensible in another, and it becomes the
immigrant's responsibility to build up and to excavate those layers
of impossible translation.

Postcolonial history is necessarily an investigation of fossils. We
are constantly discovering inexplicable factoids on the surface of
represented history that invite us to cut through the layers and connect them to their source, cutting between private recollection and
official discourse. More often than not, the investigator contracts
their infectious quality, finding that her own history is based on partial truths. The "piece of the rock" that contains our own lives, con-
stituting them both in terms of and separate from dominant history,
disintegrates into unstable, seething sands, and we have no choice
but to sift through, looking for clues.

Deleuze's hallucinatory list of the qualities of the fossil, especially its destructive potential, resonates strongly with Pietz's (and
Benjamin's; see Buck-Morss 1989) intimations that fetishes are revo-
lutions just waiting to happen. Both fossil and fetish, in the senses
I have described, carry within them histories that, once unraveled,
make the present untenable. The "radioactive" aspect of these objects is that they may arouse other memories, causing inert presences on the most recent layer of history themselves to set off chains
of associations that had been forgotten. Yet I would like to reconsider the contaminating and carcinogenic connotations of the image
of radioactivity. Certainly these image fossils from other times or
other places are volatile, and will behave uncontrollably when they
are exposed to viewers, just as radioactive materials decompose and
emit energy when they are exposed. But the danger is in realizing
that there exist histories that are contradictory to those one knows,
cultural knowledges that shake the security of one's own cultural
position in the world. This is an unsettling, de-composing experience, and it is certainly destructive of firmly ethnocentric views, for
example. But I like to think of it as a benign form of "contamination," such as what happens when a perfume blows one's way (or, to
stay with the fossil metaphor, when a long-preserved funerary un-

guent startles archaeologists with the immediacy of its fragrance). One cannot avoid smelling it, it pervades one's immediate environment and inevitably reroutes one's thoughts, it is at the same time both exigent and ambient. The cinematic fossils I examine here do indeed have an unsettling effect, but they are only as destructive as the material they assault is rigid.

Indexical Witness: Cinema as Fetish and Fossil

As I stated earlier, transnational objects are not only discursive productions; their meaning cannot be separated from their materiality.[6] Fetishes resist abstraction. They insist on the materiality of the original presence to which they refer. Hence the dismissal of Catholic "fetishism" by Protestants and commodity fetishism by Marx. Their value is not transferable. They cannot be traded for money. They do not symbolically represent power; they physically embody it. To think of the moving image as a fetish or fossil implies understanding it not as a representation, which is volatile only because of the projections brought to it, but as an emissary, which is volatile to the degree that the viewer/receiver has access to the materiality of its original scene.

The implication of the notion of contact that underlies both the fossil and the fetish is that representation and knowledge are not to be explained exclusively on the level of language, but also participate in contact with the object represented. The objects I discuss here encode material conditions of displacement as well as discursive ruptures. Representation and knowledge participate in contact with the object represented. Their substrate is not solely a "referent" but also a material touchstone. Clearly, then, in my use the tropes of fossil and fetish operate on a fairly concrete level. Both can be used simply as heuristic devices based on a notion of contact with some original, powerful object. I want to use them as more than that, however. The notion of the fetish, in particular, I find epistemologically powerful because it is constituted from a physical, rather than mental, contact between objects; it is not a metaphor.

André Bazin (1967) famously described photography as an imprint of the world, a trace of material presence like a death mask. This is the fetishlike/fossil-like quality that is at work in cinema: it is the trace another material object leaves on the surface of the film (or encodes in video's electronic witness). This fact is what gives film its representational power, just as a fetish (in the religious sense) obtains its power by carrying the trace of another material object. The use made of indexicality varies, to be sure, from evidentiary proof to mere ghostlike trace of the profilmic real. As Maren Stange (1994) notes, the essential qualities of photographic indexicality must be understood in the context of their historical use, the value placed upon indexicality at different periods. Currently there is a lot of suspicion regarding indexical evidence, at least among Western academics.[7] Yet I would like to suggest that the indexical capacities of an image or object are very important for those who have few sources of evidence, few witnesses to their stories. Thus the broad definition of documentary, as a cinema whose indexical relation to the real is of central importance (Nichols 1991, chapter 5), is still crucial to intercultural cinema. Any kind of cinema has this relation to the profilmic event, but only documentary claims this relation to the real as one of its defining qualities. By understanding the indexicality of cinema as a fetishlike or fossil-like quality, I mean to emphasize that this trace of the real in cinema is embalmed in layers of historical use and interpretation, which obscure and ultimately transform any original meaning the object might have had.

Of course, these issues are not exclusive to intercultural cinema. All cinema has a fetishistic relationship to its object. All cinema is transnational in that its audiences will not be able to decode its images perfectly, insofar as they originate from other places and times. Intercultural cinema, however, takes these issues as its explicit subject, and the stakes of whether, how, and by whom its fetish-images and fossil-images can be translated are especially high.

Film's ability to animate objects, indeed to anthropomorphize them, captivated early theorists of cinema. Béla Balász devoted a chapter of his *Theory of the Film* ([1923] 1972) to the close-up. He considered that close-ups imparted a physiognomic quality to still objects. His tender, almost maudlin tone underscores the close-up's fetishlike ability to bear witness to the invisible:

The first new world discovered by the film camera in the days of the silent film was the world of very small things visible only from short distances, the hidden life of little things. . . . By means of the close-up the camera in the days of the silent film revealed also the hidden mainsprings of a life we thought we knew very well. . . .

. . . The close-up shows your shadow on the wall with which you have lived all your life and which you scarcely knew; it shows the speechless face and fate of the dumb objects that live with you in your room and whose fate is bound up with your own. ([1923] 1948, 55)

Further on Balász notes, "Close-ups are often dramatic revelations of what is really happening under the surface of appearances" (56). Balász attributed to the image the power to materialize invisible phenomena, to put a face on them. A close-up shot of an inanimate object or space, he suggests, is capable of capturing the subtle realm of nonorganic life. This need not sound mystical if one considers objects to embody the social in their very status as objects, and not merely as discourse hardened into things (see Pels 1995; Sereme-takis 1994).

Such anthropomorphic theories fell into disfavor with the rise of semiotic analyses of cinema: they certainly seem to appeal to the qualities of the image that "exceed" the power of the sign (see, for example, Barthes [1957] 1972, for a critique of this fetishistic quality of the cinema). But for the same reason, Balász's theory is useful to a renewed discussion, not of how film fetishizes its objects, but how film can be a fetishistic medium. The physiognomic quality Balász attributes to images is echoed in Deleuze's discussion of faciality (*visagéité*) in cinema. Faciality is the intensification of affect in an image whose motor extension is limited: "It is this combination of a reflecting, immobile unity and of intensive expressive movements which constitutes the affect. . . . Each time we discover these two poles in something . . . we can say that this thing has been treated as a face [*visage*]: it has been 'envisaged' or rather 'faceified' [*visagéi-fiée*], and in turn it stares at us" (Deleuze 1986, 87–88). The facelike image is dense with affect that has been deposited in it from else-where and that resists analysis. As Patricia Pisters (1998, 93) notes, because the affection-image, of which the facial image is a subset, reduces the spatial coordinates of the third dimension, it opens up to the fourth dimension of time and the fifth dimension of spirit. A facial image, Deleuze suggests, returns the look: this is, of course, a characteristic of auratic objects, as I will discuss.

To understand how history is encoded in objects, it is useful to re-
fine Marxist theorists' discussion of fetishism and representation
with anthropological theories of exchange. The generations following Marcel Mauss's ([1950] 1990) germinal study of gift economies
have tended to focus on the process of exchange itself. However,
lately anthropologists have also been returning to the question of
the objects of exchange themselves. Arjun Appadurai (1986), Igor
Kopytoff (1986), Annette Weiner (1992), Nicholas Thomas (1991),
and C. Nadia Seremetakis (1994) all describe the movement of objects within and between cultures as not only a market exchange but
also a cultural one; this circulation produces, in Kopytoff's words, a
"cultural biography of things." Their approach permits a certain ob-
duracy of the object to remain, so that we can pay attention to the
object in its irreducible materiality in spite of efforts, by investors
and by theorists, to reduce transnational flows to simply the flows
of capital or of signs.

Anthropologists and others have worked to trouble the distinction
between the commodity and the gift (between Marx and Mauss),
and between the social systems to which they are supposed to be
proper. Common sense suggests that that only unique objects, not
mass-produced commodities, can encode memory. But these distinctions are actually quite fluid, for within commodities lurks the
(unwanted?) gift of particular histories.

Maussian theory posits a number of differences between gift and
commodity. Gifts are inalienable, that is, have no value separate
from their owner, while commodities are alienable and circulate
with no danger or loss of value; gifts have rank, or quality, while
commodities have price, or quantity; gifts are subjects in their ability
to enter into relations with people, while commodities are objects
(Thomas 1991, 14). It has often been assumed that traditional societies are gift based and modern, capitalist societies are commodity
based; where traditional societies use commodities, this is assumed
to result from colonial influence. In fact this alignment is not so
neat. Alienation, commodification, and abstract exchange do occur
in noncapitalist societies, as Nicholas Thomas (1991) points out.
Thomas's detailed historical study of exchange in Melanesia shows
that indigenous societies vary greatly in the arrangements of their

economies, some having vast categories of objects that do not enter exchange, while others are more widely commodified. In addition, this difference is not a function of the infiltration of colonialism per se, but results from the degree to which a society has relations with other societies (Thomas 1991, chapter 3).

There is no doubt that our world system is interconnected by the flows of capital and power. Similarly, there is no doubt that the postcolonial condition describes not only "third-world" situations but a space we all inhabit, interconnected as we are by global flows. Nevertheless, this process of worldwide interconnection is more complex than an inevitable process of capitalist reification, of endless commodification. It is incorrect to understand gift-type economies to operate only in "third-world" cultures while "first-world" economies are commodity based through and through. Even objects that move in the apparently sanitized flows of transnational capital encode movements of cultural translation and mistranslation. Arjun Appadurai looks at these translation processes in the social life of an object in terms of knowledge: the continuities and discontinuities in knowledge between the producer and the consumer (1986, 42–44). There may be no knowledge gap in the local movement of a quart of peaches or the transnational movement of a car, both cases in which the producer and consumer share knowledge about a commodity thanks to proximity or standardization. But large knowledge gaps mark the movement among cultures of objects that encode personal or ritual meaning.

Appadurai complicates the Marxist notion of the commodity by understanding objects to move in and out of commodity status in the course of their lifetimes. In cross-cultural movement an object's "commodity status" is highly mobile; for example, a thing that is above commodification in one society may be a commodity candidate in another, and intercultural relations heighten the likelihood that an object may enter the commodity context of another society (1986, 14–17). Objects may pass in and out of identities as commodity, gift, ritual object, or trash (Kopytoff 1986, 67). In intercultural movement this process accelerates. Through their travels and through being owned and used, objects become singular, gaining a biography. Objects contain a wealth of knowledge if only we could read them. Objects provide maps of their travels, the people who

The Cinema of Transnational Objects

Cinema, then, can follow an object in an attempt to elicit its cultural biography and to read the knowledge it embodies: to engage with the object discursively. In addition, as material objects themselves, film and video are uniquely capable of confronting the object in its material as well as its discursive meaning. Benjamin found dialectical images in the ruins of the arcades; we might look for them on the Home Shopping Channel. We may also turn to the microgenre of films and videos that trace the movement of recollection-objects among cultures, works that perform a dialectical reading of objects. These examples begin with the relatively simple transnational conversions of labor to capital, and move to more idiosyncratic and intimate travels of fetishes, fossils, and transnational objects.

First are those works that trace the movement of an object as it shakes the traces of local cultures to become a deracinated, transnational commodity. The transnational object in Amos Gitai's *Ananas* (1983) is a can of pineapple. Its contents are produced in Hawai'i, its label printed in China, its can assembled on the North American continent, and so forth. The traces of humans who smelted the steel, harvested the fruit, and ran the printing press would be utterly lost in the can of pineapple, as in most commodities, were it not for Gitai's excavation, which de-alienates their labor. Similarly, in Marta Rodriguez and Jorge Silva's *Love, Women and Flowers* (1988) the transnational object is the flowers that travel from a chemical-laden hothouse in Colombia by KLM jet to European florists. Rodriguez and Silva's film takes a flower so highly cultivated that it seems to grow right in the florist shop refrigerator—the stiff, long-lasting carnation—and endows it with haunting histories of women's labor. The flowers' low cost in Amsterdam or New York reflects successful union-busting in Bogotá; their conventional length, we learn, is ensured by women workers who mechanically lop off extra buds; their unblemished uniformity results from the same clouds of toxic fungicides that cause the workers to sicken and die. In Deleuze's terms, the carnation is a recollection-image of women's work, pain,

33. Frame enlargement from *Love, Women and Flowers.*
Courtesy of Women Make Movies.

and solidarity. In Appadurai's terms, the film fills in a knowledge gap about the conditions in which the Colombian women labor, a gap that makes it easier for northern consumers to buy the flowers. Another film about suffering extracted from flowers is Jorge Furtado's *Island of Flowers* (1989), a surrealist documentary about the extremely poor people who live around and eke their livelihood from a garbage dump ("Isla das Flores") outside Rio de Janeiro. In five minutes, the film demonstrates with wicked economy the inexorable logic of making equations between money, commodities, and lives. Like *Love, Women and Flowers, Island of Flowers* is a savage critique of the process of capitalist abstraction, recreating in reverse the accordion-like movement whereby human suffering is transmuted into value.

These films undertake the Marxist project of reconstituting human labor to powerful effect. Nevertheless, it is hard to see the traces of human presence in these objects as any sort of communication. Though the women who grow the carnations may know well who is on the receiving end of their labor, such mass-produced commodities are sufficiently deracinated that the northern carnation buyers probably have no idea where their flowers came from.

More complex intercultural movements endow objects with greater powers of memory and transformation. As global movements of capital and culture make the distinction between "first" and "third" worlds increasingly muddy, the shifts between commodity and singularity accelerate and mutate. Ordinary enough commodities become singular markers of status in Jean-Pierre Bekolo's *Quartier Mozart* (1992), where the magazine *Paris Match*—a commodity for a day, then trash, in France—becomes a rare and unique object in a neighborhood in Cameroon, making the shopkeeper of the *quartier* a local authority on Denzel Washington and Princess Di. In Kidlat Tahimik's *The Perfumed Nightmare* (1978), objects regularly move in and out of commodity status with the aid of fantasy, or, more properly, fabulation. Kidlat (the character) has the knack of finding unique objects, gifts, and fetishes among the anonymous commodities of Paris. The eggs he buys from an outdoor vendor turn out, every time he cracks one open, to have two giant yolks. Awed, Kidlat returns to the vendor, Lola, who explains that all her eggs are double-yolked because they came from the same grandfather—"not like those cheap supermarket eggs." The Filipino Kidlat, the French Lola, and the German artisans of church onion domes, whom he also visits, all marginal to the tide of international commerce, recognize objects for the human (and chicken) experience they encode. Kidlat also marvels at the vast high-tech chimneys on the city's new incinerator, big enough for three families to live in. At the end of the film, the president ex officio of the Werner von Braun Fan Club hijacks one of these vast white chimney-spaceships and flies home in it. This time, Kidlat uses his "bamboo technology" to magically reclaim the mass-produced object. A true fetishist, Kidlat turns one object to another use, as collectors turn another culture's utilitarian objects into *objets d'art.* The final leg of his triumphant journey of fabulation is a Filipino commemorative stamp of Kidlat in the chimney-spaceship, "proving" that it happened.

That humblest of commodities, the potato, is re-endowed with history and sacred powers in Alex Rivera's tape *Papapapá* (1996), whose title translates to "potato-father." Beginning with the tuber's sacred centrality to Inca culture, Rivera follows its historical journey from Latin America to Europe (in a stop-motion animated potato "race," which the brown potato unfortunately loses), up through the continent, and back to North America. As it travels, the potato acquires new cultural values and loses old ones. While the potato was as sacred to its Irish cultivators as to the Incas, its status falls dramatically on its return to the Americas. The potato's final reduction to commodity status is signaled by an interview with a spokes-

34. Still from *Papapapá.* Courtesy of Alex Rivera.

person for Tri-Sum Snacks, who explains that the company sees a vast potential market in Latin America for potato chips, as well as popcorn and pork rinds. At Tri-Sum, it is important that chips be light and uniform in color and untouched by human hands: this policy, the filmmaker suggests, reflects the unconscious racism of factory standardization. Meanwhile, the stakes of Rivera's historical quest are raised by his anxiety for his Peruvian father, now an expatriate couch potato watching Latin American television in Miami. Rivera's long-baked potato bursts its commodity frame, revealing layers of memories and forgettings, capitalist expansion and cultural recoding.

Jean Rouch has exploited the transformations that people and objects experience as they cross between cultures in many films, including *Jaguar* (1971), *Petit à petit* (1969), and more recently *Madame l'eau* (1993). His most famous experiment in the material embodiment of colonialism is surely *Les Maîtres fous* (1953), a documentary of the Hauka movement in Niger, a cult whose members become possessed by the spirits of colonial administrators. This important film has been thoroughly discussed (for example, Taussig 1993, 240–43; Stoller 1995). I would note simply that one of the striking things about the film is that it documents a fetishistic spirituality, insofar as it is not the spiritual state of the worshippers' souls but the physical state of their bodies that mediate their relation to divine power: the Haukas' spirituality is immanent and embodied. But of course what is most disturbing about the film is that

what the Hauka embody is the history of colonialism of the Songhay people; this spirituality seems to be nothing elevating but a
harsh exorcism of a colonialism that infects the spirit and the body.
Rouch's critique of colonialism is far more playful in *Madame l'eau*.
In this film what moves is windmills, from Holland to Niger, supposedly at the inspiration of Rouch's friends Damouré, Lam, and
Tallou, to relieve the drought in their region. (These three collabo-
rators first appeared in *Jaguar* more than twenty years previously.)
Rather than being a miniature model of World Bank-style development, in *Madame l'eau* the importation of windmills is marked by
magic and the mutual contamination of cultures. After the Dutch
government has agreed to donate three windmills, the three Nigeri-
ans perform a divination sacrifice on the Dutch seacoast. Perhaps
it is this ritual that invests the windmill with non-Dutch (and non-
discursive) powers, so that it causes a field of tulips to spring up
overnight on the banks of the Niger.[8]

Another sort of work that traces the movement of objects among
nations, gathering and erasing meanings as they go, is the film or
tape that reconstitutes the path of an object as it becomes commodi-
tized. Dennis O'Rourke's *Cannibal Tours* (1988) and Ilisa Barbash
and Lucien Taylor's *In and Out of Africa* (1992), for example, trace
the process of cultural translation that makes local African objects
into artifacts for export. Works like these follow not simply the process of commodification of indigenous use-values into exchange-
values, but the willful creation of fetishes in intercultural translation. *In and Out of Africa,* which follows the traffic of the Muslim
merchant Gabai Baare between West Africa and New York City,
shows how Westerners desperately desire to import not just commodities but histories, and how go-betweens pander to that desire.
Baare hires African workers to carve massive numbers of traditional
ritual objects and then age them with root-based dyes and mud. The
fake antiques prove to be recollection-objects that put the lie to the
collectors' lofty notions of the universal beauty of (certain kinds of)
African sculpture. When the American collectors buy these objects,
they think they are buying aura, human experience encoded in an
object. Yet in fact they are buying a quite different kind of experience, since these recollection-objects connect not to some authentic African ritual practice but to a quite cynical process of market
analysis. *In and Out of Africa* retraces a trade route that was built

precisely to materialize colonial desires for a primitive authenticity, as they move from European and North American galleries and collections to African construction sites. Yet in following this route, the film not only deconstructs the collectors' desire but also reveals that the African sculptural objects are precisely *intercultural* products, as in Pietz's definition of the fetish. Commissioned by the trader Baare, they are the result of their African producers' reasoned second-guessing of Western collectors' fantasies about Africa.

The European and American collectors interviewed in the tape disdain the African sculptures that implicate them in the real history of European-African relationships. *Colón* figures, sculptures of white colonists, are rejected by one collector as lacking the universality and spirituality of traditional African sculpture. The European collectors prefer works that refer to a timeless, precolonial "Africa," works that deny the coevalness of European and African cultures (Fabian 1983).[9] Ironically, it is these figures that actually *are* spiritual for their African makers; they are used in ritual practices to embody the power of the colonizers just as the Hauka dealt with their colonial history by embodying the spirits of the Europeans. The *colón* figures, like Cuna Indian figurines in the shape of General Douglas MacArthur and other foreigners (Taussig 1993, 10), materially embody spirituality: they are the radioactive fossils of colonialism.

Misguided—or dangerously knowledgeable—collectors also figure in Victor Masayesva's *Imagining Indians* (1994). The collectors Masayesva interviews are variously knowledgeable about the native objects they own, from the greedy amateurs at a weekend fair to the dealer who is well enough informed about the kachina mask he owns to be uncomfortable with its power. The latter is waiting to restore the stolen mask to the Hopi community, if it can be acknowledged that he bought it legitimately. "I talk to it and feed it cornmeal," he says, showing that he is attempting to respect Hopi custom. Yet Masayesva suggests that a little knowledge is a dangerous thing. It is safe enough for hobbyists to buy native artworks that, like Baare's fake antiques, are produced for the market. The transaction may be marked by colonial desire, but the manufacturers are practicing a pre-emptive fetishism, effectively protecting their culture by sending out decoy objects. The knowledgeable collector, however, is attempting to break through the layers of intercultural translation and to penetrate to the center of Hopi ritual practices.

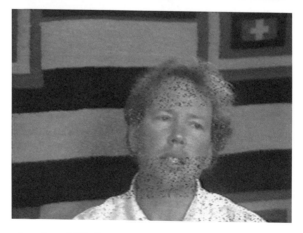

36 and 37. Stills from *Imagining Indians*

Like Masayesva, I think that another culture's spiritual identity is none of our business, and that to attempt an unmediated encounter with the most sacred objects of another culture is even more destructive than to fetishize them. As the dealer continues to speak, earnestly and rather arrogantly, Masayesva digitally erases him from the frame so that only the Navajo blanket behind him remains.

All these examples emphasize the singularity and materiality of an object, even, or especially, those objects that are supposed to be reducible to signs through exchange. The carnation, the potato, the *Paris Match,* the windmill: it is these objects' unique trajectories through time and space that invest them with a value properly called auratic. Market-based equations do not manage to capture their value. Nor, I would argue, do film theories based on Saussurean semiotics, in which any sign can equal any other. The irreducible materiality of these objects calls for a film theory that respects their aura as distillations of history. The films and videos discussed above may seem to be only films "about" transnational objects, works that take these objects as their subject matter and nothing more. But as my discussion moves to more idiosyncratic objects, I hope to show that it is the ability of film and video to make contact with these things' material presence that gives these works their unsettling power.

The Memory of Transnational Objects

Another such volatile commodity circulates in *Woman from the Lake of Scented Souls* (1994; a China-Hong Kong-Japan coproduction) by Xie Fei.[10] In this fiction film, Xiang, a Chinese village woman who runs a sesame oil factory, gets acclaim when her product is adopted by a Japanese company. The sought-after product, and the fetish in this story, is the sesame oil. It is said to get its flavor from the high-quality local sesame seeds and the clear water of the lake by which the village was built. The lake is also said to have an unusual perfume, according to the legend that two women once committed suicide by drowning themselves in the lake, rather than enter loveless marriages. Yet Xiang herself is unhappily married, and she has also forced a marriage between her mentally retarded son and a young woman, Huanhuan, despite the latter's wishes. The film suggests that the heartache of the women who run the factory is

essential to the flavor of the oil: local experience and local memory
bottled for international consumption. This extremely local product
is chosen for mass production and export by Japan, representative of
multinational capital. The Japanese characters in the film are represented as urban and rootless, in contrast to the people of the village
who live intimately with their history. What happens when what
is considered universally superior, the Platonic form of sesame oil,
turns out to be the bottled product of local memory?

The film is exhibited under two English titles: the literal translation *Woman Sesame Oil Maker,* and the more poetic *Woman from
the Lake of Scented Souls.* This double title is another case of the
mutation of transnational objects. The Chinese title refers prosai-
cally to the commercial product. The title for foreign consumption
calls up connotations of ancient, ineffable Chinese culture. The further the product (both the oil and the film) travels, in other words,
the more its meanings become rarefied and distanced from their material origin. On the other hand, distance also makes it possible to
specify the emotional source of the sesame oil's flavor, which would
have been anathema back in the village. Its manufacturers attribute
the flavor of the oil to the clear water of the lake. They are at pains
not to disclose the story of the thwarted lovers who drowned themselves in the lake, for fear of repelling their customers. But by the
time the product is at a safe distance from the village, the romantic
story only enhances its value.

Woman from the Lake of Scented Souls traces a remarkable process of concentration and displacement in the production of transnational objects: an emotional, even spiritual phenomenon becomes
the force underlying the appeal of a commodity. It should not be
surprising that what gets (literally) bottled in the film is women's
experience, whose expression is not sanctioned by the culture. The
painful relationship between Xiang and Huanhuan is built on an un-
resolvable contradiction: the former requires her daughter-in-law to
submit to a loveless marriage, as she herself did, in order to maintain the coherence of the family business. In the tense scenes between these women, the strained, truncated dialogue tends to be
confined to the household chores. Neither speaks of the bruises that
the daughter-in-law's husband has inflicted on her. A tacit understanding grows between the two when the young woman discovers
that her mother-in-law has had a lover for the entire duration of

her marriage. In these scenes, the women never meet one another's glance. Often one spies on the other from a window onto the courtyard of the house. Their final exchange takes place, in effect, through a veil: standing on the roof amid laundry hung to dry, the daughter-in-law is silhouetted behind a sheet while her mother-in-law, in a few subdued words, releases her from her bondage. In *Woman from the Lake of Scented Souls* the tragedy of the women's lives finds no verbal expression, and is muted visually as well. The longing and pain of generations of women appears only in the fragrance of the sesame oil they produce. (And the film is not a tirade against modernity: when the factory's primitive machinery is replaced by modernized equipment, an investment from the Japanese backers, the flavor of the oil is not altered. Instead, it is the specifically emotional character of the labor that affects the oil's quality.)

It is only a slight shift from the commodified objects in the works described above to noncommodified, personal objects. While those volatile commodities encode social more than individual histories, the meaning of personal objects resides in their power to release memories that are specific to individuals. These processes are not "merely" personal, however; rather, they suggest how the personal and idiosyncratic may be the only visible aspect of broader cultural histories (Seremetakis 1994, 135). The significance of the sort of transnational movement contained in personal objects cannot be underestimated. How often has it been the case that memories that were seen as "only" private proved to be the sole repositories of diasporic cultures? It is important to take seriously what seem to be isolated, idiosyncratic, or seemingly private phenomena, because they may prove to be the only level at which widespread cultural movements are able to speak.

Earlier I mentioned the piece of tar paper that is one of several objects that encode history in Tajiri's *History and Memory*. The object that Tajiri most successfully pursues to learn what it "remembers" is a wooden bird her grandmother carved in the detention camp at Poston. This colorful object, shot, like the piece of tar paper, against a black background, comes to resonate on another historical level when Tajiri finds a photo in the National Archives. Going through a box of documents from the internment camps, Tajiri comes across a photograph of a roomful of people working at long tables, labeled

38. Still from *History and Memory*

"Bird-carving class, August 1941," and there in the photo is her grandmother. The archive—in this case, the literal archive—is as ignorant of Mrs. Tajiri's private history as she is willfully amnesiac of it. Only the bird remembers. Traveling from the prison camp to the family home, the wooden bird embodies a recollection that is now lost. The carved figure that now resides in Tajiri's mother's jewelry box is material evidence of a trauma her mother has almost wholly forgotten.

Personal objects remember and attest to events that people have forgotten. Like cameraless films made by placing things directly on the negative, some works undertake to excavate the memories of objects merely by exposing them and "developing" the stories they retain. Such a work is Walid Ra'ad's short video, *Missing Lebanese Wars* (1996). Like several other expatriate Lebanese artists, among them Yasmine Khlat (*Leylouna notre nuit*, 1987), Olga Nakkas (*Lebanon: Bits and Pieces*, 1994), and Jalal Toufic (*Credits Included: A Video in Red and Green*, 1995), Ra'ad returns to his old home to ask the walls, the pictures, and the objects to recount the "missing" war and explain the marks it left on his family. The tape begins with a meditation on photography's ability both to fix and to undermine the truth of an event. "It is a well-known fact that the major historians of the Lebanese civil war were compulsive gamblers during the war period." Every Sunday, Ra'ad explains, Marxists, Islamists, and

39 and 40. Stills from *Missing Lebanese Wars.* Courtesy of Walid Ra'ad.

Maronite nationalists went to the racetrack to bet not on the horses but on what moment of the photo finish would be represented in the newspaper the next day. This scene is shot so as to deny the camera's ability to capture visible evidence. All we see of the race, in a series of blurry dissolves, are fragmented close-up shots of the crowd of spectators at the track. In the next scene, over a melancholy oboe solo from Marcel Khalifé's "Ghina'iyat Ahmed Al Arabi," a voice-over recounts how a woman named Zainab Fakhouri left her husband during the war, taking seventeen objects with her on the journey from Bir Zeit to Beirut to Amman to Free Town. To illustrate this journey, Ra'ad isolates details from still photographs of family gatherings, homing in not on the faces of loved ones but on the objects behind them. Encoding years of memories, the objects bear witness to how the war came to make itself felt in the marex-husband, historian Fadl Fakhouri, has his own memory objects: he spends his days listening to recordings of his old lectures about the Lebanese civil war and rearranging his son's bullet collection (we see the bullets lined up on the bedspread), as though the right combination would make sense of his past.

Ra'ad's oblique, seemingly dispassionate, and overtly fictionalized approach hints that to try to recover the memories these fossils contain would be too painful. Instead he moves cautiously over their surface, examining the geological forces that produced them. A later tape by Ra'ad, *Secrets in the Open Sea* (1997), makes even more explicit the power of objects to remember materially what is officially forgotten—in only three minutes. A number of photographic plates, Ra'ad explains in voice-over, were found in the intelligence headquarters of the warring militias active during the civil war. As he speaks we see the blue Mediterranean and more of those any-space-whatever Beirut streetscapes such as Ra'ad and Jayce Salloum used in *Talaeen a Junuub* (1993). He continues: the Arab Research Institute in Beirut sent these plates to labs in France and the United States for analysis, where they were found to represent group portraits; we see this series of stills, some of which are obviously newsprint half-tones. All the people in the photographs, Ra'ad explains, were members of the militias, and all had drowned at sea in the past few years. The film closes in silence with a percussive sequence of bluish rectangles. In Deleuze's phrase, something is hidden in the image: these flat rectangles are witnesses to a disappearance. The very elaborateness of the research project *Secrets in the Open Sea* purports to record hints that the whole thing is a fake. A supporting document published by Ra'ad asserts that the prints' $150,000-each development costs were defrayed by contributions from corporations, individuals, and the fictional Fakhouris of *Missing Lebanese Wars,* and that the Arab Research Institute contains 4,600 additional "indexed microfiched" documents (Ra'ad 1997). Such comfortable resources would be a fantasy for any artist, but especially one whose search for objective records of the Lebanese civil war has turned up only contradiction and denial. More wishfulness shows in the fake opening credit, "BBC and Canal+ present." In short, the story that the photographic plates hide in their blue surfaces is not true—that is, it may well be true, but they are not telling it. Yet the blue plates that briefly present their faces to the screen are radioactive, objects that look inert but contaminate the discourse of truth surrounding them.

Objects and Sense Memory

As an object decays it often changes in texture and emits odors. As a recollection-object breaks down, through the engagement with memory, memory generates sensations in the body (Bergson [1911] 1998, 179). Thus an image, insofar as it engages with memory at all, engages the memory of the senses. And as I will insist, the senses often remember when nobody else does. The memory of the senses may call forth histories of transnational objects, histories that have been lost en route. *How* can knowledge be embodied in senses other than the visual? How can one form of sense knowledge embody another? I ask the reader's patience while in the rest of this chapter I raise the stakes of such questions, which will be the subject of chapters 3 and 4.

Food and the plants on which it grows are recollection-objects in a number of intercultural films and videos. On Tajiri's visit to Poston she videotapes the date palms that the Japanese American prisoners planted almost fifty years earlier. Tall and strong, the trees attest to the presence of the people who "brought water to the desert and made things grow," and to the concentrated sweetness of the fruit they might have tasted. In Julie Dash's *Daughters of the Dust* (1992), okra and other vegetables imported from Africa act as memory-fossils for the inhabitants of Ibo Landing. Okra figures in Marlon Riggs's *Black Is, Black Ain't* (1995): it is an important ingredient in gumbo, which Riggs uses not only as a metaphor for the differences and commonalities among African diasporic people, but also a means of recreating African diasporic communities through memories of smell and taste and rituals of cooking. *Great Girl* (1994), a film by Kim Su Theiler, retraces a young American woman's journey back to her Korean birthplace. Her search for her home and mother is inconclusive, except for a couple of indexical traces. One is a scar on the young woman's forehead. A woman who may have been her mother does not recognize her, but she tells of an accident her little daughter had with the scissors that would explain the scar. The other is sweet potatoes. The narrator tells how she met Mr. Chao, the former gardener of the orphanage where she was supposedly raised,

41. Frame enlargement from *Great Girl*.
Courtesy of Women Make Movies.

when she went to the village. "He said he didn't recognize me, but he said that if I'd eaten sweet potatoes, he had planted them." The material memory of sweet potatoes connects Kim Su and the gardener, even though neither of them remembers with certainty that she lived there.

Sense memories are most fragile to transport, yet most evocative when they can be recovered. Hamid Naficy notes that it is especially important to consider the nonaudiovisual ways that exiles experience film and television: "The exiles produce their difference not just through what they see and hear but through their senses of smell, taste, and touch. Indeed, these aspects of the sensorium often provide, more than sight and hearing, poignant reminders of difference and of separation from homeland" (1993, 152–53). What is left out of expression registers somatically, in pain, nausea, memories of smells and caresses. What does not register in the orders of the seeable and sayable may resonate in the order of the sensible.

The originary fossil-image in *History and Memory*—the image that encodes lost memories—is that of a woman filling a canteen at a pump. It is Tajiri, reenacting her mother's sole recollection-image from the internment camps. A tiny puncture of pleasure in the eternal vigilance the woman must hold in order to survive in the concentration camp, it will be the only image to remain years later, when that other narrative of deprivation has been put away. The space that is beyond discourse in *History and Memory* is also one that the colonizing images from the American newsreels could not touch: a private sense memory, held in safe keeping.

As I have noted, Shauna Beharry is a ritual/performance artist. *Seeing Is Believing* (1991) was her first work in a mechanically re-produced medium. The tape expresses Beharry's frustration over her inability to express in this medium, for, paradoxically, she is using video to show the limits of vision. It begins with Beharry's camera searching a still photograph over and over. The photograph is of Beharry, wearing the sari. Her voice on the sound track is de-scribing the anger and bafflement she felt when, after her mother died, she could not recognize her in photographs. Only when she put on her mother's sari, Beharry says, did she feel that she had "climbed into her skin." The feel of the fabric awakens for Beharry a flood of memories that were lost in the family's movement from India to Europe to Canada. *Seeing Is Believing* calls upon the sort of knowledge that can only be had in the physical presence of an object—or from the indexical witness of cinema. Touch is a sense whose knowledge requires the physical presence of the object: Be-harry makes this clear in her attempt to "squeeze the touchability out of the photo" (Beharry 1996). To touch something one's mother, one's grandparents, or an unknown person touched is to be in physi-cal contact with them.

Similarly, in Mona Hatoum's *Measures of Distance* (1988), it is the skin of her mother, as well as the indexical trace of her voice on tape, that gradually activate the sense of her mother's presence as well as the painful finality of her absence. This is a tape Hatoum made in Vancouver about her mother in Lebanon. Photographs taken while her mother bathed, and tapes of their familiar conversations, punc-tuated with laughter, are overlaid by her mother's letters to her far-away daughter. The letters establish the distance of the title, their Arabic words making a scrim over the images, and their increas-

42. Still from *History and Memory*

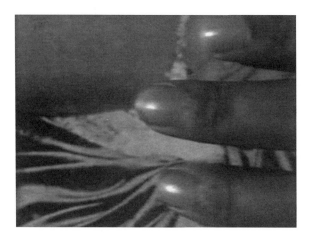

43. Still from *Seeing Is Believing*

ingly mournful content, read in voice-over, has a muffling quality
that seems to want to fill in the gap by appealing to the memory of
touch. All three of these videos call upon tactile memory to create
a communication between daughters and mothers that words, and
audiovisual images, could not. All three use sense memory to restore the history that has become fossilized in an object. Ultimately
they defetishize the object, by teasing out the story it contains.

Similarly, consider how smell is an indexical witness. Failing direct neural stimulation (olfactory hallucination), we smell because
molecules from the source of smell have reached the membranes

within our noses. Smell requires contact, molecules coming into touch with receptors. A source of smell gradually diminishes over time as its particles disperse. To smell something, then, is to participate in its gradual destruction. But it is also to share the experience of the thing with others who smelled it before. Smell is the quintessentially fetishistic and defetishizing sense: it depends upon the presence of the object, but it also destroys it.

Beharry is quite aware that the power of touch, smell, and taste lies in their transitoriness. She makes this a theme of her performance "Ashes to Flowers: The Breathing," whose title alone suggests a reverse movement of fetishism, where a live thing is reconstituted from dead traces. Participants smell incense and the food she prepares; at the end of the performance they walk on raw rice strewn in patterns on the floor, perceiving the image with the sense of touch at the same time that they destroy it. But to transfer this sense of the fleetingness of the senses to a recording medium, in both its intensity and its evanescence, requires that the fetishlike quality of the audiovisual image be acknowledged. Film and video (like any medium of mechanical reproduction) tend to fix and generalize their objects; but film is also capable of the same volatility that characterizes the fetish. Film/video is able to reactivate the presence of the fetishized object, as the (audio)visual image yields to the things it cannot represent; and in the process, as I will explain, the image ceases to exist as a fetish.

Sense Knowledge and Cultural Translation

When objects are extracted from their cultural contexts, it is often their nonvisual qualities that are the first to be forgotten. The cultural history encoded in nonvisual sense memory gets lost in any kind of intercultural movement, but especially in the diasporic movement to the modernized West, or from rural areas to metropolitan centers. This is an effect not only of Western ocularcentrism but also of commodification. Curators of visual art note that the recoding of a useful object as a high-art commodity tends to strip away its nonvisual aspects. As Laura Trippi writes, "Conventions of fine art display, taking objects out of context, stimulate a tendency to experience vision as if it operated objectively, independently of the other senses and even outside the contingencies of history" (1993).[11] Similarly, Constance Classen (1993) notes that museums' practice of storing artifacts behind glass recontextualizes these objects as primarily visual, and thus often misinterprets the sort of knowledge they provided in their traditional cultures. She uses the example of a basket from the Desana tribe of Colombia, a culture, she demonstrates, that has a complex organization of knowledge based on symbolisms of color, odor, temperature, and flavor. "Though a Desana basket, for instance, is evidently a multi-sensory object, it would never occur to the ordinary Westerner viewing one in a museum that meaning might lie not only in its form and function, but also in its texture, taste, and smell" (136).

Fetishism as an intercultural relation involves a tremendous amount of translation, decipherment, and excavation. And ultimately there is no possibility of getting to a truth about either culture, for the fetish is produced only in the movement between cultures. Beharry's excavations, for example, are not just about finding the Indian "voice" silenced by generations of life in the West. They are also excavations of many histories that get lost in cultural translation, histories that are repressed at home as well. In *Seeing Is Believing,* in the reading of the meanings fossilized in her own skin, she reveals a mixed legacy that includes a Chinese grandfather, undoing the myth of racial purity that matters both in cross-cultural "explanation" and in intracultural lineages. In the performance "Ashes to Flowers," Beharry combines humble folk rituals with Brahmin ceremony, making a carnival of Hinduism in a way that may be quite offensive to some people. When she makes chappatis with rose water and kneads rose petals into them, she is not only mixing peasant food with ritual offerings, but also allowing folk rituals and women's work to erupt into high Brahmin traditions.

Performed at (the appropriately named) Gallery Burning in Montréal, "Ashes to Flowers" addresses the difficulty of holding on to an ever-heavier object inscribed with indecipherable meaning, and undertaking the burden of translation. The earnest attempt at translation of *Seeing Is Believing* gave way, in the performance, to a dismissal of the very possibility of translation. In the early part of the performance, Beharry attempted to recite a poem she had written in Urdu. Like a child trying to remember a lesson, she stamped and tossed her head with frustration, her eyes wet with relief when she did manage to resolve a phrase. But she did not translate the poem to the group of friends gathered in the gallery, none of whom understood Urdu. It was only for us non-Urdu speakers to experience the painful difficulty of excavation. (When Beharry performs this ritual for audiences of Indian descent, the reaction is no doubt quite different—sorrow, perhaps, at the cultural atrophy evident in her effort.) Such a renunciation suggests an acceptance of untranslatability as part of the postcolonial experience.

Beharry's working process itself is antifetishistic, built on a suspicion of the reification that happens when an artwork enters discourse. (Whereas fetishes, as I have argued, are live things that can telescope back out to processes and relationships, reification reduces processes and relationships to things.) One must obtain permission from Beharry to write about her work. She does not circulate images of her performances or stills from her videos, but issues a single photograph, of her cupped hands holding a lily of the valley. Though she operates in the context of the Canadian art community, she has taken pains to work differently from most career artists. This course has been possible in part because of the still fairly generous Canadian art funding system, which enabled Beharry to pursue her practice in residencies and the like without being pressured to deliver salable products. She refuses to document her performances, preferring instead that information about her work be spread in the conversations of the people who have witnessed it. The statement she gives whenever required to represent herself in print is "My work is small, simple, and travels by word of mouth. I trust in it."

Beharry's projects typically erase their own process but leave traces of the changes that have occurred, often by substituting olfactory or tactile traces for visual evidence. They may include burying objects, burning objects (including, to this critic's consternation, videotapes), scattering a pattern carefully traced on the floor, and otherwise ensuring that the record of the event remains only in the memory of those who witness it or hear about it. She is a curator's nightmare. When Beharry was asked to create an installation at the Vancouver Museum of Anthropology around its collection of First Nations artifacts, she proposed to surround the objects in their glass cases with chappatis cut into the shapes of hands (Beharry 1996). The museum curators were horrified because the bread would have attracted insects; but as Beharry points out, the little

44. Publicity photograph, courtesy of
Shauna Beharry.

bugs are already in the walls and carpet of the museum, and her
chappatis would only have made them visible! In this way Beharry's
work carries out Classen's and Trippi's critiques of museum practice
by enabling the smelly and gustatory processes that go unseen and
disavowed in an ocularcentric culture—if only by appealing to the
sense of smell of weevils and other insects. Beharry's work, in short,
is resolutely material in that it resists representation, and yet resolutely immaterial in that she erases its traces as soon as possible.

And interestingly, the way these traces linger the longest is in the
form of smell. Paper and flowers burnt at one of Beharry's performance spaces leave their acrid fragrance for days after. Sites where
she has worked retain the scent of incense that she buried in the
walls, detectable even under a fresh coat of paint. Friends receive in
the mail poems scented with rose oil, or envelopes full of ashes that
burst onto their shirts.

The artist's grief in *Seeing Is Believing* is heightened by resentment of the Western cultural emphasis on visuality. The photographs
of her mother seem to rob Beharry of actual memories of her. As
such, the loss she is trying to address not only concerns the intimacy between mother and daughter but also has to do with a kind of
knowledge. Memory, she suggests, can be lost in translation, espe-

cially in the difference between cultures' regimes of sense knowledge. Beharry's use of video to critique photography is a pointed reference to the way visual records steal memories, precisely in their reified concreteness. Photography has a specific cultural history, which includes its ethnographic use as one of the technologies of imperial domination. Nevertheless, the Western snapshot has achieved ascendancy in most cultures, including the top echelons of "third-world" cultures, as the way of coding private representation. As Beharry has stressed, visuality is also the dominant mode of knowledge in Brahmin ritual, or the practices of the upper caste within Hinduism. It is no problem, or not such a great problem, to put a Brahmin ritual on tape, say. The rituals that get lost in the act of immigration and cultural translation are the non-Brahmin, the peasant rituals.[12]

Beharry's performances and videos excavate a form of knowledge that patriarchal cultures tend to dismiss, namely, the sensuous knowledge that pertains to Indian (diasporan) women's daily lives. These are not experiences that would be immediately accessible to any woman. It is not possible to assert a feminine kinship with Beharry, or with the women whose lives are implicit in her work, on the basis of identifying with some universal female experience. Her source of memory, the feel and smell of a sari on her skin, is quite specific to a particular group of women. However, though we the viewers may not be privy to the particular information Beharry learns from putting on her mother's sari, *Seeing Is Believing* does give us license to value other intimate, sensory experiences as sources of knowledge. Her mother's skin touched the sari, and now the sari touches her: knowledge is transmitted tactilely rather than visually. To be able to value this kind of knowledge it is necessary to think of the skin as something that can distinguish, know, and remember. What Beharry gives us in *Seeing Is Believing* is not an introduction to Indian women's sense of touch, but an awareness of the importance of the knowledge of the senses in whatever our culture of origin might be. As we begin to seek our own sense knowledges, we can evaluate how our own cultures assimilate or filter out the knowledge of the senses. In chapter 4 I will explore further how the sensorium is organized by culture.

"Sensual abandon" is a phrase of Enlightenment subjectivity, implying that the senses (except maybe vision, and possibly hearing) dull the powers of the intellect. It implies that the Orientalist desire for the sense experience of other cultures is in part a desire to stop thinking, as though sensory knowledge is radically opposed to intellectual knowledge. But when, in "Ashes to Flowers," Beharry lights incense, washes our hands with rose water, and encourages us to dance, she is not encouraging us to "abandon" ourselves to our bodies but to respect our bodies' capacities for knowledge. This is a knowledge that requires just as much effort to acquire as intellectual knowledge. The "Oriental" trip she gives us is not an opportunity to breathe in the smells and let it all hang out—an interpretation she circumvents when shortly into the performance she changes from romantic *shalwar kameez* into a frumpy slip and housedress— but a time to do a particular sort of work where bodies and minds work together. This appeal to olfactory, tactile, and other nonvisual bodily knowledges makes many participants uncomfortable, since these knowledges are little valued or cultivated in modern Western contexts, even in the art world.[13] Even if we respect them, we may not know how to make sense of them. In short, stirring up the hierarchy of the senses is not a chance to play dumb: in fact it's quite exhausting.

The Aura of the Transnational Object

Pietz's archaeology of the fetish is essential to a critique of the hierarchical organization of the senses. Enlightenment thinkers (and many before them) separated knowledge from the body, reinforcing the hierarchy of the senses whereby vision is valued as furthest from the body and closest to the intellect, while smell and taste are considered the most bodily and least intellectual of the senses. (More on this hierarchy in chapter 4.) I propose we turn those thinkers "on their heads" and attempt to practice fetishistic thinking.

The fetish, by partaking physically of the thing it represents, threatens the idea that only the distance senses lend themselves to knowledge. Fetishism is a form of belief based in and dependent upon the body. As such it is denounced in the majority of world philosophies and religions. But thinking fetishistically allows us to take embodied knowledge seriously. In addition, to be dependent upon an object affirms not only the materiality of one's body but also the incompleteness of one's self: it suggests that meaning inheres in the communication between self, objects, and others rather than in a communication mediated by the mind alone. The nontranscendence of African fetishism, as construed by Enlightenment-era Europeans, represents a strategic way of reconceiving material relations among people. Because they make the individual dependent upon bodily contact for spiritual power, fetishes, like other auratic objects, threaten the autonomy of the subject. Hence the Dutch explorer De Brosses denounced fetishism for draining the humanity from the worshipper (according to Mitchell 1986, 191): in fetishism, "humanity" or subjectivity was a function of the exchange among the worshippers and their objects. Fetishes are fellow-travelers. They are fundamentally like Balász's "dumb objects . . . whose fate is bound up with your own" ([1923] 1972) to which the close-up bears witness. Fetishistic subjectivity does not inhere in individual souls but rather is distributed among bodies, objects, and places.

Throughout this chapter I have been referring to objects that travel as auratic. Through their travels and through being owned and used, objects become unique. The transnational object is precisely auratic in that it testifies to "the essence of all that is transmissible from its beginning, ranging from its substantive duration to its testimony to the history which it has experienced" (Benjamin 1968c, 221). In the religious practices from which the word *aura* was borrowed, it meant the presence of the sacred. In this way an auratic object is a fetish. It holds within it the presence of the sacred, concentrated in the object through some initial contact or use. As I have noted, the auratic character of things is their ability not simply to awaken memories in an individual, but to contain a social history in fragmentary form. The bottles of oil in *Woman from the Lake of Scented Souls*, the carnations of *Love, Women and Flowers*, the sweet potatoes in *Great Girl*, Walid Ra'ad's precious family objects, Rea Tajiri's heirloom brooch in *History and Memory*, and the fabric whose surface Shauna Beharry searches in *Seeing Is Believing* are all auratic in that they have made physical contact with histories—histories too volatile and disruptive to be related as simple stories. The works I have described explore this auratic presence by following the objects back to their source of power.

Yet aura is not merely a human presence that narrative uncoils from the object like a ball of string. Objects also have a life independent of the human relations they encode, beyond their discursive

and narrative significance. Their materiality itself is significant. As
Peter Pels provocatively suggests,

> Things may, indeed, be enlivened by their forms, uses and trajectories with-
> out recourse to materiality, through memory, written representation, or
> other forms of symbolic action, but that is another realization of the social
> life of things than that mediated by materiality itself, in which their forms,
> uses, and trajectories are apprehended, like habitual practice, "without re-
> course to discourse" . . . or representation. (1995, 9; quoting Pierre Bourdieu)

Meaning resides in objects, as habit stores memory in the body.

How can we account for the way meaning is mediated materially? Most current Marxist criticism has deteriorated into a dry positivism on one hand, and a Baudrillardian dazzlement at the world of self-replicating signs on the other. This, I would argue, results from Marx's own campaign to demystify the commodity. Paradoxically, in making legible the social relations encoded in an object, one tends to lose the materiality of the object. The continuing appeal of Benjamin's work is partly due to his provocative effort to both de- and *re*-mystify the object, to incorporate its inexpressible and intangible properties at the same time that he read it politically. Very controversially, Benjamin fused Cabbalist and Marxist understandings of how meaning is immanent in the things of the world—immanent but veiled according to the Cabbalists, immanent but reified according to the Marxists (Buck-Morss 1989, 235–40). Benjamin was roundly criticized by Adorno, Brecht, and later critics such as Rolf Tiedemann and Jürgen Habermas for these attempts to fuse mysticism with Marxism (245–49). Most of these ideas remained unpublished, or expressed only in hints in Benjamin's published essays (Hansen 1987, Buck-Morss 1989).

But since the time Benjamin was taken to task, intellectuals' faith in our ability to read the world wholly in terms of signs has waned. Perhaps now it is possible to contemplate how objects mean in themselves—to contemplate their aura—without being accused of obfuscation. If this is mysticism, it is an attempt to account for an enchantment of the world different from the opiate aura of the commodity. It is an attempt to understand how meaning is conveyed through physical presence as well as through intellectual signification. The films and videos I have been examining demonstrate that many recollection-objects are irreducibly material and irreducibly auratic. To understand how objects mean in their materiality requires that we undertake a tactile epistemology, to which I will return in the next chapter.

The Dissolution of the Fetish

Earlier I remarked that when a recollection-object, like other kinds of recollection-image, successfully engages with memory, it engages with communal storytelling and its "radioactive" quality is neutralized. The way a fetish object accomplishes this, while it is not sexual per se, has to do with how the fetish is libidinally (autoerotically?) located upon the body. The dissolution of the fetish is accomplished by its reembodiment. When sense memory is revived in the body—when the body remembers—the recollection-object ceases to exist as such.

Borrowing from Michel Leiris's beautiful essay on Giacometti, Pietz ponders the relation of fetishes—and successful works of art—to the body:

The fetish is . . . first of all, something intensely personal, whose truth is experienced as a substantial movement from "inside" the self (the self as totalized through an impassioned body, a "body without organs") into the self-limited morphology of a material object situated in space "outside." Works of art are true fetishes only if they are material objects at least as intensely personal as the water of tears. (1985, 11–12)

Pietz suggests that the movement from the inside to the outside—the process of concretization—is what makes a fetish a fetish. Tears are an example: they are a material expression of an internal state. The thing about tears, though, is that they do not remain a concrete object; they dissolve back into the body. Pietz provocatively refers in passing to the "body without organs" as the body that produces fetishes, or art. Only a body that is not libidinally fixated in terms of particular parts can invest with desire something *outside*. I picture the Deleuze-Guattarian "body without organs" (1983) as something like a water balloon. You can willfully twist shapes onto its surface, play with them until they lose their fascination, and then undo them and make others. This sort of libidinal investment, the schizoanalysts argue, is the only one that is built around desire rather than need. The appeal of this model is that, voluntaristic though it certainly is, it allows for the strange and contingent ways subjects form attachments. The body without organs produces fetishes galore, but it does not fixate upon any one of them; they dissolve back into its undifferentiated surface. Similarly, the fetishes produced in the movement between cultures are only transitory markers of a brief relation that will probably change. (Hence the perverseness of collecting "third-world" artifacts as though they are markers of a static condition, as the collectors in *In and Out of Africa* and *Imagining Indians* do: such fetishism harks back to an impossible moment before colonial and postcolonial relations of cultural mixing and transformation.) The body without organs is playful toward the object of desire, having a "double consciousness of absorbed credulity and degraded or distanced incredulity" (Pietz 1985, 14) that permits both investment and critique.

The fetish that is produced in the movement between cultures is a concrete expression of the state of longing produced when what was inside moves to the outside, when what was taken for granted of one's culture becomes an object of contemplation. Like the fetish produced by an "impassioned body," these only exist as fetishes for as long as they contain a cultural meaning that cannot exist comfortably in the new cultural context.

Let me return to Winnicott's ([1951] 1958) theory of the transitional object to explore how the fetish is produced on the body without organs. Is the transitional object—the comforting blanket, the TV that lulls the child to sleep, for that matter, the smell of a familiar food—part of the body or not? Certainly it is part of the body without organs, the body that makes itself anew by organizing itself with relation to an external object. The subject's identity comes to be distributed between the self and the object. Yet it is the self, not the object, that is in transition. The object remains the same, although it takes on layers of meaning that later, as the subject acquires some new sort of subjecthood, dissolve away.

Recall how fetishes are produced in the space between cultures. The transnational object is a transitional object not only for the person in transition from one cultural reality to another, but also for the one whose cultural reality is entered and changed. The object becomes a means of both of their projections about the other culture. As it moves, it is bound to become a lot heavier before it gets lighter. Here is the difference between fetishes and fossils, then. Fossils retain the shape of the cultural upheaval, perpetually inviting decoding of past conflicts. Their "radioactive" quality may diminish as connections are made to the historical stratum in which they were created, but they do not go away. Fetishes, although they are similarly dense with meaning, tend to dissolve away after the need for them has dissipated.

The function of transitional objects is decidedly not to aid assimilation to another culture. For they do not simply bring an aspect of their place of origin to a new site; they also make strange the place into which they arrive. These cultural fossils are radioactive because they bring back lost histories in which both origin and destination are implicated. They reveal the radical hybridity already present at both sites.

Cinematic images, as transitional objects, retain some indexical trace of an originary event. They do not transparently reflect it, but obscure it. These images are transitional objects insofar as they are dense, sedimented, crystallized. They become unnecessary once they are dissolved. The works discussed in this chapter bring the fetishistic, auratic character of the traveling object to its apex—and then they dissolve its power, by connecting it to memory, changing fossil-images to recollection-images.

I hope to have demonstrated a combination of cinematic qualities and practices that both materializes and dissolves the fetishlike and fossil-like quality of the image. The emphasis on the nonvisual qualities of the image in *History and Memory, Seeing Is Believing,* and other works turns our attention away from the kind of fetishism most commonly (and pejoratively) discussed in cinema, visual fetishism. At the same time it calls attention to other material presences borne forth by the image, such as touch and smell: a process of sensory replacement that I will explore in the following two chapters. The "life cycle" of the fetish is also supported by Beharry's refusal to let her moving images circulate, often to the point of destruction. Her practices both acknowledge the dense aura surrounding the image and aid in its dissolution.

Let me make some generalizations about the fetishistic quality of documentary. In its use as described by Pietz, the fetish seems to *fix* the value of those crisis moments when incommensurable histories meet. But in bringing these histories together the fetish also renders each of them unstable. The works by Beharry, Tajiri, Ra'ad, and others are pointed examples of how documentary can exploit cinema's volatile, fetishlike quality, but all documentary has the potential to act in this way. All documentary images are fetishes, insofar as they are indexes of the event documented. However, they do not transparently reflect it, but opaquely encode it. When documentary is accused, as it often is, of fetishizing the people and events it represents, this is because it maintains the fetish in a state of fixity. But the fetish object may be coaxed to unfold into memory, as when these artists search a photograph, a scar, or a piece of tar paper for the history it encodes. As the fetishistic relations these objects embody are worked through, they cease to be fetishes. Another example is Shauna Beharry's chappati hands.

In "Ashes to Flowers," Beharry makes chappatis, cuts them out in the shape of hands, two right two left, smears them with the red paste used to mark a bindi on the forehead, and places them on an altar made of rice and vaguely in the shape of a woman's body. What is shocking about these actions is the significance of the red hands. I had known that brides' hands are decorated with henna in Hindu weddings. But I only learned later that, in the traditional practice of *suttee,* the last thing the widow does before she steps onto her husband's pyre is to dip her hands in henna, red like blood, and make the mark of her two red hands on a stone. So the two sets of red hands Beharry made are not only about the tactile lineage of learning, from her mother and her mother's mothers, how to make chappatis. Nor do they refer simply to the cultural dislocations that made the simple recipe, with all its concomitant responsibilities, difficult for the third-generation daughter to learn (as she tells us, "My father said, if you make nice round chappatis you'll get a husband"). They also pay homage to the generations of women in her history who have been forced to burn. For those who know about the red hands, this point in the performance is physically nauseating.

Beharry could not and did not want to embrace her Hindu heritage uncritically, for it is a heritage that includes the cruel subjugation of women. In her acts of excavation she cannot discover a lost history of women, for the women are gone for good. She can only cut through the geological layers and make inert histories volatile by crashing them into each other. Beharry is not the product of any one discourse but carries a number of irreconcilable histories with her. Her chappati hands are not the fragrant bread of nostalgia; they are radioactive fossils that destabilize everything that comes into contact with them.

3

The memory of touch

If cinema does not give us the presence of the body
and cannot give it to us, this is perhaps also because it sets
itself a different objective: it spreads an "experimental night"
or a white space over us; it works with "dancing seeds" and
a "luminous dust"; it affects the visible with a fundamental
disturbance, and the world with a suspension, which
contradicts all natural perception. What it produces
in this way is the genesis of an unknown body.
—Gilles Deleuze, *Cinema 2: The Time-Image*

In the previous chapter I wrote that Shauna Beharry's *Seeing Is Be-lieving,* a tape made in mourning for her mother, uses the audio-visual image to convey the tactile memory of her mother's skin. Here let me describe how she achieves this. The tape is built around a single still image of the artist wearing her mother's sari. While Be-harry tells her story, the camera has been looking ever more closely ("focusing" is not the right word) at the fabric of the sari in a detail of the photo, following the folds of silk as they dissolve into grain and resolve again. Eventually the tape keys in a smaller, sharp-focus image of the portrait, superimposing it on the folds of the sari.

The difference between these two ways of seeing is startling. I realize that the tape has been using my vision as though it were a sense of touch; I have been brushing the (image of the) fabric with the skin of my eyes, rather than looking at it. Beharry says she wanted to "squeeze the touchability out of the photo" (1996), and she has: the difference between the senses collapses slightly.

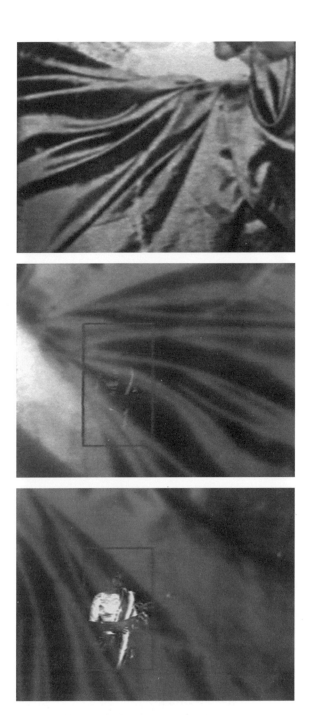

45, 46, and 47. Stills from *Seeing Is Believing*

The switch between what I will term haptic and optical vision describes the movement between a relationship of touch and a visual one. This experience of looking, together with Beharry's compelling words, makes us reflect that memory may be encoded in touch, sound, perhaps smell, more than in vision. The disparity between the searching movements of the camera and her wistful voice on the sound track, between visual and audio, creates a poignant awareness of the missing sense of touch.

Beyond the Audiovisual

I concentrate in this and the next chapter on the ways cinema can appeal to senses that it cannot technically represent: the senses of touch, smell, and taste. This focus is not some intellectual game but an extension of my concern throughout this work to show how and why cinema might express the inexpressible.

The two previous chapters began to explore the representation of memory in intercultural cinema. I suggested that cinema is able to evoke the particularly hard-to-represent memories of people who move between cultures, by pointing beyond the limits of sight and sound. The works I discussed show the dilemma that occurs when words, sounds, and images trap as much as they free: when giving expression to some things that are cinema's proper territory prevents the expression of something else. In chapter 1 I argued that the characteristic gaps of time-image cinema offer a way to represent memories that are effaced from dominant cinematic representations. I suggested, following Deleuze, that sometimes the disjunction between the visible and the verbal may point to meanings that lie between them. But, as the films I examined began to demonstrate, often meaning escapes the audiovisual registers altogether. In chapter 2, I suggested that memory is encoded in objects through contact, and examined films and videos that attempt to reconstruct those memories by engaging with the object. In this chapter, I will argue that cinema itself appeals to contact—to embodied knowledge, and to the sense of touch in particular—in order to recreate memories. A story "bears the marks of the storyteller much as the earthen vessel bears the marks of the potter's hand" (Benjamin 1968b, 92); so cinema bears the marks of sense memories that do not find their way into audiovisual expression.

Let me recall once more the originary fossil-like image in *History and Memory*—the image that is for Rea Tajiri what the madeleine was for Proust—that of the woman filling the canteen. The second time the image plays, as the woman (Tajiri, playing her mother) kneels in the dust, we hear the sound of water splashing: she rinses her face with a grimace of relief, as though this visit to the pump were her only respite from the days of imprisonment, dust, and waiting. Her mother's only memory, then, is a *tactile* memory, of the heat rising and the coolness of water on her hands and face. The film alludes to this level of perception through image and, especially, the gurgling sound of the running water: the tactile memory is encoded audiovisually.

It is not accidental that certain experiences are most likely to be "recorded" only in the nonaudiovisual registers of touch, smell, and taste. The fabric of everyday experience that tends to elude verbal or visual records is encoded in these senses. Senses that are closer to the body, like the sense of touch, are capable of storing powerful memories that are lost to the visual. Senses whose images cannot be recorded (the primitive experiments of virtual reality notwithstanding) are repositories of private memory. Leslie Devereaux writes of the experience of wearing a tight woven belt, which Zinacanteca women of Guatemala do from the very day of their birth, as an experience that is encoded only by the body. Like the fossil object/images of the previous chapter, the belt bears within it a great complex of meanings:

Without the frost under my foot, the grassy patches between forest and cornfield would not be good pasturage for sheep. Without the baa-ing of the sheep, the wool in the belt would be gone. Without the truck the colourfast red dye from German companies in Guatemala would have to come by muletrain, and would be too costly and scarce. Without the woodsmoke from the disappearing oak forests, how would the weaver cook her corn into tortillas? So it is clear that this belt is actually composed of an infinitude of non-belt elements. It has no separate existence apart from this web of non-belt elements. (1995, 57–58)

Devereaux does not attribute to the woven belt some ancient and immutable wisdom: it contains the traffic permitting German dyes, the disappearance of the forests, and other signs of changing Zinacan-

teca life within its traditional form. It is a witness to all these histories, and insofar as it is, these histories are imprinted on Zinacanteca
women's bodies (Devereaux once saw that her friend's waist bore
a permanent half-inch-deep indentation). Objects, bodies, and in-
tagible things hold histories within them that can be translated only
imperfectly. Cinema can only approach these experiences asymptotically, and in the process it may seem to give up its proper (audiovisual) being.

In what follows I emphasize the multisensory quality of perception, the involvement of all the senses even in the audiovisual act
of cinematic viewing, in order to shift the discussion of visuality
from the optical terms that usually predominate. (As I will explain,
an *optical image* in the sense that I use it, borrowing from Alois
Riegl, is different from Deleuze's term *optical image;* in fact, con-
fusing though it may sound, it is the haptic image that falls under
Deleuze's category of optical images.) My exploration of other sensory knowledges in this chapter and the next is an inquiry into
how the image calls up multisensory experience. It is not a search
for a way to reproduce multisensory imagery. I will not be looking primarily at technologies that attempt to reproduce the sense
of smell (for example, Odorama) or touch (for example, the Power
Glove)—in effect, movement-image strategies for evoking smell and
touch—but rather examining how audiovisual media evoke these
other senses within their own constraints, in a manner more conso-
nant with Deleuze's model of time-image cinema. I will argue that
intercultural cinema has especially good reason to push the media
beyond their audiovisual bounds, perverse though this may be.

Let me begin this discussion with some caveats. By now, visuality
has been blamed for as many evils as, at other times, capitalism and
the weather have been. I will argue, however, that the critique need
not be extended to all forms of visuality. It may apply to the visuality
typical of capitalism, consumerism, surveillance, and ethnography:
a sort of instrumental vision that uses the thing seen as an object
for knowledge and control. Yet it seems the critique of visuality has
come to a turning point. A number of theorists are reconsidering
vision by classifying it as instrumental and noninstrumental, objec-
tifying and intersubjective, vision aligned with mastery and vision
that allows its object to remain mysterious (see Levin 1993 for sev-

eral such thoughtful reconsiderations). Similarly, my project here is not to condemn all vision as bent on mastery, nor indeed to condemn all mastery, but to open up visuality along the continua of the distant and the embodied, and the optical and the haptic. I will suggest that a form of visuality that yields to the thing seen, a vision that is not merely cognitive but acknowledges its location in the body, seems to escape the attribution of mastery.

Also, let me note that there are good reasons for the dominance of vision in nearly every world culture. A certain degree of separation from the body is necessary in order for our bodies to function. Imagine if our perceptions were so embodied that we could feel every step of our digestive process, the twitching of our neurons. We would be so attuned to the universe within that it would be impossible to focus on the world around us. If we were aware of the functioning of our spleens, the constant activity upon the mucous membranes of our nostrils, the traffic on our synaptic highways, we would certainly not be able to drive a car, let alone distinguish perceptions most necessary for survival. Drew Leder argues in *The Absent Body* (1992) that a certain degree of "alienation" from our bodies is crucial. Vision, as the sense generally most separate from the body in its ability to perceive over distances, is the central sense to this necessary alienation. Leder's term "the absent body" makes overt use of the Latin root of *absence,* which means not a void but "being-away," a being that is away from itself. He argues that the lived body combines first-person and third-person perspectives, in order to have the distance from itself necessary for functioning.

Similarly, while I am remarking upon the rise of interest in tactile forms of knowledge, I must note that a regime of knowledge in which tactility reigned supreme would have its ethical and epistemological problems (as well as make driving a car almost impossible). Tactility cannot be a distance sense, even in the foggiest valleys and most polluted cities where one can really touch the air. A configuration of the senses that would value sense information perceived within the body, on the body's surface, and at close, middle, and far distances from the body would seem to be an ideal alternative to the current skewing of the modern sensorium in favor of distance. Vision, in fact, is capable of almost all these sorts of perception. Finally, it is worth considering that since humans have developed many prosthetic machines, from telescopes to magnetic-resonance imaging, that render the world optical for us, we have the luxury, and perhaps the necessity, to explore other sorts of visuality as we have not before.

These caveats made, I should note that in recent years artists in many mediums have taken renewed interest in the tactile and other sensory capacities of their work, often to the diminishment of its visual appeal. Scholars in philosophy, art history, anthropology, and cognitive science have begun to posit an epistemology based on the sense of touch. Theorists in many disciplines have made connections between the Cartesian privileging of vision, insofar as it is the most "cerebral" of the senses, and a destructive desire for self- and social control. Historians of vision and visuality note connections between the structure of industrial and postindustrial societies and the reconfiguration of the senses, with implications for militarism and other forms of social control.[1] The critique of ocularcentrism has a considerable legacy among feminist theorists, who link vision to the distanciation from the body and to the objectification and control of self and others. Many of the feminist critiques of vision and control are grounded in psychoanalytic theory, while others take a more historical, sometimes Foucauldian approach to the uses of visuality.[2] Other critics, such as Trinh T. Minh-ha (1989) and Fatimah Tobing Rony (1996), have noted the specifically Western character of visuality as one that objectifies others, isolates self from others, and attempts to master external and internal worlds.

A significant number of intercultural film- and videomakers embed a critique of visuality in their work. Often they draw from critiques of ethnography. This well-known critique asserts that ethnographic photography and film have objectified non-Western cultures and made a spectacle of them; they have reduced cultures to their visual appearance; and they have used vision as part of a general will to knowledge of the other as a means to power.[3] Many films and videos critique the will to visually master another culture. Some put up real or metaphoric smokescreens that obscure the view of a culture. Others suggest that the most important aspects of the culture or the story are invisible. In all cases, these works trouble the relationship between vision and knowledge. Pointing to the limits of visual knowledge, they frustrate the passive absorption of information, instead encouraging the viewer to engage more actively and self-critically with the image.

One of the most important innovators of the critique of ethnographic visuality has been Trinh T. Minh-ha. Trinh's films *Re:Assemblage* (1982) and *Surname Viet Given Name Nam* (1989), like Chris Marker's *Sans soleil* (1982), Claude Lanzmann's *Shoah* (1985), Alain Resnais's *Hiroshima mon amour* (1959), and Peter Kubelka's *Unsere Afrikareise* (1961–66), use both poetic and aggressive strategies to compel the viewer to consider the destructive effects of believing that one can know another culture or another time through visual information alone. The legacy of her experiments has nourished thoughtful reflections on the possibility of visual knowledge, as well as founding a generation of sometimes derivative works. By the time of *Shoot for the Contents* (1991), Trinh proposes a model of vision based on the Chinese game that gives the film its title: do not believe what you see, but think of the image as a box whose contents you must infer. At the same time, Victor Masayesva Jr. has been challenging the destructive effects of ethnographic filmmaking in works such as *Ritual Clowns* (1988), which shows how ethnographers depicted Hopi rituals as the childish antics of a primitive people. In *Hopiit* (1982) and *Itam Hakim Hopiit* (1985) Masayesva offered a more appropriate way to image Hopi life that protected sacred activities from the view of outsiders and represented the most important aspects of Hopi life obliquely, for example, by using the life cycle of corn, the Hopi staff of life, to structure *Itam Hakim Hopiit,* an oral history of the Hopi people.

I have already discussed, in chapters 1 and 2, how a lack of faith in the visual motivates many artists to treat the image as a mine (and a minefield) that they must excavate in order to find meaningful stories. As I noted in chapter 1, the Black British workshops Black Audio and Sankofa developed sophisticated critiques of the complicity of visual knowledge with official discourse. Works such as Black Audio's *Handsworth Songs* (1986), Reece Auguiste's *Twilight City* (1989), John Akomfrah's *Testament* (1988) and *Who Needs a Heart?* (1991), Isaac Julien's *The Passion of Remembrance* (1986) and *Looking for Langston* (1989), and others by these workshops approached the visual archive warily and interrogated it for what it could not tell. Some more recent works that begin their historical excavation with a suspicion of the image include videos "about" Palestine and Lebanon: Elia Suleiman and Jayce Salloum's *Muqaddimah Li-Nihayat Jidal (Introduction to the end of an argument)*

48. Frame enlargements from *Hopiit*. Courtesy of Victor Masayesva Jr.

Speaking for oneself . . . speaking for others (1990), Jayce Salloum
and Walid Ra'ad's *Talaeen a Junuub (Up to the South)* (1993), Salloum's *This Is Not Beirut* (1994), and Jalal Toufic's *Credits Included:
A Video in Red and Green* (1995). As the filmmakers of Black Audio
and Sankofa suspect the image's complicity with official racist discourse about Blacks in Britain, so these works suspect the ability
to represent the Middle East in a Western context already saturated
with images that derisively dismiss the Palestinian struggle and the
Lebanese war. In these works blurry images shot from moving cars,

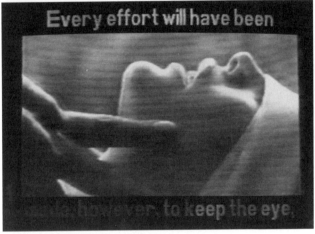

49 and 50. Stills from *Aletheia*. Courtesy of Tran T. Kim-Trang.

uninformative shots of damaged buildings, and seemingly irrelevant details challenge viewers' desire to read the truth of the Palestinian and Lebanese conflicts with Israel (and the West) from visual images alone. Another artist who initiates her works with a wry suspicion of the images that already contain her (Chinese) culture in the West is Yau Ching, in *Flow* (1993) and *Is There Anything Specific You Want Me to Tell You?* (1991). This body of work does not necessarily offer a plenitude of new sense experience, but rather, by muffling the experience of the visual, points to the possibility of less ocularcentric ways of seeing.

There are also a number of intercultural works specifically about

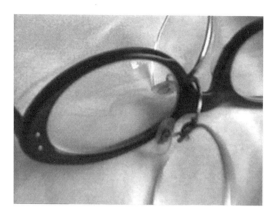

51. Still from *Ekleipsis*

Western visual technologies. In Pam Tom's *Two Lies* (1989) a Chinese American woman gets plastic surgery to widen her eyes, and the film plays on the metaphor of impaired vision. The "Blindness Series" by Tran T. Kim-Trang, thus far *Aletheia* (1992), *Operculum* (1993), *Kore* (1994), *Ocularis: Eye Surrogates* (1997), and *Ekleipsis* (1998), explores the use of visual technologies in objectification and surveillance. But even in their critique of instrumental vision, the tapes begin to present to the viewer a different kind of visuality. *Aletheia,* for example, is a tape "about" the desire to blind oneself. Yet it is dense with visual detail—it layers many visual images as well as sound tracks; it begins with a shot of a piece of Braille writing; it overlays shots from a car window with a fragment of a map of Los Angeles. The effect of this surface density is to invite a kind of vision that spreads out over the surface of the image instead of penetrating into depth. Even the long quotes from Trinh and Fanon that appear in the tape begin to dissolve into a pattern on the surface of the image. *Ekleipsis* deals with a group of Cambodian women living in Long Beach, California, all of whom have hysterical blindness dating to the experiences with the brutal Khmer Rouge regime that made them refugees. What is most striking about Tran's oblique telling of the story is that the images that illustrate it cycle by in brief intervals, separated by fades to white. Images of jewelry and watches (which the fleeing women hid in their vaginas), eyeglasses, a stupa, and a pineapple (which Tran notes Cambodians equated with the Khmer Rouge: having eyes everywhere [1997]), appear to vision for only a second and are then obscured again. Tran thus mimics the vision of one who has suffered so much that she must shield herself from perception, to whom images occur in the briefest of flashes and then are reabsorbed by an anaesthetic forgetting.

A Tactile Epistemology: Mimesis

Tactile epistemologies conceive of knowledge as something gained not on the model of vision but through physical contact. Many of the sources for tactile epistemology may be regarded as unrigorous, romantic, or downright spooky: the Cabbalistic undertones of Walter Benjamin's theories of representation (Hansen 1987, Buck-Morss 1989); the exoticizing longing of anthropologists for other cultures' ways of knowing (Jay 1993b and the lively exchange between Taussig 1994, Stoller 1994, and Jay 1994); Deleuze and Guattari's (1987) nonlinear musings on navigation and insects, viewed askance by many academics; the perceived essentialism of feminists who describe a form of representation grounded in the body (see Grosz 1994, introduction, for a rejoinder). My effort here to describe a form of cinematic representation based on the sense of touch may also be susceptible to some of these criticisms. I would like to keep those critiques in mind but hold them in check until later in this chapter.

Tactile epistemology involves a relationship to the world of mimesis, as compared to symbolic representation. Mimesis, from the Greek *mimeisthai,* "to imitate," suggests that one represents a thing by acting like it. Mimesis is thus a form of representation based on a particular, material contact at a particular moment, such as that between a child at play and an airplane (Benjamin 1978a), a moth and the bark of a tree (Caillois 1984), or a Songhay sorcerer and a spirit (Stoller 1989). Mimesis, in which one calls up the presence of the other materially, is an indexical, rather than iconic, relation of similarity. According to Erich Auerbach (1953), mimesis requires a lively and responsive relationship between listener/reader and story/text, such that each time a story is retold it is sensuously remade in the body of the listener. Auerbach was describing the relationship between reader and written text; we might expect the relationship between "viewer" and the more physical object of cinema to be more convincingly mimetic.

Mimesis is a concept thoroughly rooted in Western thought (it appears in Aristotle). Although Deleuze and the philosophers upon

whom his cinema theory is based, Bergson and Peirce, do not use
the term *mimesis*, it is quite consistent with all their conceptions of
the relationship between the world and the sign or the image. Like
memory in Bergson's theory, mimesis is mediated by the body. As
Peirce's semiotics presumes a continuum between more immediate
signs and more symbolic signs, mimesis presumes a continuum between the actuality of the world and the production of signs about
that world.[4] This excursion into increasingly bodily forms of representation is thus consistent with the theories of representation and
memory with which I began.

Mimetic representation, then, exists on a continuum with more
symbolic forms of representation. It lies at the other pole from the
symbolic representation characteristic of contemporary urban and
postindustrial society. The highly symbolic world in which we find
ourselves nowadays is in part a function of the capitalist tendency
to render meanings as easily consumable and translatable signs,
a tendency that in turn finds its roots in Enlightenment idealism.
Consequently, critics of capitalism often seek a return to mimetic
representation in order to shift the emphasis from the world of abstraction to the concrete here-and-now. Because vision is the sense
that best lends itself to symbolization, contemporary forays in Western scholarship into a tactile epistemology are generally rooted in
critiques of the current state of visuality in postindustrial, capitalist
society.

Noting that the senses are formed in a social context, Marx argued
that the modern individual's "alienation" is an alienation not only
from the products of his or her labor but from the very body and
the senses ([1844] 1978, 87–89). This observation informed many
subsequent critiques of the apparent atrophy of sensuous knowledge in industrial and postindustrial societies. British critics such
as William Morris critiqued the fact that capitalist culture alienated the "close" senses such as touch and smell, while honing the
visual sense until it acquired the character of a weapon (Classen,
Howes, and Synnott 1994, 87). Similarly, the Frankfurt School critics perceived an increasing process of abstraction stemming from
the subjugation of nature in Enlightenment science and culminating
in late capitalism. They do not confine this movement to the West,
noting that in both Homer and the Rig-Veda the separation of subject and object in representation originates in periods of territorial

domination and the subjection of vanquished peoples (Horkheimer and Adorno 1972, 13). Still, they argue that capitalism enables the domination of nature and others to an unprecedented degree. Sensuous knowledges that rely on both body and mind, according to Horkheimer and Adorno, or what Benjamin called the mimetic faculty, have atrophied in the historical context of industrialism and capitalism. The Frankfurt School critics valued sensuous knowledge as a reservoir of nonalienated experience (Horkheimer and Adorno 1972, 71 and passim). Mimesis, they argued, is a form of yielding to one's environment, rather than dominating it, and thus offers a radical alternative to the controlling distance from the environment so well served by vision.

Recall Benjamin's enormously productive suggestion (1968c) that *aura* entails a relationship of contact, or a tactile relationship. The "Artwork" essay implies that aura is the material trace of a prior contact, be it brushworks that attest to the hand of the artist or the patina on a bronze that testifies to centuries of oxidation. Aura enjoins a temporal immediacy, a co-presence, between viewer and object. To be in the presence of an auratic object is more like being in physical contact than like facing a representation. In early drafts of the "Artwork" essay Benjamin posited a form of "sensuous similarity" that would find communicative correspondences between nature and perception (Hansen 1987). Sensuous similarity describes correspondences between one's body and the world that precede representation, such as the relationship between people and the heavens described by astrology (this controversial notion disappeared from the final draft of the essay). Benjamin's essay "On the Mimetic Faculty" (1978a) also took up this theme. This essay and the unfinished *Passagen-Werk,* like the early drafts of the "Artwork" essay, attempted, always evasively, to demonstrate a mimetic understanding of material reality. Benjamin valued children's ability to relate to things mimetically (Buck-Morss 1989, 263–67), and he suspected that the mimetic relationship need not be superseded by an "adult" way of relating to things as merely objects. He also suggested that the use of the mimetic faculty varied over history. "It must be borne in mind that neither mimetic powers nor mimetic objects have remained the same in the course of thousands of years. Rather, we must suppose that the gift of producing similarities—for example, in dances, whose oldest function this was—and also the gift of recognizing them, have changed with historical development" (1978a, 333). As I will discuss below, like Benjamin (and influencing him), art historians in the early twentieth century assigned a new value to a mimetic kind of vision that drew close to its object.

Writings on mimesis have a prescriptive implication: through mimesis we can not only understand our world, but create a transformed relationship to it—or restore a forgotten relationship. Mimesis shifts the hierarchical relationship between subject and object, indeed dissolves the dichotomy between the two, such that erstwhile subjects take on the physical, material qualities of objects, while objects take on the perceptive and knowledgeable qualities of subjects.[5] Mimesis is an immanent way of being in the world, whereby the subject comes into being not through abstraction from the world but compassionate involvement in it. As Roger Caillois (1984) wrote, mimicry (he did not use the term *mimesis*) is "an incantation fixed at its culminating point," because things have been in contact leave their traces irrevocably on each other.[6]

Not all accounts of mimesis or of tactile epistemology call for a return to a state before language and before representation. They do, however, insist that symbolic representation is not the sole source of meaning. In fact, even in its most abstract forms, symbolic representation derives from a more fundamental, mimetic relationship to the world. Mimetic and symbolic representation are related in the way that the inside of a glove is related to the outside. Benjamin (1978a) argued that language is the highest form of the mimetic faculty. This does not describe language as the system of signs we have come to understand it to be. Rather it describes a language that draws close enough to its object to make the sign ignite. "The coherence of words or sentences is the bearer through which, like a flash, similarity appears. For its production by man—like its perception by him—is in many cases, and particularly the most important, limited to flashes. It flits past" (1978a, 335). Merleau-Ponty described the same flash of embodied meaning in language when he wrote, "Words most charged with philosophy are not necessarily those that contain what they say, but rather those that most energetically open upon being" (1973, 20). Language is rooted in the body, its meanings inseparable from the sounds and gestures that bore it forth. Similarly, Derrida emphasized the sensual basis of philosophy in *Glas* (1974, 161), where he describes the tactile production of speech:

shaped by the mucous membranes of the mouth, stuck together by saliva, and spat out. These accounts of symbolic production show that its embodied and mimetic moments, where the body of the speaker opens into the text and the space between speaker and listener thickens, are fundamental to its meaning. Even in the most sophisticated representational systems, such as writing or cinema, the iconic and symbolic coexist with the indexical: representation is inextricable from embodiment.

I mentioned in chapter 1 that Bergson's *Matter and Memory* inaugurated a way to understand memory as being located in the body. Nevertheless, Bergson undervalued embodied memory, in part because he assumed that memory can be easily brought forth when necessary, not acknowledging the individual and social prohibitions on the actualization of memory. More fundamentally, he undervalued it because he privileged the intellectual intervention in the bodily actualization of memory. He distinguished two kinds of memory: memory images, and modifications of the body: "the one *imagines* and the other *repeats*" ([1911] 1988, 93). The former are ultimately action, since memory can only be brought to consciousness in action. The latter are mere habitual representation" (89–91). Lumping together the memory of children, dreamers, and "African savages," he notes that all have greater access to spontaneous memory, or memory that is immediately and unselectively actualized in the body: he refers to a missionary's account that after preaching a long sermon to some Africans he heard one of them repeat the whole sermon, "with the same gestures, from beginning to end" (199). Bergson dismisses such "impulsive" bodily memory as inferior to a more selective memory that actualizes only what is useful. In arguing for the value of mimetic knowledge I am giving greater value to what Bergson called "habit," which I will argue is a knowledge of the body more highly cultivated than he acknowledges. Clearly Benjamin, in his admiration of children's mimetic capacities, was already beginning to shift the value of Bergson's hierarchy.

Benjamin might have added that the mimetic faculty not only varies historically but is cultivated differently across cultures. When the European colonists and traders dismissed African practices as fetishism (Pietz 1987), as I discussed in the last chapter, they were simply unable to recognize the mimetic knowledge that the Africans had assiduously cultivated. Anthropologist Michael Taussig (1993) closely following the Frankfurt School theory of mimesis, suggests that some cultures retain the mimetic faculty that has been devalued in the West. Taussig historicizes the notion of mimesis as a form of knowledge by analyzing a number of non-Western cultures' forms of knowledge, primarily those of the Cuna Indians of San Blas Islands and environs. These cultures reveal that knowledge is far more dependent on bodily mimesis than conventional Western science can acknowledge. Taussig posits an epistemology of touch that would be less instrumental than the predominant visual epistemology. Sensuous knowledge implies "a yielding and mirroring of the knower in the unknown, of thought in its object" (45). Horkheimer and Adorno (1972), following Freud, had compared the yielding form of knowledge that is mimesis to the death instinct, the willingness to merge back with nature. In contrast, Taussig usefully aligns mimesis not with a state of nature but with an alternative, cultivated epistemology.

Similarly inspired by the Frankfurt School theorists, especially Benjamin, Susan Buck-Morss (1992) also posits mimesis as an alternative way of being in the world, a sort of productive embrace. She is more cautious than Taussig about the capacities of mimesis. In her reading of Benjamin's (1968a) essay on Baudelaire, Buck-Morss notes that mimesis has become a way to shelter the individual from the shock of the world, such that mimesis is the form of alienation inscribed upon the body in modern culture. Echoing Benjamin's critique of remembrance, Buck-Morss notes that in modern, capitalist times perception shields the body from experience, rather than permitting sense experience to flow into the body. Factory workers who learn to coordinate their movements to those of the machines are practicing this murderous form of mimesis (1992, 17), what Horkheimer and Adorno called a "mimesis unto death" (1972, 57). Nevertheless, Buck-Morss hopes that a rediscovery of mimesis might inform a nonalienated consciousness. Like Taussig, though less optimistically, she posits a mimetic faculty that might counter the self-distanciation typical of modernity and restore the body to its senses.

One might argue that Taussig's cross-cultural comparison and Buck-Morss's call for a return to a more sensuous time, like Benjamin's admiration of children and Horkheimer and Adorno's nostalgia for a time before capitalism when the senses were not alienated, hint of a sort of prelapsarian longing (see Jay 1993b). However, I believe that these theorists are borrowing from other cultures and ages in order to "think at the edge of what can be thought," to create a new language for a mimetic knowledge that exists in a nascent and latent form in the contemporary West. It is possible to take up theories of tactile epistemology without adopting the dire diagnoses of complete cultural alienation on which these scholars' arguments rest. Sensuous forms of knowledge do not get wiped out as though by a plague. As Merleau-Ponty ([1969] 1973) argues, we humans have never ceased to cultivate mimetic knowledges. The issue is that these are not necessarily valued in a given culture. Yet cultures are diverse enough, and "development" is "uneven" enough, that different forms of sensory knowledge always exist in some form. Indeed the current Western cultural longing to rediscover sensuous knowledges, evident among scholars, artists, and consumers, is a sign of such life. These descriptions of tactile epistemology compellingly formulate the desire for a sensuously informed knowledge that is newly prevalent in the late-twentieth-century West.

I would argue, then, that rather than give in to the prelapsarian or primitivist longing for sensuous knowledge that motivates many accounts of mimesis, we acknowledge that many cultures have cultivated mimesis and other forms of sensuous knowledge. The perceived need for a mimetic visuality among the critics I have cited came as a reaction to several centuries of European ocularcentrism, in which vision alone was the ontological sense par excellence (Jay 1993a). Yet cultural traditions that do not separate vision so radically from the body have less need to deconstruct and reimagine visuality. Many of the works I discuss in this book draw on such cultural traditions and critically compare them to the predominant Western visual regime.

Theorists who call for a return to the senses often treat sense experience as prediscursive and, hence, as natural. This is a position I dispute. Theorists descended from Marxism and phenomenology appeal to the senses' basically biological function in serving needs for shelter, nourishment, safety, and sociability. Yet they tend not to acknowledge that sensuous knowledge is cultivated. This, I believe, is a result of the Eurocentric mistake of thinking that because the proximal senses of touch, taste, and smell are not accorded much importance in Western cultures, they are outside culture in general. For example, Buck-Morss argues that the senses "maintain an uncivilized and uncivilizable trace, a core of resistance to cultural domestication" (1992, 6). Similarly, Steven Shaviro attributes a raw state to sensation: "I am violently, viscerally affected by *this* image and *this* sound, without being able to have recourse to any frame of reference, and form of transcendental reflection, or any Symbolic order" (1993, 32). What Merleau-Ponty called "indirect language" would supposedly bring listeners into contact with "brute and wild being," in that it requires a mimetic relationship between the body and the word[7]: the same can be said for cinema, which would bring viewers into a mimetic relationship with the image. But just how "wild" is this being? I argue that, while much of sensory experience is presymbolic, it is still cultivated, that is, learned, at the level of the body. The senses are educated to a larger extent than these theorists acknowledge.

Thus my interest in focusing on sense experience (particularly in cinema) is to find culture *within* the body, more than to identify a "wild" strain outside culture. By paying attention to bodily and sensuous experience, we will find that it is to a large degree informed by culture. Perception is already informed by culture, and so even illegible images are (cultural) perceptions, not raw sensations. Once these primitivist understandings of the senses are put to rest, *then* we can explore what part of sensory knowledge is precultural, and thus what part of cinematic perception, if any, is universal in its visceral immediacy.

Embodied Perception and Embodied Spectatorship

Film is grasped not solely by an intellectual act but by the complex perception of the body as a whole. This view of perception implies an attitude toward the object, in this case a film, not as something that must be analyzed and deciphered in order to deliver forth its meaning but as something that means in itself. In the following, I offer a theory of embodied visuality that revalues our mimetic relationship with the world.

Often informed by a newly revived phenomenology, theories of embodiment begin with the premise that our bodies are not passive objects "inscribed" with meaning but are sources of meaning themselves (Csordas 1994, 7). This is not to deny the power of semiotics to analyze cinema, nor the existence of cinematic codes.[8] Yet most semiotic approaches cannot take into account the embodied nature of the cinematic viewing experience.[9]

A discussion of embodied vision might begin with the early nineteenth-century European physiologists' and philosophers' experiments on the subjective nature of perception (Crary 1990). They found vision to be a physiological effect—the impression of color could be produced by electrical stimulation of the optic nerve, for example—rather than evidence of a coherent, external world of objects. Goethe, Purkinje, and others recounted their experiences of retinal afterimages and other "subjective" images with a mixture of dismay and exhilaration (Crary 1990, chapter 3). Their discoveries of the degree to which vision is embodied dealt a final blow to the "Cartesian" ideal of a detached, objective observer.

The nineteenth-century experiments in perception inspired Bergson's theories of how the body mediates perception and memory. His *Matter and Memory* supports an understanding of how memory may be served by different configurations of the senses, as in different cultures. In Bergson's model, perception is not only inherently social, but also radically embodied, plastic, and instrumental, variable according to culture and local need. Memory, Bergson wrote, is actualized in bodily sensations ([1911] 1988, 130), and correspondingly is not simply a mental but an embodied process: perception appeals to the "intelligence of the body" (112). To recapitulate, for Bergson an image is not visual but multisensory, comprising all the information that one's senses perceive about an object. The difference between an objective reality and the perceived image is that the former is present in all its qualities while the latter isolates only that in which one is interested. When I perceive an object I do not perceive it as a whole but discern it with my different senses, creating for myself an image whose gaps "measure . . . the gaps in my needs" (49). Thus the definition of *image* is that which is isolated from its context by one's (interested) perception, which is informed by memory and actualized in the body. The interestedness of perception depends upon the memory of what counts as useful information: for example, what counts as useful in a given culture will inform whether one perceives an object visually, tactilely, olfactorily, or (usually) in some combination of these and other modalities.

Bergson privileged the distance senses as better able to engage with memory. He distinguished sensation from perception in that sensation involves direct action upon the body by a stimulus, whereas perception is a measure of potential action. "The more immediate the reaction is compelled to be, the more must perception resemble a *mere* contact" ([1911] 1988, 32; my emphasis). Some perceptions are more immediate: smell, taste, and touch usually fall into this category. Other perceptions provide more room to maneuver, a "zone of indetermination" (32) in which memory may intervene. Only on the body's surface do sensation and perception coincide: perception is like contact to the degree that reaction is immediate. However, these distinctions are quantitative, not qualitative. All sense perceptions allow for, and indeed require, the mediation of memory. Consequently, even the "mere contact" sensations engage with embodied memory. Memory teaches us to ignore an odor that constantly pervades our environment, for example. Culture teaches us which odors are to be avoided (for example, research on infants, as well as parents' observations, shows that they do not initially find the smell of feces unpleasant but must learn that it is: this is something that differentiates humans from other species [Engen 1991, 44]). It would seem that vision is the least immediate sense (since it does not involve contact with the body) and thus most apt to extend into memory. However, as the oeuvre of Proust, who read *Matter and Memory,* demonstrates, any sense perception can call up seemingly infinite, widening circles of memory like concentric ripples on a pond.

As I noted in chapter 1, a Bergsonian form of film spectatorship involves a viewer's "attentive recognition" of the images onscreen. Perception takes place not simply in a phenomenological present but in an engagement with individual and cultural memory. Attentive recognition, I suggested, is thus a participatory notion of spectatorship. We move between seeing the object, recalling virtual images that it brings to mind, and comparing the virtual object thus created with the one before us. This viewing process reactivates a viewer's complex of memory-images at the same time that it creates the object for perception. Therefore it is consistent with the theory that the image is multisensory, since Bergson's model of perception, upon which Deleuze relies, engages all sense perceptions. When Deleuze writes, toward the end of *Cinema 2,* that cinema cannot give us a body, but it can give us "the genesis of an 'unknown body,' which we have in the back of our heads, like the unthought in thought" (1989, 201), he suggests that cinema may indeed be capable of bringing us to our senses. Given the nature of memory, the audiovisual image necessarily evokes other sense memories, perhaps even memories that belong to that "unknown body." For example, when I am watching a scene shot in a garden in Shani Mootoo's *Her Sweetness Lingers* (1994), close-ups of magnolia flowers remind me of how they feel and how they smell, and the buzzing of insects reminds me of the heat of summer. For me the tape calls up associations with gardens I have known in my ancestral Alabama, associations that are probably somewhat different from the artist's and other viewers' associations with them.

Memory is a process at once cerebral and emotional, and this is especially evident with smell. Research suggests that we cannot remember an odor unless that odor is waved in front of our noses again (Engen 1991, 80). I would love to be able to dispute this, because it *seems* that I can remember just what a magnolia smells like, though this may be only the stirring of my other sense memories and associations around an empty center of magnolia fragrance. In any case, an audiovisual image evokes bodily associations, so that when I hear crickets and see a magnolia I remember the prickle of sweat on my skin, and (nanoseconds later) the *words* for the smell of a magnolia— *pungent, sap-like, always about to rot* (!)—emerge from the emotional associations I formed with magnolias when I did smell them.

Merleau-Ponty ([1945] 1992) significantly developed the ground laid by Bergson, loosening up the relationship between perception, body, and memory that was still rather stiff in the work of his predecessor. In Merleau-Ponty's account, time and space are thick, almost viscous, with experience. "Memory is built out of the progressive and continuous passing of one instant into another, and the interlocking of each one, with its whole horizon, into the thickness of its successor." Our perceptions fold us into this thick world at the same time that they demarcate us from it ([1945] 1992, 215). For Merleau-Ponty, our relationship to the world is fundamentally mimetic.

If cinema is perceived by a whole body, vision is inextricable from the other senses. As Merleau-Ponty argued, vision, by virtue of being a distance sense, allows us to "flatter ourselves that we constitute the world"; whereas tactile experience "adheres to the surface of our body; we cannot unfold it before us, and it *never quite becomes an object*. It is not I who touch, it is my body" ([1945] 1992, 316; my emphasis). Yet, echoing Bergson, he goes on to argue that touch is only "effective," that is, is only a perception, insofar as it links with memory (317). Luce Irigaray criticizes Merleau-Ponty for privileging vision as the model of all other perceptions (Grosz 1994, 104–6; Vasseleu 1998). She argues that touch, as the first sense experienced by the fetus and by the infant, should be the model of a mutually implicating relationship of self and world. Certainly, touch seems to be the foundation upon which subsequent sensuous experience is built (Montagu 1971, 270). More than any other sensory deprivation, the loss of the sense of touch creates a feeling of being an orphan in the world. Irigaray's question, "How to preserve the memory of the caress?," rests on a fundamental sense of loss: of a world of tactility experienced by the fetus and the infant, before language and vision organize its sensorium.

Despite Irigaray's critique, I find that Merleau-Ponty shares her ethical insistence on defining a relationship between self and world that is symbiotic, indeed mimetic. They both emphasize that in embodied perception the perceiver relinquishes power over the perceived. The proximal senses are more capable of such a mimetic relationship than vision is, for while looking tends to be unidirectional, one cannot touch without being touched. Yet vision too, insofar as it is embodied, is able to relinquish some of the power of the perceiver.

As Merleau-Ponty insisted that language is not a substitute for but an extension of being, so Vivian Sobchack (1992) argues that the cinema is not an illusion but an extension of the viewer's embodied existence. In theories of embodied spectatorship, such as Sobchack's, the relationship between spectator and film is fundamentally mimetic, in that meaning is not solely communicated through signs but experienced in the body. The phenomenological model of subjectivity posits a mutual permeability and mutual creation of self and other. Cinema spectatorship is a special example of this enfolding of self and world, an intensified instance of the way our perceptions open us onto the world. Sobchack's phenomenology of cinematic experience stresses the interactive character of film viewing. If one understands film viewing as an exchange between two bodies—that of the viewer and that of the film—then the characterization of the film viewer as passive, vicarious, or projective must be replaced with a model of a viewer who participates in the production of the cinematic experience. Rather than witnessing cinema as through a frame, window, or mirror, the viewer shares and performs cinematic space dialogically (10–15). This work is an important complement to Deleuze's theory, drawing upon Bergson, of the temporal relationship between viewer and film: Sobchack, drawing on Merleau-Ponty, emphasizes the spatial relationship between them.

I must mention the apparent incongruity between Deleuze's cinema theory and phenomenology. Deleuze found phenomenology particularly inadequate to the understanding of the cinema, noting Merleau-Ponty's objection that the cinema creates a world that exceeds natural perception, while phenomenology is modeled upon a notion of natural perception (1986, 57). In addition, Deleuze doubted the usefulness of phenomenology to understand perception, arguing, to state it simply, that phenomenology privileges consciousness over the world ("a beam of light which drew things out of their native darkness"), whereas for Bergson (and Deleuze) consciousness and the world, that is, the image, are indistinguishable (1986, 60–61). Yet, as I have argued, Merleau-Ponty's phenomenology did in fact inherit and expand Bergson's implication of perception in the body. More centrally, it seems that phenomenology builds a bridge to explaining how a viewer experiences images. Deleuzian cinematic philosophy is not a theory of spectatorship. To talk about the states, histories, and circumstances of the individual people experiencing cinema, we need a phenomenology of individual experience. Deleuze says "Give me a body, then," but his interest is not in exploring how cinema relates to the bodies we have already been given.

And although they cannot be utterly reconciled, both Merleau-Ponty's "consciousness of the world" and Bergson's "the world is consciousness" work against the psychoanalytic understanding that "consciousness misrecognizes the world." Theories of embodied spectatorship counter at their root theories of representation grounded in the alienation of visuality from the body, in particular Lacan's theory of the mirror phase, which has been so influential in cinema studies. The mirror-phase theory of subjectivity is based upon a fundamentally alienated selfhood that is constructed visually, when the infant comes into awareness of being seen from the outside.[10] In contrast, Merleau-Ponty posits a primordial subjectivity, an immanent knowledge of the body, that "fleshes out" specular alienation. Rather than an encounter between two lacks (the

fundamentally lacking subject of Lacanian psychoanalysis and the
fundamentally lacking object of the film), the phenomenological encounter is an exchange between an embodied self-in-becoming (the
viewer) and its embodied intercessor (the cinema). Theories of embodied visuality acknowledge the presence of the body in the act of
seeing, at the same time that they relinquish the (illusory) unity of
the self. In embodied spectatorship the senses and the intellect are
not separate. Sobchack writes, "The lived-body does not have senses
[which require a prior separation and codification of experience].
It is, rather, sensible" (77). Even pornography, a form of cinema in
which the image is generally thought to be utterly objectified, can
be the site of embodied and intersubjective spectatorship, as Linda
Williams (1995) has demonstrated.

Another recent theory of embodied spectatorship, Steven Shaviro's (1993), is less rigorous and more polemical than Sobchack's.
He argues that film does not (or not only) provide pleasure by ap-
peasing the spectator's ego, fixing him or her in a position of dominance, but also through "decentered freeplay, the freedom from the
constraints of subjectivity, that editing and special effects make possible" (42). Yet given that he draws his examples from *Blue Steel*
(Kathryn Bigelow, 1990) and the famous eye-slicing image from
Un chien andalou (Luis Buñuel and Salvador Dalí, 1928), Shaviro's
violent formulation of the tactile image would be more accurately
called propulsive or projectile.[11] Shaviro's assaultive and masochistic model of spectatorship maintains a radical alterity between self
and film, merely switching the poles of who does what to whom.
Unlike Shaviro, I would suggest that "the [Deleuzian] gap is a
wound at the heart of vision" (50) only if we equate vision with mastery. We need not respond with dread to cinema's threat/promise to
dissipate, or even to wrench away, our unified subjectivity. A tactile
visuality may be shattering, but it is not necessarily so.

In the following I explore how cinema may reconfigure, rather
than shatter, a subjectivity that may not be cast in stone in the first
place. Tactile visuality draws upon the mimetic knowledge that does
not posit a gulf between subject and object, or the spectator and the
world of a film. The theory of haptic visuality I advance should allow
us to reconsider how the relationship between self and other may
be yielding-knowing, more than (but as well as) shattering. In intercultural cinema, haptic images are often used in an explicit critique

of visual mastery, in the search for ways to bring the image closer to the body and the other senses.

Let me repeat that I am exploring sense experience in cinema not to seek a primordial state of sensory innocence, but to find culture *within* the body. A valid critique of phenomenology is that it mistakenly believes that all of experience is accessible to consciousness; it is just a matter of being in the present and perceiving. Merleau-Ponty's benign examples of embodied perception in *The Phenomenology of Perception*—his dawning perception of the solidity of the ashtray, the roundness of the bowl, the blue of the rug—suggest that it is indeed easy for one to participate bodily in the world from the comfort of one's study. The fact that the experience of the body is informed by culture, implicit in Merleau-Ponty, is explicated by recent returns to phenomenology informed variously by feminism, Foucault, and cultural anthropology. These studies show that our bodies encode history, which in turn informs how we perceive the world. When we speak of embodied perception, we must include the embodied *blocks* to perception and to full participation in the world: such are the sense of feminine embodiment as confinement (Young 1990), rape trauma (Winkler 1996), or the redirection of suppressed political resistance into the Chinese martial art *qigong* (Ots 1994). Embodiment involves a level of trauma that phenomenology did not initially recognize. This critique of phenomenology might be phrased in Bergsonian terms (even though, as we have seen, Bergson has a similar blind spot). Merleau-Ponty is perhaps insensitive to the fact that perception is subtractive. For Bergson, the subtractive nature of perception is the animal response of screening out all that does not meet our immediate needs. But perception can also be subtractive because of learned response (I tend not to distinguish among the smells of spices) or the affective responses of trauma (I block out the sound of voices that remind me of shouting fights I overheard as a child). Thus, if we consider that perception is subtractive, we can respect the fact that perception is not an infinite return to the buffet table of lived experiences but a walk through the minefield of embodied memory. Ultimately phenomenology can account for how the body encodes power relations somatically. It can acknowledge that embodiment is a matter of individual life-maps as well as cultural difference. These matters are important for understanding intercultural experience, where traumas and more ordinary histories become encoded in the body. When intercultural films and videos appeal to the different power relations involved in looking and in touching, they remind us that these power relations are built into cultural organizations of perception. As I will argue at greater length in the next chapter, embodied responses to cinema vary not only individually but collectively.

The cinematic encounter takes place not only between my body and the film's body, but my sensorium and the film's sensorium. We bring our own personal and cultural organization of the senses to cinema, and cinema brings a particular organization of the senses to us, the filmmaker's own sensorium refracted through the cinematic apparatus. One could say that intercultural spectatorship is the meeting of two different sensoria, which may or may not intersect. Spectatorship is thus an act of sensory translation of cultural knowledge. For example, when a work is viewed in a cultural context different from that in which it was produced, viewers may miss some multisensory images: many viewers will miss the implications of references to cooking, dance, and hairstyle in Julie Dash's *Daughters of the Dust* (1992) that are more likely to be clear to an African diasporan viewer. Paul Stoller writes optimistically that "a more sensual gaze will not enable us to see what the ethnographic other sees, but it will produce texts that correspond more closely to the experience and perception of the ethnographic other" (Stoller 1989, 68). Similarly, a more embodied perception of intercultural cinema may not make those sensory experiences available to the viewer, but it will at least give us a sense of what we are missing. And then again, viewers in the intercultural encounter may discover sense information that was not obvious in the original context.

The Memory of Touching

A number of intercultural works engage sense memories, and memories of touch in particular, by exploiting the relative weakness of the visual image—the lack of things to see. In chapter 1 I discussed several works that "mind the gaps" in grainy, faded stock footage or consumer-format video to search for unrepresentable memories: films such as *Handsworth Songs, Bontoc Eulogy,* and *Calendar. Seeing Is Believing,* as we "saw" earlier, finds a way to touch the image when seeing is not enough. Mona Hatoum's videotape *Measures of*

Distance (1988) breaks down the visual relationship in order to appeal to a personal and cultural memory of touch.

Measures of Distance begins with still images so close as to be unrecognizable, overlaid with a tracery of Arabic text. Warm reds and purples and curving shapes suggest that it is a close-up of parts of a body, but the large grain of the images and the (to non-Arabic readers) decorative letters effectively break down any figure-ground relationship. As the tape continues, the images are shown from a greater distance and revealed to be a naked woman whose large, voluptuous body is still veiled in the image's graininess and the layer of text. Meanwhile, Hatoum's mother's letters, translated and read in voice-over, convey her deep love and longing for "my dear Mona, the apple of my eye" and let us infer that she and her husband, originally Palestinian, are living in Lebanon during the civil war, while their children are dispersed all over the world. Undated but probably written in the mid-1980s, the letters testify to the increasing difficulty of communication—no phone, and later no post—as the shelling of southern Lebanon worsens. At the same time, the letters make us realize that these images are photographs that her daughter took of her on her last visit; further, they tell that Hatoum's father was very jealous of his wife's body and the idea of another, even/especially his daughter, being in intimate proximity to it.

Images of the most intimate places in the home; the figure of a naked woman, nearly obliterated by marks on the surface of the image; a daughter's desperate desire to make contact with her parents, as war makes communication ever riskier: these elements are eerily prefigured in an earlier video work by Hatoum, *Changing Parts* (1985). There, quiet shots of the clean interior of the bathroom of her parents' house in Beirut are intercut with a performance by the artist in London. Hatoum, naked, is imprisoned inside a polyethylene-walled container, whose sloping sides and floor prevent her from standing up. The bottom of the container appears to be covered with mud. As Hatoum struggles to rise, her limbs mark the sides of the container until they—and thus the surface of the image, since the container parallels the camera screen—become a palimpsest of muddy traces. At times she scratches on the plastic walls in a kind of incoherent writing. As this performance becomes increasingly frenzied, the tape cuts to the calm of home, represented in the humblest things: a toothbrush balanced by the sink, the clean white tiles, the pipes along the bathroom wall. On the sound track,

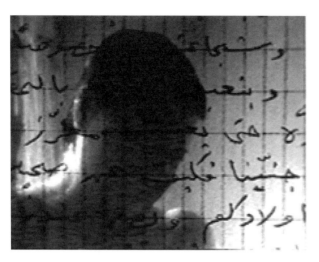

52. Still from *Measures of Distance.* Courtesy of Video Out.

53. Still from *Changing Parts.* Courtesy of Video Out.

a Mozart concerto gradually gives way to a radio broadcast from Beirut. The words of the broadcast are barely intelligible, but the BBC-accented reporter appears to be describing another bombing of the city where her parents live. In both these works by Hatoum, the ill-fated desire to make contact with home is expressed in tactile markings on the surface of the image, which obscure the image of a woman's naked body. Here the haptic image is suffused with sadness and desperation, the inadequacy of one kind of touch substituting for another. (Hatoum also seems to have a sustained interest in *plumbing:* the bathroom pipes documented in *Changing Parts,* other kinds of pipes in *Corps étranger,* which I discuss later.)

Like these works by Hatoum, Sami Al-Kassim's film *Far From You* (1996) uses the disintegration of the image to meditate on the painful knowledge of the exile: a knowledge that is ever more rarefied, ever further from the beloved things of home. The mother imaged in Al-kassim's *Far From You* is not her own but a national mother figure, the singer Umm Kholtoum. Kholtoum was beloved throughout Arab countries and the Arab diaspora, her dignified image and powerful voice signifying a pan-Arab nationalism for her generation. Yet, as Al-kassim points out in voice-over, Kholtoum as a representation of the Arab nation is deeply ironic, as her powerful voice is a reminder of the 1967 defeat of Egypt by Israel, her association with Nasser, and the blame she received for "numbing the masses." Although her powerful singing remains intact on the sound track, her image is reduced almost to an abstract pattern by the tenth-generation images on a TV screen. Together they call up bittersweet and conflicting memories: the longing of exiled Egyptians for a past life that she represents, yet the political turmoil she also represents. At first, Al-kassim's processing of the film suggests a television's poor reception of a foreign broadcast, or the bootleg videos so treasured by emigrants. Later, the multigenerational, color-processed image renders the images of Kholtoum grotesque, pink and purple blobs barely indicating the singer's strong-featured face and regal movements. These distorted images call to mind Hamid Naficy's (1993) warning that exiles will ruin their chances at creating a new life in diaspora if they fetishize the signifiers of their homeland. At the same time, the decaying image makes the viewer reflect on how much of perception is generated by memory and longing, rather than engagement with a crisply available visual object.

Another provocative example of how cinema can express embodied knowledge is the short video *I Wet My Hands Etched and Surveyed Vessels Approaching Marks Eyed Inside* (1992) by Roula Haj-Ismail. A philosophy student in Lebanon, Haj-Ismail made this tape in a workshop taught in Beirut by Walid Ra'ad. It attempts to give form to the "inner scars" of both the artist and the artist's grandmother, a Palestinian from Haifa, by exploring the visible scars on people and buildings. "Death cannot be made visible or cast the shadow of its presence," Haj-Ismail says, as the camera slowly

54. Frame enlargement from *Far From You*

pans images of suffering bodies: Gustav Klimt's emaciated women, a Gilles Peress photo of a child with its face covered with flies. Such images cannot give a sense of the living with wounds that is her and her neighbors' experience: this is an experience that can only be touched. Shots of bomb-pocked walls are common in films and videos about Lebanon, but Haj-Ismail's camera treats them like bodies, caressing the buildings, searching the corners of shutters and stone-latticed windows like folds of skin. Shot thus, these exterior scars increasingly resemble the image with which they are paired, a close-up of a woman's fingers, with red-enameled nails, repeatedly pressing into her cesarean scar. "Everything around me is imperfect, broken, shattered, destroyed. Holy wars, broken windows, jagged edges. My world and I, we echo each other. We reflect upon each other: two broken pieces of another broken part." As her scars are compared to the scarred buildings, so other shots pair the woman's shifting eyes with the windows facing so close to her house. "We are forced to enter into the lives of others," Haj-Ismail says with rising frustration. "We hear them fighting, singing, showering; I see them cooking, eating, and cleaning. One is never alone, I am never alone." The devastation of Beirut, the brokenness and incompleteness of each person, family, and house, has forced a greater porousness among them. To make scars speak, Haj-Ismail suggests, requires acknowledging one's lack of wholeness. Haj-Ismail elicits individual and communal memories by appealing to the way those memories are embodied.

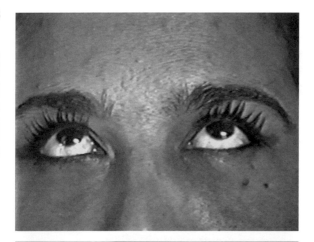

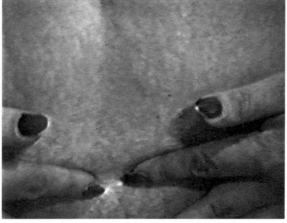

55 and 56. Stills from *I Wet My Hands Etched and Surveyed Vessels Approaching Marks Eyed Inside*

What Haj-Ismail evokes in condensed, poetic form is evident in narrative form in a video by Yasmine Khlat, *Leylouna notre nuit* (1987), a documentary of the everyday lives of women in a Beirut apartment building during the worst years of the Israeli bombings of Lebanon. Here too we witness the porosity of a neighborhood where women's lives mingle, where the world comes in through the many open windows. Even when the windows are closed one can hear the bombs exploding. The television too is like another window connecting the women's lives with other Lebanese. It brings news of more deaths, which registers on their bodies, as they weep, as well as in their talk. The difference between the narrative *Ley-*

Iouna notre nuit and the experimental *I Wet My Hands . . .* is one of degree. The former gives a sense of the what the women of Beirut suffered (in the senses both of undergoing pain and of having experience) during the years of the Israeli shelling through narrative, more than through appeals to sensory experience. The latter evokes this suffering by embodying it in the image, more than through narrative. *I Wet My Hands . . .* and other works appeal to embodied memory by bringing vision as close as possible to the image; by converting vision to touch. They also work by bringing vision close to the body and into contact with other sense perceptions; by making vision multisensory. They do this in part by refusing to make their images accessible to vision, so that the viewer must resort to other senses, such as touch, in order to perceive the image.

A Note on Sensory Difference

The reader will notice that many of the haptic films and videos I discuss in this chapter are made by Arab and Arab-diaspora women. Though this is a topic I will take up at length in the next chapter, it is worth considering whether these artists have a specific cultural interest in tactile or embodied knowledge. We might consider that, in the sensuous geographies of Arab and North African cultures in particular, touch and smell play relatively important roles. Whereas in most other cultures touch and smell are considered private senses, in Arab societies they are means of public communication (Rodaway 1994, 79). It is commonly noted that touch is a social sense in Arab cultures: for example, that men embrace and walk arm-in-arm in public. Since touching other people is considered a private activity in other cultures, especially northern ones, this is often interpreted as public intimacy and affection; but it is better understood as a carefully negotiated system of establishing trust (Hall 1969; Griffin 1990, 110; Rodaway 1994, 56–59). Also, fragrance has a long-standing importance in Arab countries, even given recent incursions of olfactory consumer culture such as the use of brand-name perfumes. There is plenty of anecdotal evidence for the social importance of smell, such as the striking fact that Chinese musk was incorporated in the mortar of the mosques of Kara Amed and Tabriz built in Persia in the twelfth century (Stoddart 1990, 155). In the contemporary United Arab Emirates, one of the most traditional and wealthy Arab societies, elaborate use is made of perfumes for social occasions, including the offering of perfumes to guests at the end of a meal (Classen, Howes, and Synnot 1994, 125–29). Compared to the urban geography of European or Chinese cities, for example, a less visual and more tactile and olfactory relationship to space informs the dense, cellular geography of Arab cities, organized around public/private spaces rather than vistas (Rodaway 1994, 59). In *I Wet My Hands,* the densely interconnected city is an extension of the body. In *Far From You, Measures of Distance,* and other works, the tactile image does seem to reflect a greater cultural awareness of knowledge gained through touch, to the point of substituting touch for vision.

Nevertheless, I wish to be careful in arguing that art necessarily expresses cultural predispositions, for the connection is not self-evident. As she points out in *I Wet My Hands . . . ,* Haj-Ismail is a Western-educated artist, "always feeling out of place: my hairy body and my world's strategic position; my black hair and its diverse identities, my acne and its civil war, my accent and its francophone, Anglo-Saxon ties, my name and its religious beliefs." Her tape represents a tactile relationship to the world that is traditional in Arab cultures, but she does this in a self-aware, even somewhat ironic way. Most intercultural artists have grown up in Western, or hybrid, cultures. They may not have learned the organization of the senses typical of their traditional cultures. Their explorations may be firmly couched in the Western critique of ocularcentrism, like those of other Western artists: Tran (1997) describes her work as based in a feminist critique of ocularcentrism more than in any traditional Vietnamese sensory practice. They may be perceptual experiments in the tradition of video art, which is how Seoungho Cho identifies his work, rather than in terms of his Korean heritage—although he has written, "In Korea, a person opens his heart through opening his eyes" (1994), suggesting that in his cultural tradition vision can be aligned with respect rather than mastery. Or these explorations may be selective combinations of a critique of Western visuality and a self-conscious exploration of other cultural traditions.

Beharry (1996), for example, says that her interest in touch comes from a strong desire to rediscover and reinvent her Indian heritage, as well as from more personal reasons. *Seeing Is Believing* attempts to rediscover a traditional Indian sensuous knowledge, but critically and self-consciously. When we look to traditional Indian conceptions of vision, we do find that vision is considered to be a means of knowledge by analog to hearing and touch more than in its own right (Pinard 1990). The spoken word is at the heart of Vedic worship, embodied by the high-caste Brahman who is the vessel of sacred knowledge. Written language and visual representations are determined by the images contained in the chants (Pinard 1990, 78). As Stella Kramrisch describes it, the traditional Hindu conception of vision startlingly parallels the tactile visuality imagined by the pre-Socratic philosophers. In it, vision entails "a going forth of the sight toward the object. Sight touches it and reveals its form. Touch is the ultimate connection by which the visible yields to being grasped. While the eye touches the object, the vitality that pulses in it is communicated" (Stella Kramrisch, quoted in Pinard 1990, 84). Thus it would seem that the tactile image reflects a traditional Indian organization of perception.

Of course one must take such accounts with a grain of salt, or a spot of *masala,* for as descriptions of high-culture, high-caste religious practices, they still cannot describe the everyday Indian sensorium. Religious practices find their everyday expression in rituals around eating and bathing, for example, and it is here that the conceptual universe would seem to be embodied in daily life. The complex relationships between temperature, flavor, and color in Indian tradition (see, for example, Daniel 1987), reflected in Ayurvedic medicine, are also found in cooking, a women's activity whose theory is embodied rather than explicit. Concluding his sketch of the Indian sensorium, Sylvain Pinard avows that in fact taste is the sense modality that structures all others. Eating, he argues, assimilates all the other modalities: the orality of significant sound, the tactility of vision, the discrimination of touch (1990, 93). These aspects of the Indian sensorium are reflected in Beharry's tape, but they are incorporated critically, by an artist who is cognizant of the cultural uses of the senses as only the culturally hybrid can be. In short, I believe it is important to show how cinema *may* respond to different cultural organizations of the senses—for example, by appealing to the sense of touch—without insisting that it always does.

Let us examine how cinema may evoke the sense of touch by appealing to haptic visuality. Haptic *perception* is usually defined by psychologists as the combination of tactile, kinesthetic, and proprioceptive functions, the way we experience touch both on the surface of and inside our bodies (see, for example, Heller and Schiff 1991). In haptic *visuality,* the eyes themselves function like organs of touch. I derive the term from nineteenth-century art historian Aloïs Riegl's distinction between haptic and optical images. Riegl borrowed the term *haptic* from physiology (from *haptein,* to fasten), since the term *tactile* might be taken too literally as "touching" (Iversen 1993, 170). His use of a physiological term indicates that he was aware of the experiments in the subjectivity and physiology of vision that also informed Bergson. Like Bergson, he argued that subjectivity is involved in perception: perception requires "the supplementary intervention of thought processes" (Riegl 1927, 28; quoted in Iverson, 77). Haptic visuality is distinguished from optical visuality, which sees things from enough distance to perceive them as distinct forms in deep space: in other words, how we usually conceive of vision. Optical visuality depends on a separation between the viewing subject and the object. Haptic looking tends to move over the surface of its object rather than to plunge into illusionistic depth, not to distinguish form so much as to discern texture. It is more inclined to move than to focus, more inclined to graze than to gaze.[12] I am changing Riegl's definitions somewhat. He associated the haptic image with a "sharpness that provoked the sense of touch," while the optical image invites the viewer to perceive depth, for example, through the blurring of chiaroscuro ([1902] 1995, 30–31). Most important in Riegl's distinction is the relationship the different kinds of images create with the viewer. Because a haptic composition appeals to tactile connections on the surface plane of the image, it retains an "objective" character; but an optical composition gives up its nature as physical object in order to invite a distant view that allows the viewer to organize him/herself as an all-perceiving subject (31).

To distinguish more terms, a film or video (or painting or photograph) may offer haptic *images,* while the term haptic *visuality* emphasizes the viewer's inclination to perceive them. The works I propose to call haptic invite a look that moves on the surface plane of the screen for some time before the viewer realizes what she or he is beholding. Such images resolve into figuration only gradually, if at all. Conversely, a haptic work may create an image of such detail, sometimes through miniaturism, that it evades a distanced view, instead pulling the viewer in close. Such images offer such a proliferation of figures that the viewer perceives the texture as much as the objects imaged. While optical perception privileges the representational power of the image, haptic perception privileges the material presence of the image. Drawing from other forms of sense experience, primarily touch and kinesthetics, haptic visuality involves the body more than is the case with optical visuality. Touch is a sense located on the surface of the body: thinking of cinema as haptic is only a step toward considering the ways cinema appeals to the body as a whole. The difference between haptic and optical visuality is a matter of degree. In most processes of seeing, both are involved, in a dialectical movement from far to near. And obviously we need both kinds of visuality: it is hard to look closely at a lover's skin with optical vision; it is hard to drive a car with haptic vision.

Haptic images are actually a subset of what Deleuze referred to as optical images: those images that are so "thin" and unclichéd that the viewer must bring his or her resources of memory and imagination to complete them. The haptic image forces the viewer to contemplate the image itself instead of being pulled into narrative. Thus it has a place in Deleuze's time-image cinema. Optical visuality, by contrast, assumes that all the resources the viewer requires are available in the image. Accordingly, the optical image in Riegl's sense corresponds to Deleuze's movement-image, as it affords the illusion of completeness that lends itself to narrative.

The haptic image, like other sensuous images, can also be understood as a particular kind of affection-image that lends itself to the time-image cinema. Recall that the affection-image, while it usually extends into action, may also force a visceral and emotional contemplation in those any-spaces-whatever divorced from action. Thus the haptic image connects directly to sense perception, while bypassing the sensory-motor schema. A sensuous engagement with a tactile or, for example, olfactory image is pure affection, prior to any extension into movement. Such an image may then be bound into the sensory-motor schema, but it need not be. The affection-image, then, can bring us to the direct experience of time *through* the body.

Haptic cinema does not invite identification with a figure—a sensory-motor reaction—so much as it encourages a bodily relationship between the viewer and the image. Consequently, as in the mimetic relationship, it is not proper to speak of the *object* of a haptic look as to speak of a dynamic subjectivity between looker and image. Because haptic visuality tends less to isolate and focus upon objects than simply to be co-present with them, it seems to correspond, if only formally, to Trinh T. Minh-ha's example (in *Reassemblage,* 1982) of "speaking not about, but nearby" the object she is filming.

In revaluing haptic visuality I am suggesting that a sensuous response may be elicited without abstraction, through the mimetic relationship between the perceiver and a sensuous object. This relationship does not require an initial separation between perceiver and object that is mediated by representation.

Haptic Visuality and Cultural Difference

Though Riegl was concerned to show the relation between sensory organization and cultural expression (as opposed to a universal ideal of art), he presumed a teleological development in which the haptic must necessarily give way to the optical, in order to realize the achievements of Renaissance perspective. This teleological view required Riegl to ignore optical illusionism in early Roman painting and to otherwise rewrite the history of art. Thus it is all the more interesting to examine the cultural biases that would have caused him to so value the optical over the haptic.

Cultural difference in the representation of space was of great interest to Riegl and some of his contemporaries. They needed both to take these differences into account and to argue that European art was superior to other cultural traditions. Riegl's student Wilhelm Wörringer noted that historians were having to revise their assumptions when confronted by "cultures of import" (1928, 81; quoted in Lant 1995, 49)—probably the Near Eastern, Asian, African, and Oceanic art that entered European markets in the wake of colonial adventures.

Riegl was one of several art historians who were reevaluating the spatial qualities of visual art around the time that the new medium of cinema was impressing its audiences with the apparent physical immediacy of the moving image. Riegl and Adolf Hildebrand, in books each wrote in 1893, were the first art historians to theorize spatiality in art with an eye to cultural variations in the representation of space. Soon after, other art historians, including Bernard Berenson (1896) and Wörringer ([1908] 1948), drew attention to the tactile quality of vision. In *The Florentine Painters of the Renaissance* (1896), Berenson argued that the quality most essential to painting was "the power to stimulate the tactile consciousness" (5). Like Bergson, he was influenced by new research in perceptual psychology, and argued that touch is the first sense an infant experiences (4). Through retinal impressions, a painting can stimulate perceptions of volume and movement in the imagination, even the body, of the viewer. According to Berenson, in terms that sound like a volumetric version of the mirror stage, tactile values simply make life better. "The stimulation of our tactile imagination awakens our consciousness of the importance of the tactile sense in our physical and mental functioning, and thus, again, by making us feel better provided for by life than we were aware of being, gives us a heightened sense of capacity" (11).[13]

These early theorists of tactility in visual art generally considered it to appeal to the viewer's kinesthetic sense, and thus to recreate, through reception, a sense of the three-dimensionality of the depicted object. But in addition Riegl made an important distinction between the materiality of haptic representation and the abstraction of optical representation, as when he wrote, "With an increased space and three-dimensionality the figure in a work of art is also increasingly dematerialized" ([1927] 1985, 74). This distinction between concrete and abstract describes a cultural difference as well. Riegl's history of art turned on the gradual demise of a physical tactility in art and the rise of figurative space. He observed this development from the haptic style of ancient Egyptian art, which "maintain[ed] as far as possible the appearance of a unified, isolated object adhering to a plane," to the optical style of Roman art, in which objects relinquished a tactile connection to the plane (Iversen 1993, 78–79; quoting Riegl [1927] 1985). His theory dwelt on the moment in late Roman art when figure and ground became thoroughly imbricated (Riegl [1927] 1985).

According to Riegl, the rise of abstraction in late-Roman works of art (sculpture, painting, and especially metal works) made it possible for a beholder to identify figures not as concrete elements on a surface but as figures in space. Optical images arose with the distinction of figure from ground, and the abstraction of the ground that made possible illusionistic figuration. Listen, for example, to Riegl's description of the difference between late Roman and Byzantine mosaics. The aerial rear plane of Roman mosaics

remained always a plane, from which individual objects were distinguished by coloring and [relief]. . . . However, the gold ground of the Byzantine mosaic, which generally excludes the background and is a seeming regression [in the progress toward depiction of illusionistic space], is no longer a ground plane but an ideal spatial ground which the people of the west were able subsequently to populate with real objects and to expand toward infinite depth. ([1927] 1985, 13)

It is important to note that the creation of abstract space in Byzantine art made it possible for a beholder to identify figures not as concrete elements on a surface but as figures in space. By contrast, haptic space is concrete, in that it seeks unity only on a surface. The rise of optical representation marked a general shift toward a cultural ideal of abstraction, with significant consequences. Abstraction facilitated the creation of an illusionistic picture plane that would be necessary for the identification of, and identification *with,* figures in the sense that we use "identification" now. In other words, optical representation makes possible a greater distance between beholder and object which allows the beholder to imaginatively project him/herself into or onto the object. Antonia Lant notes this implication as well when she writes, "Riegl's understanding of the relation of viewer to art work is not derived from his or her identification with a represented human figure, but rather operates at the level of design, suggesting an additional avenue for discussing film figuration besides narrative and plot" (1995, 64).

The revolution in visual styles Riegl observed coincided with a revolution in religious thought. The Barbarian invasion of the Roman Empire precipitated a clash between the belief that the body could be the vehicle for grace and the belief that spirituality required transcending the physical body.[14] Barbarian notions that the spirit transcends the body seem to be reflected in the development of a figurative picture plane that transcends the materiality of the support. Hence the origin of modern illusionistic representation can be traced to the cultural clash between beliefs in transcendent and immanent spirituality, represented by the late Roman battle of the optical and the haptic.

Both Riegl and Auerbach were tracing the history of a shift in the nature of Western figurative representation. According to Auerbach (1953), in the figural tradition (for example, in the Christian Old Testament), the symbolic characters are *figures* of transcendental events, existing not on the horizontal plane of earthly history but on the vertical axis of divine teleology.[15] Both were concerned with how the means of representation become more transparent in order to awaken sensuous response in the viewer/listener. That is, both described how Western art came to achieve sensuous similarity to its object through representation, rather than through contact. Riegl, especially, argued that increasing abstraction, or increasing membership in the symbolic, characterizes the history of Western art. As Margaret Iversen (1993, 125–26) points out, Riegl's theory of the relationship between subject and object is based on Hegel's *Aesthetics,* in that he argues that the increased disembodiment of painting, its existence as pure appearance alone, corresponds to a disembodied subject represented by (optical) vision alone. In his 1902 essay on the Dutch group portrait, Riegl wrote, "The history of mankind up to the present is intelligible in this regard in terms of two simple extremes: in the beginning, the conception that every subject was at the same time an object—that is, only objects exist; today, the opposite whereby there are hardly any objects and only a single subject" (quoted in Iversen, 125; Iversen's trans.).

Obviously my project here contrasts absolutely with Riegl's teleological assumptions. What these historians of Western art and literature saw as a necessary development was in fact only typical of a particular (albeit long) period in a particular (claimed as Western) history of representational practice. They were unable to acknowledge aspects of Western art that did not fit into their teleology, a teleology that was founded in the first place on assumptions of Western cultural superiority. Riegl's bias, for example, leads him to ignore early signs of the modernist revaluation of tactility, such as the visible brushstrokes in works before 1825 by artists such as Goya, Géricault, and Delacroix.

Both Riegl and Auerbach were writing about their respective fields on the cusp of modernism, which could be characterized as the return of materiality to the mediums of art and literature. Paint became opaque again, words became dense, and meaning came to reside in the embodied and intersubjective relationship between work and viewer or reader. After modernism it is easier to conceive that contact, and not only representation, is the source of sensuous similarity between a subject and an object (or between two subjects). Meaning occurs in the physical, sensuous contact between two subjects before, and as well as, it occurs in representation. The current intellectual embrace of embodiment, and the increased interest among artists in haptic and sensuous work, repudiate Riegl's teleology of disembodied and singular subjectivity (or, if one interprets Riegl more generously, they demonstrate a shift in his proposed dialectic). These recent changes reflect a revaluation of the non-Western and "minor" Western cultural traditions of material and sensuous art that Riegl saw as inferior.

Deleuze and Guattari appropriate Riegl's findings to describe a "nomad art" (appropriate to the idea of the small, portable metalworks of the late Romans and their Barbarian conquerors) whose sense of space is contingent, close-up, short-term, and lacking an immobile outside point of reference (Deleuze and Guattari 1987, 493). Riegl described the effects of figure-ground inversion in hallucinatory detail in *Late Roman Art Industry* (1927). But where he saw this viral self-replication of the abstract line as the last gasp of a surface-oriented representational system before the rise of illusionistic space, Deleuze and Guattari take the abstract line as a sign of the creative power of nonfigurative representation. "The organism is a *diversion* of life," they write, whereas the abstract line is life itself (497). Where Riegl justifies the tactile image as a step on the way to modern representation, Deleuze and Guattari see it as an alternative representational tradition. I concur with them insofar as haptic representation has continued to be a viable strategy in Western art, although it is usually relegated to minor traditions.

Interestingly, Riegl was initially a curator of textiles. One can imagine how the hours spent inches away from the weave of a carpet might have stimulated the art historian's ideas about a close-up and tactile way of looking. His descriptions evoke the play of the eyes over non- or barely figurative textures. The surface of video (generally more than film) is itself like a loosely woven fabric. I have come across a handful of works that use images of fabric to appeal to memory, to invite a more tactile kind of vision, and to call upon specific cultural knowledges associated with specific fabrics. Shauna Beharry's silk sari should be quite familiar by now. Another memory-fabric is a roll of silk in Leila Sujir's *India Hearts Beat* (1988), which the artist electronically processes to become an electronic tapestry, weaving together three women's stories of homesickness. And a work in progress by Palestinian-born scholar and videomaker Alia Arasoughly uses the close-up image of an Oriental carpet as the ground for an excursion into the memory of exile. It recalls how one might lie on a carpet and stare at its patterns, daydreaming; or, how patients might have gazed at the patterns on the carpets covering Freud's couch.

Riegl observed tactile modes of representation in traditions generally deemed subordinate to the procession of Western art history: Egyptian and Islamic painting, late Roman metalwork, textile art, and ornament. One can add Western high-art traditions such as medieval illuminated manuscripts, Flemish oil painting from the fifteenth to seventeenth centuries, and the surface-oriented, decorative rococo arts of eighteenth-century France. I would also include the "low" traditions of weaving, embroidery, decoration, and other domestic and women's arts as a presence of tactile imagery that has long existed at the underside of the great works.

All these traditions involve intimate, detailed images that invite a small, caressing gaze. Usually art history has deemed them secondary to grand compositions, important subjects, and a correspondingly exalted position of the viewer. However, a number of art historians have suggested alternative economies of looking that are more appropriate to tactile images, and, not incidentally, more embodied. For example, Svetlana Alpers (1983) and Naomi Schor (1987) describe ways of seeing seventeenth-century Dutch still life, in which the eye lingers over innumerable surface effects instead of being pulled into centralized structures. Mieke Bal (1991) proposes a way to read paintings not around the phallic Barthesian *punctum* but a gender-neutral *navel.* Jennifer Fisher (1997) proposes a haptic aesthetics that involves not tactile visuality so much as a tactile, kinesthetic, and proprioceptive awareness of the physicality of the art object. As I am here, Fisher is concerned to redeem aesthetics from their transcendental implications by emphasizing the corporeal and immanent nature of the experience of art.

Finally, there is some temptation to understand haptic visuality as a feminine kind of visuality; to follow, for example, Irigaray's assertion that "woman takes pleasure more from touching than from looking" (1985, 26). Nevertheless, rather than embrace the notion of tactility as a feminine form of perception, I prefer to see the haptic as a visual strategy that can be used to describe alternative visual traditions, including women's and feminist practices, rather than a feminine quality in particular. The arguments of historians such as Bal, Buck-Morss, and Schor supplant phallocentric models of vision with a vision that is more ambient and intimate. Yet their arguments do not call up a radically feminine mode of viewing so much as suggest that these ways of viewing are available and used differently in different periods. To trace a history of tactile looking offers a strategy that can be called upon when our optical resources fail to see.

Haptic Cinema

Whether cinema is perceived as haptic may be an effect of the work itself, or it may be a function of the viewer's predisposition. Any of us with moderately impaired vision can have a haptic viewing experience by removing our glasses when we go to the movies. More seriously, a viewer may be disposed to see haptically because of individual or cultural learning. The works I describe here have intrinsic haptic qualities, to which a viewer may or may not respond. Similarly, there may be historical periods when cinema is perceived more or less optically or haptically.

In its early years cinema appealed to the emerging fascination with the instability of vision, to embodied vision and the viewer's physiological responses (Gunning 1990, Lastra 1997). Like the Roman battle of the haptic and the optical, a battle between the material significance of the object and the representational power of the image was waged in the early days of cinema (at least in the retrospection of historians). The early-cinema phenomenon of a "cinema of attractions" (Gunning 1990) describes an embodied response, in which the illusion that permits distanced identification with the action on-screen gives way to an immediate bodily response to the screen. Noël Burch (1986) also notes this connection, suggesting that early cinema appeals to the viewer not through the analog representation of deep space but more im-mediately. As the language of cinema became standardized, cinema appealed more to narrative identification than to bodily identification. In theories of embodied spectatorship, we are returning to the interest of modern cinema theorists such as Benjamin, Béla Balász, and Dziga Vertov in the sympathetic relationship between the viewer's body and the cinematic image, bridging the decades in which cinema theory was dominated by theories of linguistic signification.

The term *haptic cinema* has a brief history. The first attribution of a haptic quality to cinema appears to be by Noël Burch, who uses it to describe the "stylized, flat rendition of deep space" in early and experimental cinema (1986, 497). Antonia Lant (1995) has similarly used the term "haptical cinema" to describe early films that exploit the contrast between visual flatness and depth. She notes the preponderance of Egyptian motifs in such films and posits that early filmmakers were, like Riegl, fascinated with Egyptian spatiality. Deleuze uses the term to describe the use of the sense of touch, isolated from its narrative functions, to create a cinematic space in Robert Bresson's *Pickpocket* (1959). He writes, "The hand doubles its prehensile function (as object) by a connective function (of space): but, from that moment, it is the whole eye which doubles its optical function by a specifically 'grabbing' [*haptique*] one, if we follow Riegl's formula for a touching which is specific to the gaze" (1989, 12). To me, Deleuze's focus on filmic images of hands seems a bit unnecessary in terms of evoking a sense of the haptic. Looking at hands would seem to evoke the sense of touch through identification, either with the person whose hands they are or with the hands themselves. The haptic bypasses such identification and the distance from the image it requires. A writer whose use of "haptic cinema" is most similar to my own is Jacinto Lejeira (1996), who discusses the relation between haptic and optical visuality in the work of Atom Egoyan. He notes that Egoyan uses different processes, such as speeding up video footage in the film, enlarging the grain, and creating *mises-en-abîme* of video within film, to create a more or less optical or haptic sensation. "These techniques function in such a way that the overall image . . . seems to obey an instrument capable of bringing the spectator's opticality or tactility to a vibratory pitch of greater or lesser intensity" (1996, 44). I agree with Lejeira that these visual variations are not formal matters alone but have implications for how the viewer relates bodily to the image (46).[16]

How does cinema achieve a haptic character? Many prohaptic

properties are common to video and film, such as changes in focus, graininess (achieved differently in each medium), and effects of under- and overexposure. All of these discourage the viewer from distinguishing objects and encourage a relationship to the screen as a whole. Haptic images may raise ontological questions about the truth of photographic representation: this is the effect of the reproduced image in films such as *Blow-Up* (1966, Michelangelo Antonioni), *Sans soleil* (1982, Chris Marker), and works by Atom Egoyan that employ video within the film (for example, *Family Viewing,* 1987, and *Calendar,* 1993). Haptic images may also encourage a more embodied and multisensory relationship to the image in films that use haptic imagery in combination with sound, camera movement, and montage to achieve sensuous effects, such as *The Piano* (1993, Jane Campion) and *Like Water for Chocolate* (1993, Alfonso Arau).

Both film and video become more haptic as they die. Every time we watch a film, we witness its gradual decay: another scratch, more fading as it is exposed to the light, and chemical deterioration, especially with color film. Video decays more rapidly than film, quickly becoming a trace, a lingering aroma with few visual referents remaining. As the tape demagnetizes, lines drop out, and in analog video color becomes distorted. Video decay is especially significant for emigrants and exiles who treasure old, hard-to-get, or bootlegged tapes from "back home." Because they are so hard to find, these videos quickly lose their status as mechanically reproduced media and become rare, unique, and precious objects.[17] A tape that deals poignantly with video decay is *Sniff* (1996) by Ming-Yuen S. Ma, who has used haptic imagery in several works, including *Aura* (1991) and *Slanted Vision* (1995). In this short tape, the decay of the video image evokes the failure of memory. A man, played by Ma, crawls naked on his bed, bending to the sheets to search for traces of smells. Repetitively, Ma's voice-over describes his one-night stands: "M came over last night. He had two scoops of ice cream, and some chocolate." Though the telling is coy, the increasing desperation of his search makes this a work not only about the transience of love, but also about loss in the time of AIDS. Optical images of Ma crawling on the bed give way to tactile close-ups, for example, of the individual hairs gleaming on his shorn scalp. Finally, through analog dubbing, the image begins to break down: it loses its coherence the way smell particles disperse, taking memory away with them.

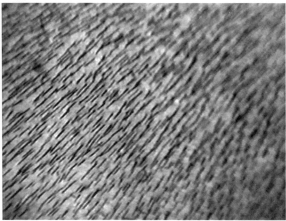

57 and 58. Stills from *Sniff*

Other haptic effects are medium-specific. In film, techniques such as optical printing, solarization, and scratching the emulsion work with the physical surface of the medium. For this reason it is commonly argued that film is a tactile medium and video an optical one, since film can be actually worked with the hands. My definition of visual tactility, however, has little to do with physical texture and mainly to do with the way the eye is compelled to "touch" an object in the way I have described. The techniques noted above do not necessarily make a film look tactile. However, optical printing can build up many layers of images on the film, producing a thicket of barely legible images. Many experimental filmmakers have used optical printing and physically worked the emulsion to achieve effects that

59. Frame enlargement from *Girl from Moush*. Courtesy of Canadian Filmmakers Distribution Centre.

can be described as haptic. The works of a relative newcomer to the tradition, Canadian filmmaker Gariné Torossian, *Visions* (1991), *Girl from Moush* (1993), and *Drowning in Flames* (1994) make a nod to postmodernism in that the images they draw from are already once-reproduced: photographs, reproductions of artworks, images shot from a video monitor. However, Torossian physically reworks these images in a way that thoroughly restores their aura, or endows them with another aura. Every frame contains two or more optically printed images and more images that Torossian cuts out and glues onto the film. Many frames are scratched for additional texture, or discolored and bubbled by the glue she uses. Her sound tracks are similarly layered and dense. To look at these works is to be drawn into a world where scale is completely different, as though one has to become miniaturized like Alice in Wonderland in order to perceive the complex texture of the films. These richly textured, miniature scenes compel a viewer to move close, yet they also multiply points of visual contact all over the screen. At the same time, they inhibit identification with the pictured objects, so that in *Girl From Moush* the icons of the artist's ancestral country, Armenia, including churches like those featured in Egoyan's *Calendar,* are ever more difficult to distinguish, let alone to fetishize as the photographer of *Calendar* does. Torossian says that the densely worked surfaces of her films pay homage to her Armenian aunts' and grandmothers' knitting and crocheting (Hoolboom 1997, 149, 151; Torossian 1998). Like the sweaters and doilies they produced, her films embody hours of women's labor in the complexity of their textures.

For 16mm and 35mm film, the contrast ratios (ratios of light to dark areas of the image) approximate human vision, or about 300:1 (Belton 1996, 71). Their grain is not visible under normal conditions (unless you sit too close to the screen). However, the grain of 8mm film is easily visible, as is the grain of higher-gauge film shot at high speed or in low light. Graininess certainly produces a tactile quality, as the eye may choose between concentrating on figures and ignoring the points that make them up or bracketing the figures and dissolving among the points. Interestingly, it can also be the high resolution of film that gives it a tactile quality. Films that, like Torossian's, seem to contain more visual texture than the eye can apprehend, have the effect of overwhelming vision and spilling into other sense perceptions.

The main sources of haptic visuality in video are more varied: they include the constitution of the image from a signal, video's low contrast ratio, the possibilities of electronic and digital imaging, and video decay. The video image occurs in a relay between source and screen. As Ron Burnett (1995) and others note, the video image's status as index is less secure than that of the film image, since it does not originate from a material object (of celluloid/acetate). Hence variations in image quality, color, tonal variation, and so forth occur in the space between source and viewer, affected by conditions of broadcast or exhibition as well as (literal) reception. Control of the image is much more open to negotiation in video, while in film the qualities of the image are chemical effects that cannot be significantly changed after the film has been processed.[18]

Another source of video's tactile, or at least insufficiently visual, qualities is its pixel density and contrast ratio. VHS has about 350,000 pixels per frame, while 35mm film has twenty times that (Bordwell and Thompson 1997, 31). The contrast ratio of video, or ratio of dark to light areas in the image, is 30:1, or approximately one-tenth of that of 16mm or 35mm film (Belton 1996, 71). Thus while film approximates the degree of detail of human vision, video provides much less detail. When vision yields to the diminished capacity of video, it must give up some degree of mastery; our vision dissolves in the unfulfilling or unsatisfactory space of video. The same effects can occur in multigenerational or badly recorded video images—but their implications are quite different, for in these works the viewer is more likely to find the image's blurriness merely a frustration and not an invitation to perceive in a different way.

A third intrinsic quality of the video medium, and an important source of video tactility, is its electronic manipulability (see Herzogenrath 1977). The tactile quality of the video image is most apparent in the work of videomakers who experiment with the disappearance and transformation of the image due to analog and digital effects. Electronic effects such as pixellation can render the object indistinct while drawing attention to the perception of textures. Pixelvision, the format of the discontinued Fisher-Price toy camera that used audiocassete tapes,[19] is an ideal haptic medium. Pixelvision, which cannot focus on objects in depth, pays a curious attention to objects and surfaces in extreme close-up. As a result, some of the best Pixelvision works focus on scenes of detail. Yau Ching's three *Video Letters* (all 1993) take advantage of the medium's visual poverty to suggest all that cannot be conveyed in a letter, using simple still lifes to create recollection-objects. Azian Nurudin's lesbian s/m scenes in *Sinar Durjana (Wicked Radiance)* (1992) and *Bitter Strength: Sadistic Response Version* (1992) become elegantly abstract in Pixelvision; she uses the high contrast of the medium to echo the effects of Malaysian shadow plays.

In utter contrast to McLuhan and the many critics who followed him in asserting that video is a "cool" and distancing medium, I argue that video's tactile qualities make it a *warm* medium. It is the crisp resolution into optical visuality that makes an image cool and distant.

Uses of Haptics

The haptic qualities I have described can be found in many works. Independent film- and videomakers have experimented with haptic visuality throughout the history of the media. Borrowing these techniques, commercial movies also make occasional use of haptic visuality. The opening-credit sequences of many movies take place over haptic images, as though to slowly ease the viewer into the story. I have noticed this, for example, in the opening sequences of *Casino* (1995, Martin Scorsese), where big blurry colored lights eventually reveal themselves to be the marquee of a casino; *The English Patient* (Anthony Minghella, 1996), in which the camera moves over a skin-like surface that turns out to be a close-up of rough watercolor paper; and *The Usual Suspects* (1995, Bryan Singer), which begins with a very dark ground with wavy colored shapes, reflections of lights in the harbor. Films like these are predicated on the audience's uncertain or false knowledge, and so it seems appropriate to begin them with haptic images that make viewers unsure of their relationship to the image and the knowledge it implies.

Intercultural films and videos take advantage of the haptic qualities of their media in a number of ways. Fundamentally, haptic images refuse visual plenitude. Thus they offer another of the Deleuzian time-image strategies to prevent an easy connection to narrative, instead encouraging the viewer to engage with the image through memory. As fetishes protect their memories, haptic images can protect the viewer from the image, or the image from the viewer. It is fairly common for experimental ethnographic films and videos to use haptic images to counter viewers' expectations of informative or exotic visual spectacle. Hatoum's *Measures of Distance* (1988) protects its images from viewers' realization that we are gazing upon a naked woman, until it resolves into an optical image. Works that mediate between cultures, such as Trinh's *Re:Assemblage* (1982), Marker's *Sans soleil* (1982) and Edin Velez's *Meta Mayan II* (1981), occasionally "clothe" their ethnographic images in soft focus or electronically processed textures. Portia Cobb's videos *Species in Danger Ed* (1989) and *Drive By Shoot* (1994) and Lawrence Andrews's *"and they came riding into town on Black and Silver Horses"* (1992) represent young Black urban men, people who are usually subject to ethnographic scrutiny on the nightly news, but swathe their images in digital graininess and layers of multiple exposure. Ken Feingold's faux-ethnography *Un Chien Délicieux* (1990) shifts to tasteful digitization for the only truly "documentary" portion of the tape, in which the Burmese villagers he is taping kill and cook a dog. *New View/New Eyes* (1993), a tape made by Gitanjali on her first visit to her ancestral country, India, is symptomatic of the reluctant-tourist strategies of experimental documentary. Unwilling to subject the

60. Frame enlargement from *Chimera.* Courtesy
of Canadian Filmmakers Distribution Centre.

land and its people, especially the very poor, to her camera, the artist seeks blurry images, like the reflection in puddles of "untouch-
ables" sweeping a wet courtyard on a misty morning. Many of the
works I discuss in this book make similar protective gestures toward
the people and places they represent.

Haptic images can give the impression of seeing for the first time,
gradually discovering what is in the image rather than coming to the
image already knowing what it is. Several such works represent the
point of view of a disoriented traveler unsure how to read the world
in which he finds himself. Bill Viola's *Chott el-Djerid (A Portrait
in Light and Heat)* (1979), for example, gives a view of the Tuni-
sian Sahara not with the certain knowledge of Baedeker-clutching
tourists but with disorientation and wonder, the shimmering desert
reflected in the air. Phil Hoffman's *Chimera* (1995) is composed of
shots at dozens of sites around that world that begin and end in
blurred motion, so that a "cut on blur" reproduces the tourist's experience as a sea of uncertainty punctuated by moments of clear
perception. In *Brasiconoscopio* (1990), Mauro Giuntini sees anew
his town of Brasilia, the prototype of the chilly, optical city, with
haptic eyes, in a series of scenes that use slow motion, painterly
digital effects, and blurring and blossoming colors to blur its inhabitants together in a great flow of life. Another artist who sees mirages
is Seoungho Cho, who writes, describing *The Island with Striped*

61. Still from *The Island with Striped Sky.* Courtesy of
Seoungho Cho.

62. Still from *Identical Time.* Courtesy of Seoungho Cho.

Sky (Seoungho Cho and Sang-Wook Cho, 1993): "Prolonged exposure and thirst may induce one to experience a mirage in the desert.
The mirage is filtered through undulating waves of air. In this video,
the mirage of the city is captured through its reflection" (Cho 1994).
The island of the title is Manhattan, and the tape reflects a profound
sense of the traveller's disorientation. Meanings float loose from
objects and merge; reflections in puddles, windows, and revolving
doors are at least as palpable as the insubstantial figures of moving
people and vehicles.

The first image in Cho's *Identical Time* (1997) is light coming through curving white filaments, with bright spots of red and green light behind them. As the focus shortens, it turns out we are looking through the window of a subway car in which somebody has scratched a name. *Identical Time,* shot in the New York subways over the course of a year, wrings beauty out of the ordinary things most riders ignore, by rendering them first as haptic images. The images are paired with an exquisite score for string instruments by Steven Vitiello, which ranges from a gentle melody on a guitar to the harsh scraping of cello strings in an aural echo to the lines scratched into the window. During the course of the tape, words at the bottom of the screen read:

Today I am alive and without nostalgia
the night flows
     The city flows
I write on this page that flows
     I shuttle with these shuttling words

. . .

            I am
     one pulsebeat in the throbbing river

. . .

Is not beauty enough?
         I know nothing
I know what is too much
         not what is enough

. . .

There is another time within time
still
    with no hours no weight no shadow
without past or future
         only alive
like the old man on the bench
indivisible identical perpetual
We never see it
         It is transparency

They are excerpts from a translation of Octavio Paz's poem "El Mismo Tiempo" (1961). The tape, like the poem, is a song for the sort of travelers who become "one pulsebeat in the throbbing river"

63. Still from *Identical Time.* Courtesy of Seoungho Cho.

when they enter the subways, travelers who, looking up from their newspapers, might lose their gaze in a delicate pattern of vertical lines that turns out to be droplets of rain and dust, dried on the subway window. Such contemplative opportunities are not as rare as one might think, even, or especially, on the subway.

Cho's videos dwell on the tactile qualities of seeing, at the same time that they question the ability of vision to yield knowledge. He connects this kind of baffled vision with the experience of cultural displacement—both the displacement of a Korean-born person living in the United States and the general displacement of the tourist, or anyone living with the daily sensory barrage of Manhattan (Cho 1997). Figures cannot be clearly distinguished, and layers of images move in an uncertain relation to the plane of the lens. Unsure what he or she is seeing, the disoriented viewer suspends judgment (unless he or she makes a snap judgment, hastening the images into intelligibility), and tests the images by bringing them close. The viewer's vision takes a tactile relation to the surface of the image, moving over the figures that merge in the image plane as though even faraway things are only an inch from one's body. Looking in such a way requires of the viewer a certain trust, that the objects of vision are not menacing but will patiently wait to be seen. Yet one might ask whether Cho trusts his senses: in his work all materiality seems to disappear, and the images that swirl to the screen's surface do not necessarily attest to the existence of objects.

Some intercultural works use the shift between haptic and optical ways of seeing to emphasize the makers' tactile connection to their environments. Rather than represent well-known and beloved places in the harsh light of optical vision, they begin with the intimate look of one who already knows what he or she is going to see (though viewers may not share this familiarity). Victor Masayesva's *Hopiit* (1982) uses haptic images to touch affectionately the ordinary things that are the center of his Hopi community. The tape is structured by the annual life cycle of corn, and by the special celebrations and everyday acts related to it. Like Cho, Masayesva often changes exposure or focus very slowly, allowing the object of vision to emerge gradually from its environment. The green leaves of corn plants, apple blossoms, and a spider working on its web emerge into focus gradually, as though to stress that all these things, including the viewer, are interconnected. The videomaker uses a similar strategy in *Itam Hakim Hopiit* (1985) and *Siskyavi: The Place of Chasms* (1991) in a gesture toward his environment that is simultaneously loving and protective. Masayesva's use of soft focus implies an affectionate and intimate relationship with things too familiar to require the close scrutiny of the optical.

Similarly, Philip Mallory Jones's videos, installations, and digital works use haptic imagery in a conscious effort to convey the multisensory environment of the places he visits throughout the African diaspora. Composed of scenes from villages in Burkina Faso, his "music videos" *Wassa* (1989) and *Jembe* (1989) are electronically processed to enhance their texture and rich color. *Wassa* moves in dreamlike slow motion to the music of Houstapha Thiohbiano: from the combination of rhythm, color, and video texture, the viewer gets a sense of warmth and fragrance emanating from shots of boys playing in a dusty street and a woman moving languidly in a dim room. Jones's search for a pan-African aesthetic, which has developed into the multimedia work in progress *First World Order,* makes him less a tourist than an inhabitant of a global Africa: I will return to Jones's work on the "African sensorium" in the next chapter.

Haptic Sound

Although this book remains largely silent on the question of sound, I find it interesting to note that sound operates along a dialectic similar to that of haptic and optical visuality. Of course we cannot literally touch sound with our ears, just as we cannot touch images with our eyes; but as vision can be optical or haptic, so too hearing can perceive the environment in a more or less instrumental way. We *listen* for specific things, while we *hear* ambient sound as an undifferentiated whole. One might call "haptic hearing" that usually brief moment when all sounds present themselves to us undifferentiated, before we make the choice of which sounds are most important to attend to. In some environments the experience of haptic hearing can be sustained for longer, before specific sounds focus our attention: quiet environments like walking in the woods and lying in bed in the morning, or overwhelmingly loud ones like a nightclub dance floor or a construction site. In these settings the aural boundaries between body and world may feel indistinct: the rustle of the trees may mingle with the sound of my breathing, or conversely the booming music may inhabit my chest cavity and move my body from the inside. In sound cinema, the relationship between aural textures and aural signs can be as complex as the relationship between haptic and optical images to which I have devoted my attention.

Haptics and Erotics

Haptic visuality requires the viewer to work to constitute the image, to bring it forth from latency. It resembles what Sobchack (1992, 93), using the terms of existential phenomenology, calls *volitional, deliberate* vision: the act of viewing is one in which both I and the object of my vision constitute each other. In this mutually constitutive exchange I find the germ of an intersubjective eroticism. By "intersubjective" I mean capable of a mutual relation of recognition, in this case between a beholder and a work of cinema. Regardless of their content, haptic images are erotic in that they construct an intersubjective relationship between beholder and image. The viewer is called upon to fill in the gaps in the image, to engage with the traces the image leaves. By interacting up close with an image, close enough that figure and ground commingle, the viewer relinquishes her own sense of separateness from the image—not to know it, but to give herself up to her desire for it.

This description will suggest that haptic visuality is somewhat different from the Brechtian stance of the active viewer often invoked in theories of experimental film and in 1970s semiotic and psychoanalytic "screen theory." Certainly haptic visuality requires an active viewer. As in modernist cinema, the haptic viewer relates simultaneously to an illusionistic image and a material object, and thus implicitly refuses to be seduced by the cinematic illusion. But the Brechtian active viewer is an explicitly critical viewer, indeed a suspicious viewer, while the haptic viewer is quite willing to pull the wool over her eyes. Put otherwise, haptic visuality does imply a critique of mastery, the mastery implicit in optical visuality, but it is through a desiring and often pleasurable relationship to the image that this critique is bodied forth.

Voyeurism relies on maintaining the distance between viewer and viewed. Eroticism closes that distance and implicates the viewer in the viewed. As Emmanuel Levinas writes, "The seeking of the caress constitutes its essence by the fact that the caress does not know what it seeks. This 'not knowing,' this fundamental disorder, is the essential. It is like a game with something slipping away, a game absolutely without project or plan, not with what can become ours or us, but with something other, always other, always inaccessible, and always still to come" (1989, 51). The erotic for Levinas, and for Irigaray, is not the possessing of the other but a "delight in the resistant alterity of the erotic other" (Davies 1993, 268). Visual erotics allows the object of vision to remain inscrutable.[20] But it is not voyeurism, for in visual erotics the looker is also implicated. By engaging with an object in a haptic way, I come to the surface of my self (like Riegl hunched over his Persian carpets), losing myself in the intensified relation with an other that cannot be possessed.

Again, let me exaggerate the dichotomy between optical and haptic visuality to make a point. The ideal relationship between viewer and image in optical visuality tends to be one of mastery, in which the viewer isolates and comprehends the objects of vision. The ideal relationship between viewer and image in haptic visuality is one of mutuality, in which the viewer is more likely to lose herself in the image, to lose her sense of proportion. When vision is like touch, the object's touch back may be like a caress, though it may also be violent, as Steven Shaviro argues—a violence not toward the image but toward the viewer. Violence may occur in an abrupt shift from haptic to optical image, confronting the viewer with an object whole and distant where she had been contemplating it close-up and partial. Haptic visuality implies a tension between viewer and image, then, because this violent potential is always there. Haptic visuality implies making oneself vulnerable to the image, reversing the relation of mastery that characterizes optical viewing.

These qualities may begin to suggest the particular erotic aspect of haptic cinema.[21] As the metalworks and carpets of which Riegl wrote engage with vision on their surface rather than drawing it into an illusionary depth, so haptics move eroticism from the site of *what* is represented to the surface of the image. Eroticism occurs in the way a viewer engages in a dialectical movement between the surface and the depth of the image. In short, the form of visuality I am describing is itself erotic; the fact that some of the images are sexual is, in effect, icing on the cake. Nevertheless, let me describe a work that is erotic both in its use of haptic visuality and in its content, namely *Her Sweetness Lingers* (1994) by Shani Mootoo—the tape with the magnolia. Mootoo is a poet, and the love poem she reads on the sound track is responsible for much of the sensual quality of the tape: not only its evocative words, but the rich voice that carries each phrase on a current of breath. "I'm afraid," are her first, whispered words; "I'm afraid of dying. . . . Why else would I be afraid to touch you, when I have not allowed my mind to lie fallow beneath this fear? I know the texture of your lips, inside of mine. I have already tasted your tongue, and smelled your face and neck, again and again, without ever having touched you—I don't want to—because, I'm afraid of dying." As she speaks, we see a group of women in a beautiful garden. One is captured in slow motion jumping on a trampoline, the impact echoing in a deep boom that emphasizes her phallic intentness; another laughs and turns her lovely face as though unaware of the camera's gaze. Like Mootoo's words, the camera tentatively circles around this woman, and then it drifts away across the grass; then the tape cuts to a circling close-up of a half-open magnolia. On one hand, this and similar cuts, to images of flowers and a gushing waterfall, evoke the lover's averting her eyes from the beloved; on the other, given the sexual symbolism of the images, they are outrageously explicit, a kind of poet's Production Code for erotic contact. Keyed-in, digitally colorized shots of scarlet quince blossoms, grape hyacinths with a wandering bee, and yellow forsythia against the bright blue sky recall the dense textures and vivid colors of Persian miniatures. The intimacy of these shots, suf-

64. Still from *Her Sweetness Lingers.* Courtesy of
Video Out.

fused with the buzzing sounds of insects in the garden, overwhelms
the viewer with their immediacy, with even a sense of humidity on
the skin. Mootoo's voice continues to erotically proclaim the value
of keeping a distance:

Watching you, desiring you for so long, I know that at the moment when
our skins will finally come together—unite—our melting passion will pulse
like an unborn wave, at first imperceptible, then slowly gathering, gathering itself up, to make a show of fearless strength before bursting apart in
momentary splendor—then heedlessly pushing on, uncaring that ahead is
its pathetic demise. Wave after wave, not one wise enough to see the pattern, and seeing, hold onto life by refusing to be born.

At one point the camera slowly pans the beloved woman's body
as she reclines naked in a dim room, digital effects denaturalizing
her brown skin to a luminous pale green, a sort of video veil over
the body of the beloved. Finally, after the poet's reasoning has come
full circle, the two women in the garden ever so slowly approach
each other, brief shots from different angles capturing the long-
anticipated meeting; and just as they bring their lips together, the
tape ends. But another consummation has already been achieved,
in the video's tactile, sensuously saturated caresses. *Her Sweetness
Lingers* embroiders its colorful and sumptuous optical images with
the intimacy of tactile images: it expresses the greedy desire of a

lover to know the beloved through every sense all at once, to admire the beloved from a distance and at the same time bring her or him close. Mootoo's words—the passion to be united with the beloved in "momentary splendor," even if this should herald the lover's demise —describe the self-eclipsing desire that propels haptic visuality.

Haptics and Identification

Haptic visuality implies a familiarity with the world that the viewer knows through more senses than vision alone. Changes of focus and distance, switches between haptic and optical visual styles, describe the movement between a tactile relationship and a visual one. I noted that in Hatoum's *Measures of Distance,* as the grainy image gradually resolves into figuration, we realize that the stills are of a woman's body, and then that they are of the artist's mother. This pulling-back powerfully evokes a child's gradual realization of separateness from its mother, and the accompanying ability to recognize objects: to recognize the mother's body as a separate body that is also desired by someone else. It parallels the developmetal shift from the "close" senses to the distance senses. It also describes a movement from a haptic way of seeing to a more optical way of seeing: the figure is separate, complete, objectifiable, and indeed already claimed by another, Hatoum's father. It is perhaps not coincidental that a number of haptic images are made by daughters of their mothers. Another example is Beharry's *Seeing Is Believing,* in which the artist's camera searches a photograph of her mother, following the folds of the silk sari in the photograph as they too dissolve into grain and resolve again. Such images evoke a tactile mirror stage in which the infant's awareness of belovedness and separation is learned in terms of touch. At the moment that the viewer forgets the body, haptic images fill in for the missing body (Lejeira 1996, 46), as the tactile folds of the sari fill the screen. But at the point where the image becomes recognizable as that of a woman in a sari, narrative rushes in: to use Deleuzian terminology, the movement-image returns.

These observations about infant's-eye vision lead to some suggestions about identification and the haptic. As I have argued, haptic media encourage a relation to the screen itself before the point at which the viewer is pulled into the figures of the image and the exhortation of the narrative. Haptic identification is predicated on closeness, rather than the distance that allows the beholder to imaginatively project onto the object.

The haptic is a form of visuality that muddies intersubjective boundaries, as I have been arguing in phenomenological terms. If we were to describe it in psychoanalytic terms, we might argue that haptics draw on an erotic relation that is organized less by a phallic economy than by the relationship between mother and infant. In this relationship, the subject (the infant) comes into being through the dynamic play between the appearance of wholeness with the other (the mother) and the awareness of being distinct. As Parveen Adams (1991) suggests, to define sexuality in terms of the relation to the mother is also to understand it as organized around a basic bisexuality. This seems to corroborate a kind of visuality that is not organized around identification, at least identification with a single figure, but that is labile, able to move between identification and immersion. In a sexual positioning that oscillates between mother- and father-identification, it seems that haptic visuality is on the side of the mother. Haptic visuality might seem to represent the "over-closeness to the image" that Mary Ann Doane (1987) and others have attributed to female spectatorship, while optical visuality implies the ability to stand coolly back that characterizes "regular" spectatorship. I can only remind the reader that I base haptic visuality on a phenomenological understanding of embodied spectatorship, which is fundamentally distinct from the Lacanian psychoanalytic model that castigates the "over-close" viewer for being stuck in an illusion. Though, as I have mentioned, the use of haptic images may be a feminist strategy, there is nothing essentially feminine about it.[22]

This excursus aside, my concern is not to anchor the definition of haptic visuality in certain psychoanalytic positions. I find it more compelling to suggest how haptic visuality works at the level of the entire body. The engagement of haptic visuality occurs not simply in psychic registers but in the sensorium. The longing communicated by *Measures of Distance* and *Seeing Is Believing* cannot be explained solely by an analysis of the cultural dynamics they exploit or the psychic states they bring into play. The eroticism of *Her Sweetness Lingers,* the sense of connectedness to the community in Haj-Ismail's and Masayesva's works, and the experience of the place-

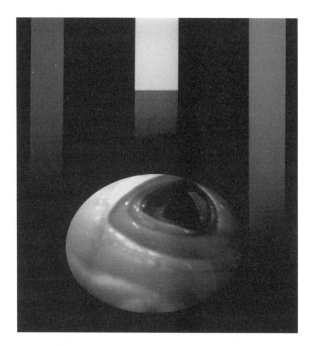

65. Installation view, *Corps étranger.* Photo: Philippe
Migeat. Courtesy of Mona Hatoum.

less traveler in Cho's tapes also appeal to the body and not only the
psyche. To describe the effects of such video works requires paying
attention to the viewer's body, specifically what happens when the
video image dissolves out toward the viewer and invites the viewer
to invest all his or her senses in the act of seeing.

A later work by Mona Hatoum demonstrates disturbingly the difference between embodied visuality and vision that enters the body.
To make *Corps étranger* (1996), the artist used an endoscopic camera, attached to a medical probe that can be inserted into the body's
orifices. The camera begins by traveling over the surface of Hatoum's
body, expanses of skin and looming facial features and nipples. Then
it (and in a kind of *Incredible Journey,* the viewer too) moves over
her teeth and plunges down her throat, taking us on a visceral journey into her (healthy-looking) esophagus. The camera takes a similar
voyage into her intestine and her cervix, making visible an archi-
tecture of glistening walls and pools of visceral fluid. The piece was
conceived as an installation in which the tape loops, so the viewer
is never "brought back out" from Hatoum's insides.

The question of identification in this tape is perplexing. As my wording suggests, it is easier to identify with Hatoum's camera than with her body, which becomes a terrain through which we travel. When we do identify with her body the effect is deeply unsettling, I believe because it is impossible to function when we are aware of our bodies' noncognitive processes such as digestion and respiration. Medical technologies such as X rays, ultrasound, CAT scans, and colonoscopy render our viscera visible. They offer not an embodied visuality, but a visuality that makes our bodies objects to us.

In a way *Corps étranger* seems a logical sequel to *Measures of Distance*. While the earlier tape attempted to use video to touch the surface of the body, the later work plunges into the body. The feeling of longing conveyed by *Measures of Distance* disperses abruptly with the later tape, when vision pushes through the covering of the body. Now it is just any body, not a loved one the image would caress. While the haptic image in *Measures of Distance* tenderly veils and tentatively touches the loved one's body, the optical image of *Corps étranger* makes the body more naked than ever. Another difference is that while in *Measures of Distance* the body was literally far away in space and time—Hatoum's mother, photographed years ago in Lebanon—in *Corps étranger* the body, her own body, is utterly familiar. Hatoum can "afford" to treat her body as an object; the effect of this work would be quite different if it were performed with any body but her own.

Tactile Epistemology: A Return

I have discussed how haptic cinema appeals strongly to a viewer perceiving with all the senses. Let me return to the notion of tactile epistemology with which I began, to think further about the significance of haptic visuality. Tactile epistemology involves thinking with your skin, or giving as much significance to the physical presence of an other as to the mental operations of symbolization. This is not a call to willful regression but to recognizing the intelligence of the perceiving body. Haptic cinema, by appearing to us as an object with which we interact rather than an illusion into which we enter, calls upon this sort of embodied and mimetic intelligence. In the dynamic movement between optical and haptic ways of seeing, it is possible to compare different ways of knowing and interacting with an other.

The above exploration of haptic visuality permits us to reconsider the now-common critique of visuality as bent on mastery. Evidently this critique need not be extended to all forms of vision. A form of vision that yields to the thing seen, a vision that exceeds cognition, seems to escape the critique of mastery. Haptic visuality may "fasten" on its object (according to its etymology), but it cannot pretend fully to know the thing seen. Instead, haptic visuality inspires an acute awareness that the thing seen evades vision and must be approached through other senses—which are not literally available in cinema. Haptic visuality implies a fundamental mourning of the absent object or the absent body, where optical visuality attempts to resuscitate it and make it whole. At the same time that it acknowledges that it cannot know the other, haptic visuality attempts to bring it close, in a look that is so intensely involved with the presence of the other that it cannot take the step back to discern difference, say, to distinguish figure and ground. A visuality that is so engaged with the present that it cannot recede into cognition would seem to inform the kind of "yielding-knowing" of which Taussig (1993, 45), following Horkheimer and Adorno's plea (1987) for a form of knowledge that did not bend its object to its will, writes.

The various ways theorists have written of vision/knowledge as an act of yielding, of giving over to its object, can be critiqued as exoticizing, organicist, romantic—Taussig's summoning of Cuna ritual practices; Levinas's seemingly occult attribution of cognition-arresting power to "the face of the Other"; even Trinh's call to "speak not about, but nearby." But perhaps these potential criticisms can be averted if we accept that it is necessarily through metaphor that we approach such models of knowledge. It is difficult to describe such a state, except indirectly. Hence the power of cinema to offer a way of speaking not about, but nearby, its object: a power of approaching its object with only the desire to caress it, not to lay it bare.

A videotape by Brazilian artist Ines Cardoso, *Diastole* (1994), uses haptic visuality to poetically approach an ineffable object. Dedicated to a loved one who died, *Diastole* is a brief and moving meditation on death, occupied with only a few images. It makes use of the wide range of resolution possible in video, and manipulates color with extreme subtlety, from naturalistic to digitally altered. The image of the moving hands of an old-fashioned clock appears in clear focus, in the subtle tones of a daylit interior. An image of two children

laughing and rolling on a bed is slightly pixellated, giving a pointil-
list effect to the dark expanse of their hair and the glowing edges
of the tumbled sheets. Other images, shot through various filtering
devices, play overtly with the inability to see what you are looking
at: a barely recognizable, sunlit outdoor scene turns out to be shot
through a sheet of bubble wrap; a hand is shot through a fine plastic
screen.

What captures me most is this last image. The hand gently presses
against the screen, and as it does its boundaries blur and merge
with the even mesh of the screen, which in turn merges with the
digital texture of the video image. Colors shimmer around it in the
camera's reaction to overexposure: pastel, barely there colors, blue-
green, a pinkish flesh tone, edged with darkness but dissolving into
light. As the image of the hand dissolves into the double grain of the
screen and the video image, the sound track carries the voice of a
child reading a poem about death (translated from Portuguese into
English subtitles). The tape ends with the words, "How can we ever
understand death?" Perhaps this seems a diagrammatic illustration
of a haptic medium: a verbal text about the limits of knowability reinforcing a visual play with the limits of visibility. Nevertheless, the
result is an expression of respect and relinquishment at the border
of the unknowable experience of death. The optical image dissolves
into the intimacy of the haptic, in a reverent nonunderstanding in
the face of death.

Tactile visuality is still not touch. Often there is a mournful quality
to the haptic images I have described, for as much as they might
attempt to touch the skin of the object, all they can achieve is to
become skinlike themselves. The point of tactile visuality is not to
supply a plenitude of tactile sensation to make up for a lack of optical image. Similarly, when in the next chapter I discuss images that
evoke senses such as smell and taste, it is not to call for a "sensur-
round" fullness of experience, a total sensory environment, to miti-
gate the thinness of the image. Rather it is to point to the limits of
sensory knowledge. By shifting from one form of sense-perception
to another, the image points to its own asymptotic, caressing relation to the real, and to the same relation between perception and
the image.

What is erotic about haptic visuality, then, may be described as a
respect of difference, and concomitant loss of self, in the presence of

the other. Unlike the alterity posed by Freud or Lacan, or Hegel for that matter, this difference is not the means of "shattering" the subject. The giving-over to the other that characterizes haptic visuality is an elastic, dynamic movement, not the rigid all-or-nothing switch between an illusion of self-sufficiency and a realization of absolute lack. It is with the same recognition that Sobchack describes the relation between perceiver and perceived as one of mutual embodiment, dynamic rather than destructive.

It may be more obvious now why intercultural works deploy haptic visuality. The apprehension of being seen, categorized, and killed into knowledge informs many works that speak from a place between cultures, given the ethnographic (in the broad sense) tendency to fix its object in a harsh light, or conversely to flatten its object into a broad projection screen. The critique of visual mastery in such works speaks from an awareness about the destructive and literally imperialist potential of vision. For the same reason, intercultural cinema is one of the most important sites of work on nonmastering visuality. From an impulse to protect the objects (people, cultures) represented from the prying eyes of others that informs much intercultural cinema, some works also begin to experiment with a visual erotics: one that offers its object to the viewer but only on the condition that its unknowability remain intact. As I will explore further in the next chapter, some works stretch the medium's ability to represent the valued senses, including touch, that slip beyond the capacities of a Western-style apparatus. And finally, haptic visuality, in its effort to touch the image, may represent the *difficulty* of remembering the loved one, be it a person or a homeland.

4

The memory of the senses

Any hint of flavor, just a hint, leads through a tunnel back
to a light: the memory of my favorite stew. I never had words for it
in the first place, although, when I am inebriated with memory,
emotions about the ghostly meal rattle around.
—Jeff Weinstein, "Thyme and Word Enough"

Seeing is not eating. —Hausa proverb

There has been increasing interest in the past several years among
film- and videomakers and "visual" artists to supplement vision with
the experiences of hearing, touch, smell, taste, and kinesthesis. Especially in documentary, this turn to the nonvisual senses has been
in part a response to the perceived imperialism of vision, the alignment of visual information with knowledge and control (although,
as I argued in the last chapter, vision need not be synonymous with
mastery). In some cases, documentary appeals to what escapes the
visual altogether but can be known, for example, through the sense
of touch, or of smell. The knowledge of the other senses is sought,
not necessarily to create a sort of multisensory *gesamtkunstwerk,*
but to show the limits of any of these knowledges.

Throughout these chapters I have been suggesting that unrepresentable memories find their expression in the characteristic gaps
of experimental cinema, or what Deleuze calls time-image cinema.
The "shattering of the sensory-motor schema" (Deleuze 1989, 55)
that characterizes time-image cinema describes a suspension of the
usual relations among the senses and their automatic extension into
movement. I suggest that the very perceptual forms that encode

memory may be revealed, by this shattering effect, to be culturally specific. Film's "physical shock effect" (Benjamin 1968c, 238) is its potential to disrupt the commonsense patterns of sense experience, making room for new cultural organizations of perception. Cinema can be the site of new configurations of sense knowledge, produced in (or in spite of) the encounter between different cultures.

The cinema of cultural displacement often focuses on loss: of language, of custom, of one's place in a community. However, a discourse of loss alone cannot explain the transformations and new productions of culture and consciousness that occur in diaspora. These chapters have moved from discourses of loss and unknowability to new conditions of knowledge: a shift that reflects the move in intercultural cinema in the last ten years or so from works of protest to works of synthesis, from excavation to transformation. When language cannot record memories, we often look to images. When images fail to revive memory, we may look to the well-kept secrets of objects. Unpacking the secrets encoded in images and objects, we find the memory of the senses. This final chapter explores the representation of sense knowledge in intercultural contexts. Yet the films and videos I examine here must still deal with loss, for when the memory of the senses fails—when there are no people who can awaken the knowledge of an object in their own bodies— the loss itself becomes an element of public culture (Seremetakis 1994, 8). Intercultural artists cannot simply recreate the sensory experience of their individual or cultural past. Instead, intercultural cinema bears witness to the reorganization of the senses that takes place, and the new kinds of sense knowledges that become possible, when people move between cultures.

In this final chapter, then, I will argue that the senses are a source of social knowledge. This will require an excursion into the psychology and neurophysiology of sense memory, in which I focus on the sense of smell. I will point out that the organization of the senses, that is, the sensorium, varies culturally as well as individually; thus we would expect cinema to represent the sensorial organization of a given culture. Often the sensorium is the only place where cultural memories are preserved. For intercultural cinema, therefore, sense experience is at the heart of cultural memory. All this evidence of the rich cultivation of sense experience is only useful for understanding cinema if we can understand the cinematic experience to be multisensory: I will argue that it is, even beyond devices like Odorama, given a viewer's mimetic and synesthetic inclinations. One would expect that artists would be somewhat suspicious of the cinematic apparatus's ability to represent their precious, and often nonaudiovisual, sensory knowledges: I will look at a number of works, particularly by aboriginal artists, to see how they stretch the apparatus to express these knowledges. A look at Julie Dash's *Daughters of the Dust* and related works explores how intercultural artists use the medium to represent the importance of sensuous and bodily memories.

Of course, with intercultural cinema, there is not only one sensorium at work. Diasporan people inhabit at least two: that of their culture of origin, and the new sensory organization in which they find themselves. Consequently, I will suggest that many intercultural works are ambivalent about their ability to represent the traditional sensory experience; this distinguishes them from the exoticizing films that serve their eager audience the sensuous life of another culture on a platter.

The work of Black Audio Film Collective was what first drew my attention to the way cinema calls upon the senses when other sources of history/memory are inaccessible. I have mentioned Black Audio's interest in using rituals and evocative tableaux in their stylized documentaries. Reece Auguiste's *Mysteries of July* (1991), in particular, evokes the knowledge of the senses in order to intensify a social protest. The short film begins with the fact that an inordinate number of young Black men in England die in police custody. As do many Black Audio films, it begins where the known facts end, for, not surprisingly, there are no official records of the circumstances of these deaths. The film reconstructs one of the deaths, making it clear that it was the result of the British police's institutionalized racism. But it does not stop here. Auguiste recognizes that the decisive laying of blame, when there is no legal recourse to convict the killers, cannot heal the pain in the Black community. Instead, *Mysteries of July* enacts an elaborate ritual of mourning. Candles and incense burn at a memorial altar decorated with flowers and rich satin, which reflects their light in pools of intense color. Mourners walk slowly, in silence, carrying candles. In a scene of grief and rage, these colors, textures, and imagined smells take on an intensity that cannot be expressed verbally or visually.

66. Frame enlargement from *Mysteries of July.* Courtesy of Black Audio
Film Collective.

Four years after I saw *Mysteries of July,* I watched a short videotape
that seemed to reduce all my ideas about cinema and sense experience to a one-liner. Toronto videomaker Steve Reinke's project "The
Hundred Videos" (1992–95) is a collection of very short pieces, many
of which are exquisite, condensed theses, almost haikus, about the
impossibility of representing truth in documentary cinema. One of
these tapes consists of a close-up of the lower half of a man's (pale,
stubbly) face. He extrudes his tongue and uses it to insert small
pieces of canned fruit cocktail into his nostrils, first one, then the
other. Then he does the same with canned peas and carrots. That's
all. The tape is called *Instructions for Recovering Forgotten Childhood Memories* (1993).

Part of Reinke's joke is that the banal and slightly disgusting act of
putting canned fruit up your nose is supposed to have the power to
reach deep levels of the psyche. Part of it is a joke on psychoanalysis:
one wishes it could be so easy to recover forgotten memories. But
also Reinke raises the issue of how memories are embodied in the
senses. Using your tongue to put pieces of canned fruit in your nose
calls upon many kinds of sensory awareness: taste; smell; the inimi-
table feeling of a slimy canned pear sliding up your face from one
sensitive membrane to another; the physical dexterity required to

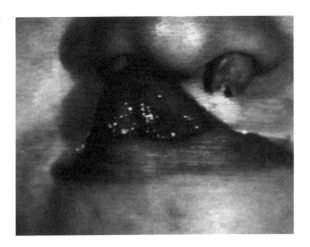

67. Still from *Instructions for Recovering Forgotten Childhood Memories.* Courtesy of V Tape.

do this. It is a rich multisensory experience that many children and surely a few adults have had. But Reinke is also calling upon a particular cultural memory, common to those of us who regularly ate canned fruits and vegetables as children. Not everybody can identify with this act.

This short tape raises some of the questions I will approach in this chapter: What experiences are so beyond cinematic representation that they require extra-audiovisual means? How does one represent sense memory? Is it a process of narrative identification, of bodily identification? Can the mere audiovisual representation of a gustatorial act successfully arouse lost memories; or, as Reinke's title ("Instructions") suggests, must one physically carry out the act oneself? And what are the intercultural limits of such memory: can one identify with sense memories one has never had?

In this chapter I continue to explore works that push the visual limits of cinema, and to appeal to the authority of nonvisual perception. I argue that in many cultures the sense of sight, while important, is not as paramount as it is in postindustrial metropoli. Thus the antivisual turn often entails an appeal to cultures that cultivate the proximal senses. However, let me caution at the outset that, much as one might like, one cannot put on a sensorium like a suit of clothes and instantly be washed with new sensory perceptions. Sense knowledge is embedded in culture. It is more productive to look for the latent sensory abilities that already exist within a culture, the tactile, smelly, and gustatory knowledges and pleasures that exist alongside the more "elevated" distance knowledges. Also, the seeker of sensation should know that sense knowledge, like any cultural knowledge, is always migrating and transforming.

Once more, let me point to some of the limits of this extravisual exploration. Vision is the primary sense in most cultures for good reason. Everybody needs senses that operate over distance, which vision and hearing do best. There are interesting exceptions: for example, the Umeda people of the New Guinea rainforest use smell as a distance sense, for they hunt in dense forests where it is not easy to see or hear one's predators or prey (Classen, Howes, and Synnott 1994, 98). My project is not to attempt to overthrow the visual altogether, but to relativize the uses of the senses according to different cultural organizations of the sensorium.

Sense Memory as Social Memory

As I suggested in chapter 1, attempts to reconstruct experience by digging in archives of public and private memory are full of pitfalls, since often these experiences are normalized upon interpretation into film language, rather than remaining destabilizing and "radioactive." How to allow experience to retain its strangeness and *un*translatability? Even the oral history, which is held to be one of the least invasive ways to represent social memory, tends to determine the shape of its responses by fitting the interviewee into the framework of dominant history (Connerton 1989). Paul Connerton suggests that these stories may be discovered not in narrative form but in the evidence of ritual, gesture, and other embodied forms of memory. These memories are especially crucial as repositories of knowledge for people whose experience is not represented in the dominant society. The memory of the senses, a nontransparent and differentially available body of information, is important to everybody as a source of individual knowledge. For cultural minorities, it is an especially important source of *cultural* knowledge. The histories recorded in the body reveal other patterns than those signaled by elections, the passage of laws, national credit ratings, and other big-ticket signs of shifts in the global sociopolitical sphere. I suggested in chapter 2 that the intercultural travels of seemingly idiosyncratic and "private" objects are often signs of political events that do not register on public scales. Embodied memories and experiences may well be some of the most important registers of global shifts in power and the emergence of new subjectivities. And as Elaine Scarry points out, the body remains a political witness despite efforts to "reeducate" it. She retells Bruno Bettelheim's story from the concentration camps in which a German soldier recognizes a woman who used to be a dancer and orders her to dance for him. "She did so, and as she moved into the habitual bodily rhythms and movements from which she had been cut off, she became reacquainted with the person (herself) from whom she had lost contact; recalling herself in her own mimesis of herself, she remembered who she was, danced up to the officer, moved her hand with grace for his gun, took it, and shot him" (1985, 347; referring to Bettelheim 1960).

Arthur Jafa (aka A. J. Fielder), cinematographer for *Who Needs a Heart?* and *Daughters of the Dust* (among other films), accepts the term "materialist retentionist" to describe his aesthetics:

> What that means is that I have a belief in certain levels of cultural retention. Nam June Paik, the godfather of video art, has this great quote: "The culture that's going to survive in the future is the culture you can carry in your head." The middle passage is such a clear example of this, because you see black American culture particularly developed around those areas we could carry around in our heads—oratorical prowess, dance, music, those kinds of things. (1992, 69)

Of course, Jafa's examples of "culture you can carry in your head" include knowledges that, like dance and music, are also carried in the body.

C. Nadia Seremetakis devotes a chapter of *The Senses Still* (1994) to a peach that was once cultivated in the region of Greece where she grew up. The *rodhákino* did not travel well and was not known outside of the places it grew. The rise of mass agricultural marketing in Greece, capped by that country's entry into the European Union, made the peach practically disappear from the market. Now, Seremetakis writes, it exists only in the memory of those who used to eat it—"Ah, that peach, what an aroma! and taste! The breast of Aphrodite we called it. These (peaches and other food) today have no taste when their stimulus has disappeared.

Seremetakis argues that the memory of the senses is itself a cultural artifact. Sense memories and material artifacts work in the same way; both are emissaries of cultural experience. She describes a cultural communion with the sense memories inscribed in objects. These artifacts are often traveling fetishes, of the sort I described in chapter 2: they might include the Zinacanteca women's tight sash that Leslie Devereaux (1995) describes, Shauna Beharry's mother's sari in *Seeing Is Believing,* the distinct smell of carnations for the Colombian women who grow them in *Love, Women, and Flowers,* or canned fruit cocktail up the nose for a North American child in *Instructions for Recovering Forgotten Childhood Memories.* Fetish objects are used to extend bodily experience into memory: Seremetakis's peach, like these other objects, is a prosthesis for memory.

Clearly the sense memories Seremetakis describes are not only individual, but shared. Her example underscores the argument that social memory is carried in individual bodies. Many artists and theorists claim sense experience as a site of "freedom" from cultural constraints—Stan Brakhage's desire to "free the eye" (1963) from cultural constraints, Susan Buck-Morss's (1992) suggestion that the body has a "wild," unalienable core of sense experience. But in fact the senses are also sites of cultural expression. Sense organs are the sites where culture crosses the body.

I have emphasized throughout this book that cinema can activate inert presences, such as historical archives and fetish objects, and make them volatile so that they intervene in the present. Now I would like to add sense memory to those presences. Seremetakis writes that the Greek etymology of *nostalgia* is *nostó,* I return, plus *alghó,* I feel pain (1994, 4). Nostalgia, then, need not mean an immobilizing longing for a lost past: it can also mean the ability of past experiences to transform the present.

Perceptual Plasticity and Intersensory Perception

To understand how the senses encode culture, it is necessary to examine how this process takes place in the body. First we must acknowledge that all the senses may be vehicles of memory, and that bodies encode memory in the senses in quite varied ways. As I have noted, Henri Bergson ([1911] 1988) anticipated later research on perception when he emphasized that the use of the senses is not given but learned. Perception in Bergson's model is plastic; implicitly it is variable according to culture and local need. Thus it provides a way to understand the wide range of possible organizations of sense memory. Some perceptions are more immediate: smell, taste, and touch usually fall into this category. Other perceptions provide more room to maneuver, a "zone of indetermination" (32) in which memory may intervene. However, these distinctions are merely quantitative. All sense perceptions allow for, and indeed require, the mediation of memory.

We are "wired" for great variation in the way we use our senses. Our sensorimotor cortex, or the outer layer of the brain where most sensory information is processed, is a map of our sensuous relationship to the world (Finkel 1992, 399). Everybody's cortex is configured differently, since sense perception, like other mental capacities, is reinforced on the basis of use and must be reinforced by continuous practice. Cooks have stronger synaptic connections between the sensorimotor cortex and tongue and nasal receptors than the average person. Violinists are found to have a larger cortical representation of the fingers of the left hand than are (presumably right-handed) nonstring players (Elbert et al. 1995, 305). Other sense capacities tend to adjust accordingly: one would not expect a cook to have an extremely discriminating sense of hearing, for example. The cooperation among the senses is especially evident in the many studies of perception that show that one sense modality can learn to respond to information normally headed for another modality. Consider the acute hearing of blind people. When I used to rent movies with two blind friends (one congenitally, the other from later in life), their aural perceptiveness astonished me. In the movie a door would open and a new character step into the room; Chris would say, "That's the bad guy," and a couple of scenes later I would find that he was right. Blindness made my friends exquisite aural semioticians.

In cognitive science there is growing interest in the idea that the mind, not the environment, is the source of representation. This need not be a solipsistic argument if we understand the mind itself to be formed through experience. Francisco J. Varela, Evan Thompson, and Eleanor Rosch (1991) argue that the meanings of sense experience are not given by the world but learned through embodied action, through the complex interaction of cultural and bodily processes. Our perception of color categories, for example, is not a reaction to wavelength and intensity of light, nor is it wholly subjective: they argue that it is both based on apparently physiological universals and culturally specific (168–71). This would suggest that while there may be physiological bases for everybody's agreement that a certain red is the exemplary red, or that a certain smell is noxious, there is also great cultural variation in the cortical representation of this information. One culture may not have a word for that exemplary red; people in another culture may be oblivious to the noxious smell.

The implications of this research for intercultural experience are several. First, our sensorium is formed by culture: it produces a map of the "objective" world that reflects our cultural configuration of the senses. Second, our sensorium creates the world "subjectively" for us. Thus, one would expect that in an ocularcentric culture, people will experience and produce the world as a primarily visual world. And a person whose sensorium reflects the cultural importance of smell will produce a world in which smell matters. Third, given the plasticity of neural networks, it is possible to learn a new configuration of the senses—although learning the memories that accompany it is another matter.

The Nose Knows

I want to focus on the sense of smell to pursue my argument that the sensorium is malleable, that the sense modalities work in concert, and that all sense experience is informed by culture. Foreign cultures tend to be both vilified and exoticized in terms of smell. It appears to be universal, and is certainly understandable, that every culture prefers its own world of smells to any other (Classen 1993, 79–80): as Freud said, our own shit never stinks. But the association of smell with primitivism has served the ends of cultural imperialism, in the name of civilizing and controlling the perceived odorous excesses of other cultures. Hence my concern to "abase" vision and "elevate" smell, by showing that the one is embodied and intimate, the other cognitive and cultivated. By pulling at these two ends of the sensory hierarchy, I hope to realign all the sensory modalities that lie "between" them in value, in order to reconfigure this hierarchy from a scale of values to a wiggle of intensities.

Everyone agrees that learning is verbal, and correspondingly that words are a medium of knowledge. Most will agree that vision can be educated as well; hence the term "visual literacy" (which reduces the visual to the symbolic). But the senses of hearing (exclusive of the verbal), taste, touch, and smell are less often accepted as senses that can be educated, that is, as sources of knowledge. Yet I would argue that olfaction, like the other senses, may be cultivated; therefore the sense of smell can be a source of cultural knowledge.[1] If this case can be made for the lowly sense of smell, then it must be accepted that other senses are knowledgeable as well.

First we must ask, do human smell preferences have some genetic core or are they entirely learned? It is a common argument that we have an innate, that is, genetic, attraction to odors associated with sexuality, and an innate aversion to odors of danger and death (for example, Stoddart 1990). The latter might explain why, especially in dualistic cultures, smell has been considered a primitive and dangerously sensual sense. This primitivism might also be explained by Freud's hypothesis that the sense of smell is repressed both phylogenetically and ontogenetically: the first, when humans adopted upright carriage and distanced themselves from their smelly anogenital areas; the second, when a child yields to socialization and abandons its pleasure in its own feces (Freud 1985, 279).

Humans' famous phylogenetic standing-up may well explain the repression of sensory awareness of sexual and other bodily odors. Now, when we use perfumes, we layer culture onto smell's biological substrate, sublimating sexual odors into these more symbolic scents, olfactory signs for sexuality. Nevertheless, despite this mimicking of biology by culture, I would argue that Freud collapsed the cultural aspects of smell onto the genetic. Sexual sublimation does not explain the complexity with which smell is deployed in different cultures, for example.

The proximal senses of touch, smell, and taste are more central to the experience of most nonhuman creatures, be they chimpanzees or paramecia, than they are to humans. These senses are also more important in the early years of human infancy and childhood: infants can identify their mothers and other important people through smell before they recognize them visually (Engen 1991, 63). The distance senses of vision and hearing are more developed in higher animals, and they also develop with human maturity. All this would seem to support the assumption that the "close" senses are primitive both in the life of the species and in the life of the individual, and that the distance senses are the most "evolved" in both implications of the word. Hence, I believe, the unwillingness of many cultural theorists to broach these topics, from fear of being accused of primitivism and essentialism. Yet it is worth venturing further to test these assumptions.

While most creatures have strong genetic codings for the smells of sex, food, danger, and death, for the most part it appears that humans do not (Hines 1997, 79). Instead we are genetically wired to learn strong but *contextual* responses to smells. Centers in the brain for processing different kinds of sensory information develop at different points in the growth of the fetus and infant. Cognition takes place in the cortex, the youngest and most evolved part of the brain (Stoddart 1990, 34). The hypothalamus, which is noncognitive, is the oldest part of the brain both phylogenetically and ontogenetically: it was once referred to as the rhinencephalon, or "smell brain." This and other parts of the limbic system (notably the amygdala) deal with memory and emotion. Olfaction is the only sense perception whose neural pathway leads directly to the hypothalamus: this means that olfaction alone has a fundamentally noncognitive component.[2] Yet simultaneously another neural pathway leads from the nose (strictly speaking, the olfactory bulb) to the cortex. This means that smell is processed cognitively at the same time that it awakens deep-seated, precognitive memories. Memories of smell endure much longer, even after a single exposure to an odor, than visual or auditory memories. Yet smell is difficult to verbalize and visualize (Schab 1991, 243). Smells are easier to identify through personal memory associations than by name (and Schab's article invests these associations with nostalgia: "grandma's kitchen" vs. "floor wax"; "the tobacco grandfather used to smoke" vs. "Prince Albert tobacco" [245, 246]). We respond emotionally to a smell first, and then we name it: asphalt, magnolia, grandma's kitchen. Since we process smell both cognitively and precognitively, we *learn* emotional responses to smell. We learn to love our mothers' smell, be it sweat or perfume (Engen 1991, 63–74), to identify the smell of home, be it fish sauce or mildew, and to build new associations with the new smell environments we come across. Margaret Morse writes most evocatively of the associations of smell with home, even when sense memories are aroused by completely different stimuli, as when the sea near Athens—"fresh like watermelon, with funky undertones"—takes her back years to a duck pond in Ohio (1999, 66).

All this suggests that, despite the "deepness" of smell centers in the brain, smell preferences and abilities can be developed in an individual lifetime. The nose, then, is not merely a gonadal gondola. The sense of smell is cultivated far beyond its "animal" associations. Given the malleability of human sensory capacities, it seems necessary to recognize the cultural dimension of smell. Where more symbolic languages tend to strip private memory away, the proximal senses are where memory remains in the body.[3]

The Cultural Sensorium

Not only cooks, musicians, and blind people develop specialized configurations of their sensoria. More profoundly, studies of the sensorium suggest great cultural differences in the way the nervous system organizes the senses. As Walter Ong first pointed out, a given culture will teach us to specialize our sensorium in particular ways by paying more attention to some types of perception than others. "Given sufficient knowledge of the sensorium exploited within a specific culture, one could probably define the culture as a whole in virtually all its aspects" (Ong [1967] 1991, 28). Since Ong wrote this, a number of anthropologists have begun to devote themselves to describing different cultures according to their organization of the sensorium.[4] This is a fascinating body of work that only begins to suggest the great variation in the uses of perception of which the body is capable, and the survival, customary, ritual, aesthetic, and other purposes that inform human sensoria. It also raises methodological questions: for example, is the sensorium best described by long-standing ritual practices, or by informal, everyday practices? I will draw on some of these anthropologists' findings below, as I did in the previous chapter, to show how cultures use the senses as sources of information and understanding in extremely different ways, and how these different sensoria can be translated into, and translate, cinematic languages.

This recent interest in cultural difference at the level of the sensorium is spurred by many anthropologists' and cultural theorists' perception of an atrophy of sensuous knowledge in Western post-industrial societies. This anxiety echoes the concern among neo-Marxists that I discussed in the last chapter. Often these critics argue that "we in the West" need to relearn how to inhabit our bodies, appealing to the embodied knowledges of non-Western cultures. Such arguments imply a kind of primitivist longing for another culture's sense knowledge; hence one must examine them critically.

Predating by decades the recent comparative cultural mappings of the sensorium, Marcel Mauss's "Techniques of the Body" ([1934] 1992) proposed an ethnology of bodily "techniques," namely, actions that are "effective and traditional," that differ according to culture, age, gender, work, and other variables. He stressed that all these techniques were learned from authority figures such as elders (as Connerton describes how social bodily memories are transmitted from old to young). Mauss fondly described non-European cultures' ability to preserve the children's posture of the squat:

The child normally squats. We no longer know how to. I believe that this is an absurdity and an inferiority of our races, civilizations, societies. An example: I lived at the front with Australians (whites). They had one considerable advantage over me. When we made a stop in mud or water, they could sit down on their heels to rest, and the "*flotte*," as it was called, stayed below their heels. I was forced to stay standing up in my boots with my whole foot in the water. The squatting position is, I believe, an interesting one that could be preserved in a child. It is a very stupid mistake to take it away from him. All mankind, excepting only our societies, has preserved it. (463)

Mauss's envious account of Australians' bodily conventions (and of course squatting is a posture also cultivated in Asian countries) reflects a fear that the body's functions would atrophy under the pressures of industrialized society and outmoded European proprieties. He seemed to have faith that the learning of bodily techniques is a simple matter, a change that could be effected in one generation. This is perhaps a more difficult sort of change to effect than Mauss hoped, given that bodies learn easily but cultural norms change much more slowly.

Following in Mauss's footsteps, the work of anthropologists such as C. Nadia Seremetakis, Constance Classen, E. Valentine Daniel, David Howes, and Paul Stoller are full of examples of experiences that appeal to many senses and to embodied aesthetic, social, or ritual experience. Howes deplores the separation of the senses and overvalorization of the visual in Western societies in a way that is partly accurate and partly romantic. For example, he compares two images: one is a Dürer engraving of an artist looking through an Albertian pespectival grid in order to make a drawing of a woman; the other is an abstract-looking design used by shamans of the Shipibo-Conibo Indians of eastern Peru. The former image translates all experience into the visual, while the latter embodies many forms of sensory experience: the designs are said to embody songs sung by the shaman, which, "on coming into contact with the patient, . . . once again turn into designs which penetrate the body and heal the patient's illness" (Howes 1991b, 5). The Shipibo-Conibo visual image, then, is only one aspect of a multisensory experience involving sound, touch, and fragrance, whose function is mimetic rather than representational, while the Albertian grid translates visual data into visual representation.

Examinations of a particular cultural organization of the senses are valuable, but implicit comparisons with the sensory devaluation of a monolithic "West" are counterproductive. When Howes suggests that the dissociation of the senses in the West is why "there is nothing healing about most Western contemporary art" (6), he merely displays his ignorance about art. Healing does imply a closeness to the body, while vision is the sense that permits the greatest distance between the body and the object. Yet, as I have argued throughout these chapters, there are many examples of more or less Western art that offer healing precisely in their appeal to the senses as a whole. Mauss's and Howes's longing for a more well-rounded sensorium resonates with Marxist critiques of the alienation of the senses, and with the disaffection with the visual that I discussed in the previous chapter. Yet they make the primitivist and exoticizing mistake of ascribing the fullness of sensory experience only to "non-Western" cultures (and to children). It is a mistake to believe that only some people have sense experience, and that only some objects have sensory histories. Also, especially given the cosmopolitan mixing of cultures in most societies, it is important to acknowledge that people's individual sensoria overlap only unevenly with their cultural sensoria. This may amount to a difference between the sensorium, or the individual's sensory wiring which is informed by

culture, and the sensuous geography, or the world of sensuous experience in a given place. Even in an ocularcentric culture, there are
always differences in the ways people engage sensuously with even
the most visual of objects. Thus, while taking different sensoria into
account, I want to avoid totalizing descriptions of given cultures'
sensuous engagement with the world.

While Mauss envied the half-sitting posture, artist Simon Leung
notes that diasporan Asians are ambivalent about the squat. While
Vietnamese refugees squat unselfconsciously to wait for the bus in
San Jose, assimilated Asians like Leung have unlearned the habit
of squatting. "An assimilated immigrant child's observation of the
squatting everyday shifted into something remarkable in the violent process of dis-identification with newly-foreign bodies, which
to others' (i.e., Americans') eyes probably resembled his own" (1995,
94). Leung points out that intercultural experience is violent at the
level of the body, for the recent immigrant must choose whether to
keep his or her bodily habits, at the cost of being considered primitive or exotic, or to shed them, at the cost of shedding the memory
these habits encode. This hard (and not necessarily conscious) decision underlies the ambivalence toward sensory traditions characteristic of much intercultural cinema.

A controversial film that explicitly examines different cultural
styles of embodiment is Ngozi Onwurah's *And Still I Rise* (1995).
Onwurah invites a number of African diaspora women to confront
the stereotype that Black women are more physical, more sensual
than whites. Rather than demur that there is no difference, most of
her interlocutors take pride in Black female embodiment. We see
Black women of all ages exemplifying the words of the poem by
Audre Lorde that the film takes for its title, "I walk as though I have
diamonds between my thighs": they wear sexy outfits, walk together,
laugh together, and dance at a street party. Their proud embodiment
is contrasted with the shoals of white commuters wearing suits that
efface their bodies and their individuality. This is Onwurah's strategic move to reclaim the Black female body from the legacy of
enslavement, dramatized in the film by scenes of an African woman
who is captured as a slave and raped by her white owner. The writers,
artists, and activists she interviews do more than reclaim a cultural
tradition of embodiment, however. At least one, writer Buchi Echehmeta, states that people of the diaspora have genetic links to the Afri-

68 and 69. Frame enlargements from *And Still I Rise*

can continent, and that Black people's physical expressiveness is not a learned form of embodiment but an expression of the genes. This controversial claim places Echehmeta at one pole of a continuum of African diaspora women who take pride in their physicality and argue that it makes them fundamentally different from the Europeans who have learned to separate mind and soul from body.

Multisensory Cinema and the Mimetic Apparatus

It would seem that smell can have no part in the audiovisual image, and cinema studies has, for the most part, understandably dismissed it. Christian Metz ([1975] 1982) maintained that cinema reproduces the aesthetic hierarchy between the distance senses of vision and hearing and the proximal senses, such as touch, taste, and smell. "It is no accident that the main socially acceptable arts are based on the senses at a distance, and that those which depend on the senses of contact are often regarded as 'minor' arts" such as cuisine and perfumery (59–60). Yet the less acceptable senses can also be cultivated aesthetically.

How can the audiovisual media of film and video represent non-audiovisual experience? There are no technologies that reproduce the experiences of touch, smell, taste, and movement. There are technologies that attempt to simulate the effects of these experiences, such as virtual reality's audiovisual synthesis of movement or IMAX movies, whose disorienting audiovisual cues induce vertigo in viewers. But there is no way to mechanically *reproduce* the smell of a peach, the texture of concrete, or the feeling of falling off a cliff.[5]

How, then, does cinema mediate the place of the body in culture, and of culture in the body? To answer, let me begin by noting that the embodied viewing experience discussed in the previous chapter extends to the physical and social spaces of the viewing environment. We take in many kinds of "extradiegetic" sensory information, information from outside the film's world, when we "watch" a film. Compare the experience of a few people watching a video on a six-foot home video screen; a lot of people gathered around a small TV to watch a bootleg import tape; the talking, picnicking audiences at Chinese theaters; the Friday night action movie packed with libidinous young couples; viewers huddling for warmth in nonprofit art spaces to squint at 16mm film. These examples should begin to suggest the wide range of ways spectatorship is "embodied."

Especially at a public movie theater, sensory information of all sorts abounds. We are aware of the movement and warmth of the other people in the theater, as well as their whispered or shouted comments on the activity on screen or elsewhere. Smells of popcorn and all sorts of other food, perfume, cigarette smoke (in the old days), body odor, cleaning products, or mildew from musty theater seats: any of these may address the sense of smell so insistently that it is hard to pay attention to the audiovisual image on screen. And of course these extra dimensions to the audiovisual experience differ greatly in different neighborhoods, and not in predictable ways. For example, while bringing a family picnic to the movies is traditional in Chinese and Indian cultures, in big North American cities it is also becoming common for nine-to-fivers to eat takeout meals at the movies after work, inciting complaining letters to newspapers about crackling aluminum foil, odors, and spilled food. Home video viewing, too, has its own individual and collective sensory rituals. In short, the cinema viewing experience, taken as a whole, is already multisensory.

A number of filmmakers have directly introduced smell to the cinematic experience. D. W. Griffith had incense burnt during screenings of *Intolerance* (1916), as Marcel Pagnol did for the premiere of *Angèle* (1934). John Waters's infamous Odorama gimmick in *Polyester* (1982) coordinated the smells of roses, farts, gasoline, and so forth, corresponding to the activity on screen, with scratch-n-sniff cards. Experimental filmmakers Yervant Ghiankian and Angela Ricci Lucci diffuse subtle scents into the room in the course of screenings of their films. A number of North American theaters have organized screening series of famous food movies, including *Tampopo* (Juzo Itami, 1986), *Like Water for Chocolate* (Alfonso Arau, 1992), *Babette's Feast* (Gabriel Axel, 1987), and *Eat Drink Man Woman* (Ang Lee, 1994), which are followed by recreations of the meals in the films at local restaurants.

Such extradiegetic sense experience amplifies the multisensory appeal of a movie, but it is not essential to it. Indeed, actual smells can supplant the mediated experience of the audiovisual image with a much more immediate response. When Pagnol diffused scents in the movie theatre at the premiere of *Angèle,* there was a public panic.[6] Associations with actual smells are so haphazard and individual that even the commonest odors incite reactions from relaxation to arousal, disgust, or horror.

The experience of viewing a film is multisensory, then, not because of actual odors in the theater, but because the sense perceptions work in concert. Movies themselves only appeal to sound and hearing, the sense modalities most accessible to symbolization and verbalization. However, Deleuze fans will note that the cinema will necessarily offer a multisensory image to the viewer, since Bergson's model of perception, upon which Deleuze relies, is multisensory. Deleuze's optical image is one that requires the viewer to complete the image by searching his or her own circuits of sense memory. Thus the audiovisual image necessarily evokes other sense memories.

Certainly, the simplest way for movement-image cinema to appeal to the viewer's senses is through narrative identification. Characters are shown eating, making love, and so forth, and we viewers identify with their activity. We salivate or become aroused on verbal and visual cue. Beyond this, it is common for cinema to evoke sense experience through intersensory links: sounds may evoke textures; sights may evoke smells (rising steam or smoke evokes smells of fire, incense, or cooking). These intersensory links are well termed *synesthetic.*

Synesthesia is the perception of one sensation by another modality, such as the ability to distinguish colors by feel. Artists have written provocatively of the synesthetic experience of colors. For Wassily Kandinsky, yellow calls to mind the unbearably sharp sounds of a trumpet's rising notes, and is more odoriferous than violet ([1938] 1968, 347–48). Derek Jarman wrote *Chroma* when he was losing his sight due to AIDS, which makes his vivid associations with colors, informed by the painter's love for precious pigments, all the more powerful.

Mad Vincent sits on his yellow chair clasping his knees to his chest—bananas. The sunflowers wilt in the empty pot, bone dry, skeletal, the black seeds picked into the staring face of a halloween pumpkin. Lemonbelly sits swigging sugar-stick Lucozade from a bottle, fevered eyes glare at the jaundiced corn, caw of the jet-black crows spiralling in the yellow. The lemon goblin stares from the unwanted canvasses thrown in a corner. Sourpuss suicide screams with evil—clasping cowardly Yellowbelly, slit-eyed. (1994, 90)

Clearly, colors have rich sensory associations. How much these are cross-cultural is a different question. Yellow, in the complex color-olfactory cosmology of the Desana people of the Colombian Amazon, is associated with male procreative power and with the "merry" melody of a flute played by Desana men (Classen 1993, 131–33). Yet in all these examples, a single color has multiple sensory associations and varying degrees of symbolic codification.

Color is but one example of the ways our experience is always synesthetic, always a mingling of our senses with one another and of our selves with the world. In the previous chapter I dwelt on how perception is embodied and inextricable from memory. When I smell a magnolia, I do not distinguish as separate perceptions the act of bending to meet it, its waxy pink-and-whiteness, its unmistakable yet indefinable fragrance, the cool touch of petals on my face, and the wave of associations from my memory. Our experience of the world is fundamentally mimetic, a completing of the self in a sensory meeting with the world. Smelling the magnolia, I mingle with it sensuously; I take on some of its qualities. Watching a bird eat a berry, or a novice cyclist teeter and fall, the sympathetic ecologist David Abram describes how he tastes the acidic burst in his own mouth, feels the impact of the asphalt against the side of his body (1996, 126). This sensuous meeting with the world is not merely an act of identification, but a function of the interplay of the senses.

As Benjamin and Merleau-Ponty argued in different contexts, a mimetic and synesthetic relationship to the world underlies language and other sign systems. Once that relationship is mediated through an image, multisensory experience is condensed into visual form. It does not vanish but is translated into the image. Thus it is not necessary to think that literate and audiovisual (as opposed to oral) cultures are fundamentally alienated from our material world. Abram argues that "many Westerners become conscious of this overlapping of the senses only when their allegiance to the presumably impartial, analytic logic of their culture temporarily breaks down," as when on drugs (1996, 61). Again, rather than blast "Western" sensory alienation, I would suggest that the mimetic traces of the world are harder to recognize in the demanding systems of signs that constitute the technological world, but they are still at work in our understanding of it. We are constantly recreating the world in our bodies, even as our representational systems become more abstract. Even when language is mediated through printed words, an invocatory trace of speech and its mimetic relationship to the world remains. Cinema, by virtue of its richer and muddier semiotic relationship to the world, is all the more an agent of mimesis and synesthesis than writing is. It has long been held that part of the magic of cinema is that some of its meaning evades codification. In fact, cinema is a mimetic medium, capable of drawing us into sensory participation with its world even more than is written language. Images are fetishes, which the reader can translate—more or less, depending on how her own experience is embodied—into sensuous experience.[7]

Rather than assume that technology alienates people from their sensuous being, intercultural filmmakers stretch the apparatus to accommodate their own sensuous and mimetic relationship to the world. Any representational technology can be more or less symbolic or mimetic, but I believe that in our uneven global emergence from literate to audiovisual cultures (see McLuhan 1962), we may be witnessing a gradual return to more mimetic technologies: technologies that call upon, or attempt to recreate, our pre-existing sensuous relationship to the world. Intercultural films and videos do show ambivalence toward representational technologies, including the very media in which they are produced. I believe this ambivalence is a testing of technologies that reduce experience to the visible and quantifiable, be they writing, photography, or cinema, for their mimetic capacities.

Experimental filmmakers have been exploring the relationships between perception and embodiment for years, offering a mimetic alternative to the mainstream narrativization of experience. However, the use of the apparatus in order to represent embodied culture is relatively recent.[8] Teshome Gabriel (1988), for example, suggests that Western filmic conventions are inadequate to the embodied time and space of "nomadic" experience, arguing that time and space are physically experienced, rather than abstractions, in nomadic experience. "[In nomadic orientations,] the conception of space is . . . relative to seeing, feeling, and touching" (66). Arthur Jafa sharpens Gabriel's speculations into detailed suggestions for how the cinematic apparatus might reflect the cultural sensorium. He suggests, for example, that the hand-crank camera would be a good tool for expressing African diasporic sensibilities: it is "a more appropriate instrument with which to create movement that replicates the tendency in Black music to 'worry the note'—to treat notes as indeterminate, inherently unstable sonic frequencies rather than the standard Western treatment of notes as fixed phenomena" (1992, 70). As cinematographer, he experiments with using the apparatus mimetically in *Daughters of the Dust* (1992), when he uses a high-speed camera in order to portray certain scenes, and in his recent short film, *Slowly, This* (1995). *Slowly, This* follows a conversation in a bar between an Asian and an African American man about racism, anger, and self-image. Reflecting Jafa's comments on the problems of lighting people of color with an apparatus designed to show off white people, the good-looking people in the bar are each lit to bring out their individual skin tones. During the conversation the camera lingers on small things—beads of moisture on a glass or a hand gesturing with a cigarette—as though to convey the men's characters through the atmosphere and objects that surround them. Jafa avoids an analogical relationship to time, instead using slow motion and freeze frames, in an attempt to evoke the intensity of embodied experience.

Philip Mallory Jones more radically intervenes in the video apparatus's capacity to represent what he calls the "African sensorium" (Zippay 1991, 121). His multimedia work in progress *First World Order* uses electronic media to find (or create) common elements of culture and aesthetic among African peoples in the Americas, Africa, Europe, Asia, and the Pacific Islands ("Festival News" 1995, 31). Using digital morphing, Jones literally stretches the medium in order to show these commonalities, for example transforming an Egyptian sphinx into a Carribean woman playing a drum. I find morphing a rather rhetorical way of demonstrating the relationships between African diasporic cultures, but Jones's conviction that this technique is superior to a narrative account of relationships among cultures is nevertheless provocative.[9]

Gabriel's characterization of nomadic aesthetics is a bit essentialist, but it does usefully describe ways that film- and videomakers use cinema to express a specific cultural sensorium. They capture some qualities of Igloolik Isuma Productions's videos, which recreate the nomadic lives of the artists' forebears. (The company consists of Zacharias Kunuk, Paulossie Quilitalik, Norman Cohn, and Paul Apak.) *Qaggig* (1989), *Nunaqpa* (1991) and *Saputi* (1994) have been mistaken for ethnographies, but in fact they are historical dramas about the Inuit community of Igloolik as it was fifty and one hundred years ago. In these works, true to Gabriel's characterization of "Third Aesthetics" (1989), the stories are not carried by individuals but by the activity of the group. The habitat of snow and tundra is as much a character in Igloolik Isuma tapes as the actors are, in long shots and pans that depict the people as a group and embedded in their landscape. In *Saputi* and "Avamuktalik" (an episode of Igloolik Isuma's television series, *Nunavut,* 1995), some magical or dreamlike events occur as well, as when a young boy is spooked by a spirit who lingers

70. Still from *Qaggig*. Photo: Zacharias Kunuk.
Courtesy of V Tape.

71. Still from *Saputi*. Courtesy of V Tape.

in front of him for a moment (with electronically distorted singing on the sound track) and then vanishes. For those familiar with this collective space, magical occurrences convey a sense of the fullness of the apparently deserted landscape. Also implicit is a fullness of sensory experience: awareness of the temperature and dryness of the air, for example; a keen sense of the distance vision and hearing necessary for hunting on vast treeless areas; the pleasure of warmth and food. The screen of vast landscape and quiet real-time activity may look sparse to outsiders, but is full of implicit presence.

Hopi videomaker Victor Masayesva Jr. (1995) critically assesses the difference between traditional, embodied knowledges and new, technologically mediated knowledges, including the cinema. Masayesva describes the ways indigenous peoples have constructed and inhabited space on the North American continent, inhabited the time of the seasons, and experienced sacred spaces. Like Gabriel, he asks what aspects of indigenous people's cultural experience might be approximated by cinema. Masayesva posits a Native American cinematic aesthetic that would speak directly to Native viewers. For example, it might introduce alternatives to cuts; the use of special optical effects; the use of 360° pans, dolly shots, and so on, not to draw attention to the facility of the cinematographer but to tell a story; editing in order to express "the rhythms of a unique order" rather than clichéd transitional shots; and of course the use of Native languages.

Masayesva has made a number of works that turn on the difference between Hopi people's knowledge of their culture and outsiders' knowledge, often expressed in terms of the Hopi sensuous geography. Meaning is embedded in the places, people, and objects of Hopi life in ways that will be opaque to others. Chapter 3 showed how Masayesva uses haptic images to give a sense of relationship to place. His *Siskyavi: The Place of Chasms* (1991) shows the difference between visually analyzing an object from outside and knowing it in lived, embodied experience. The tape is about a Hopi schoolgirl whose grandmother forbids her to join a class field trip to the Smithsonian Institute in Washington. Instead she stays home to learn how to make pots. While Smithsonian experts show the schoolchildren how they use high-tech methods to study and classify ancient fragments of Hopi ceramics found at the burial site called Siskyavi, the old woman teaches her granddaughter to dig clay, form pots, paint them, and use them in the baby-naming ceremony (she also makes pots to sell to tourists). The history of the clan as told by the grandmother is illustrated by ceramic paintings that seem to come to life as her voice populates them with interclan intrigues. By contrast, Smithsonian curators use electron microscopy, X-ray diffractometer, and neutron activation analysis to date and locate the pottery samples that the young people have brought from Siskyavi. The sincerity of the Smithsonian scientists and conservationists, their obvious love of their object of study, their enthu-

72. Production still from *Siskyavi.* Courtesy of
Victor Masayesva Jr.

siasm in working with the Hopi children, and their concern to find
the best pots "to be included in the film" make it clear that they are
not simply antagonists.

In one way *Siskyavi* witnesses the dying of traditional culture,
through the loss of people who can awaken the knowledge of cultural objects in their own sensory engagement. The grandmother
is depressed to hear how the museum uses Hopi pottery. A Hopi
student writes a report based on the museum trip, employing the
past tense to describe her people as though they were vanished. Yet
Masayesva suggests that the battery of technological and hermeneu-
tic approaches the museum experts apply to the Hopi pots cannot
penetrate the Hopi culture. The dialogue in the grandmother's home
is only partly translated, emphasizing that cultural knowledge can
only come from daily life. Shots of plants, flowers, and insects on
the land around the house give a hint of the life that infuses the pots,
a life that is tactile and olfactory as much as visual. By animating the
figures on the Smithsonian pots, Masayesva gives a sense that there
are spiritual presences witnessing or partaking in human activities: the animations liberate the painted creatures, hands, and spiral
paths to metamorphose into other forms. Beautiful vessels spiral
like constellations through the dreams of the girl who stayed home.
Ultimately *Siskyavi* suggests that visual and instrumental representations cannot "touch" Hopi culture, but that Masayesva can use the

apparatus to engender a mimetic, embodied representation of his culture.

A more corrosive critique of the difference between First Nations people's traditional way of embodying culture and imported technologies (in this case writing) is *And the Word Was God* (1987) by Ruby Truly. As it begins, a Native woman sits naked in an office reading a "found poem": a guide from 1954, part grammar lesson and part sermon, used by missionaries working among Cree people in northern Saskatchewan. She violently intones the crisp English words. "I see you. I hit you. I shoot you. I fetch you. You see men. You are shooting men. . . . They are lost in sin." During this depressing litany, her voice is accompanied by bleak shots of the office and the reservation. Yet the images gradually change, to loving shots of a river through trees and close-ups at the edge of the water, as the lesson changes to a dialogue about fishing. "He accompanies him. It is beside our home," the woman reads gently. . . . *And the Word Was God* shows that the Church did terrible damage to the Native people but did not break their connection to the land, where language gives way to a deeper knowledge of the familiar and beloved landscape.

The videomakers of Igloolik Isuma Productions critically test the new technologies for their capacity to express an Inuit sense of time, place, and community. In the last episode of *Nunavut,* called "Happy Day," the Igloolik community celebrates the newly incorporated holiday of Christmas. The people's attitudes toward the holiday, as toward the white priest who shows up in earlier episodes, seem to range from enthusiasm to suspicion. The camera also seems to view the innovation dubiously, since this last episode is the only one shot in black and white. One of the grandmas wakes every member of the household with a handshake, saying "Christmas" (pronounced "Karishimase") while others reluctantly and sleepily join in. The group takes up Inuktitut hymnbooks and begins a mournful-sounding rendition of "Oh Come All Ye Faithful." Usually in Igloolik Isuma videos, the cinematography complements the feeling of shared and social space: the camera seems to be a participant in groups of people, moving and changing focus gently in order to include everybody over the duration of a shot. In the hymn scene, however, the camera pans along the singers, lined up as though in church, stiff and uncomfortable. (Their hymn-singing is by no means as lustily embodied as it is among some congregations to the south.) Things begin to look up when the bannock is ready to eat, a woman takes up the accordion and begins to play, and the men of each household exchange gifts. With gusto, some of the men and women take turns drumming and singing traditional songs. As in *Qaggig,* the camera swings around the performers as though dancing with them, quite differently from its hands-off relationship to the hymn. The episode concludes with a lively square dance, shot from a low angle to capture as much activity as possible in the tight space: people debate the steps, and someone instructs "Say yee-hoo!" With some ambivalence, "Happy Day" shows that the Inuit of 1946 could incorporate new ways—white ways—selectively, without destroying traditional culture; and that the ways that will make it into tradition are those that make it into the body.

Such works critically compare traditional, embodied knowledges with technologies that abstract knowledge from the body, be they writing (and the Christian teaching it enables) or electron microscopy. None completely condemns the technological and instrumental (and visual) methods. With a little encouragement, these artists show, the new technologies of film and video can indeed take part in a mimetic and bodily relationship to the world.

I mentioned in the last chapter that the recent interest in using the medium mimetically harkens back to the early days of cinematic practice and theory. Early film theorists were aware of cinema's capacity to collapse the gap between the distance and proximal senses. Sergei Eisenstein noted that "in our new perspective—there is no perspective" (1970, 97; quoting René Guilléré), as Benjamin remarked upon cinema's ability to satisfy the masses' desire to "bring things closer" (1968c). Eisenstein's writings on the synchronization of the senses, though mostly devoted to relationships between the visual and sound image, acknowledge the synesthetic quality of any single sense perception, as when he quotes Lafcadio Hearn:

. . . Because [people] are insensible to the phosphorescing of words, the fragrance of words, the noisesomeness of words, the tenderness or hardness, the dryness or juiciness of words,—the interchange of values in the gold, the silver, the brass and the copper of words: —

Is that any reason why we should not try to make them hear, to make them see, to make them feel? (1970, 92–93)

Eisenstein speculated that Hearn's nearsightedness "sharpened his perceptiveness in these matters."

Hearn's poetic plea underscores the argument that a mimetic form of representation underlies language and other sign systems. By appealing to one sense in order to represent the experience of another, cinema appeals to the integration and commutation of sensory experience within the body. Each audiovisual image meets a rush of other sensory associations. Audiovisual images call up conscious, unconscious, and nonsymbolic associations with touch, taste, and smell, which themselves are not experienced as separate. Each image is synthesized by a body that does not necessarily divide perceptions into different sense modalities.

All this is evident—to a fault—in the Vietnamese film *The Scent of Green Papaya* (Tran Anh Hung, 1994), whose title states a challenge to the audiovisual medium. It is indeed a fragrant film, less because we identify with characters who taste and smell than because it makes sound and vision synesthetic. The main character is Mui, a young woman who travels from the country to Saigon to become a servant in a prosperous household. In many scenes, Mui takes pleasure in her sensuous connection to her daily work. When she cuts open one of those papayas, the image and sound, tied to her perspective, convey the slight effort of her knife and the wetness of the translucent seeds under her fingers. Frequent close-ups (with closely miked sound) linger on the papaya leaves dripping with rain, frogs plopping in the small pond, and ants tortured by the young son of the house, engaging the viewer's recollective imagination of the cool smell of rain and the harsh sizzle of a burning insect. Unconnected from any character's point of view, the camera seems to drift along currents of odor as it moves smoothly between the interconnected spaces of the courtyard, where the servant women prepare meals, and the cool dim rooms of the house.

Even though the smells and textures of this place may be unfamiliar to many viewers, the film encourages us to engage with them; viewers who themselves have lived in a Vietnamese house and have prepared and eaten green papayas will have a sensuous experience that is all the richer. Put otherwise, the more one is able to engage with the sensuous memories called upon by the film, the more its audiovisual medium becomes merely a means of access to an ultimately synesthetic experience. Tran Ahn Hung, who was born in Vietnam but grew up in France, has said, "The smell of green papaya is for me a childhood memory of maternal gestures" (Maslin 1994). The film's sensuous intensity thus embodies the exile's nostalgia, in which sense memories are all the more affectively charged than they would be for someone who still smells green papayas every day. I would criticize the film because it suggests that Mui, a peasant, has access to sensuous experiences that the urbanites do not: it compares her to the Westernized, bourgeois fiancée of her employer, and finds her "deeper" and more sensuous than the other woman, who is seen as shallow and frivolous. This is problematic, because it assumes that peasants and "non-Westerners" have a more sensuous relationship to the world than Westernized, urban sophisticates do. It thus connects the atrophy of sensory knowledges to (Western) sophistication, as anthropologists such as Ong and Howes do.

Sense Memory in *Daughters of the Dust*

Any film or video is capable of calling on the memory of the senses in order to intensify the experience it represents. But in some cases it is more crucial for cultural history to reside in the memory of the senses. This is the case particularly when official histories cannot comprehend certain realms of experience, or when they actively deny them. For example, compare Julie Dash's *Daughters of the Dust* (1992) with the recent rash of dramas based on novels by Jane Austen, Henry James, and Edith Wharton. All these fiction films are, effectively, ethnographic reconstructions of cultures that no longer exist, namely, the British aristocracy of the early nineteenth century, the late-nineteenth-century American aristocracy in Europe, and the Manhattan aristocracy of the late nineteenth century. Dash's film depicts life among the Gullah people of Ibo Landing, on one of the Sea Islands off the coast of Georgia, circa 1902. All these films use a wealth of "ethnographic" detail, especially centering on ritual, clothing, and food. They richly, even fetishistically detail the exquisite costumes that women and men in these societies wore. But these customs are differentially available in recorded history. In short, both the Austen-James-Wharton films and *Daughters of the*

Dust record bygone cultures, but the former draw intertextually on many sources, corroborating and elucidating known histories, while *Daughters of the Dust* translates into an audiovisual medium knowledges that have survived largely as oral history and sense memory.

Let us look at the example of hairstyle (see Mercer 1990). Pictorial histories of African American hairstyles are rare, and probably nonexistent for the small Gullah society. Hairstyling is a tactile and embodied form of knowledge, passed between generations by demonstration. The women of the Peazant family in the film wear elaborate and individual hairstyles: braided, twisted, swept into sculptural arrangements. These styles represent the continuity between African hairstyle traditions and the varied and elaborate fashions in hairstyle among African Americans now. Significantly, the women from the mainland do not wear their hair in elaborate styles; Yellow Mary's hair is long and "natural," as is her lover Trula's, and the Christian Aunt Viola wears her hair in a modest bun. The suggestion is that tactile knowledges such as hairstyling are harder to maintain in an urban and Euro-American setting.

Several shorter films and videos have drawn on the ways memory is encoded in African-diaspora hairstyles. The harsh judgments about "good" and "bad" hair, subjects of *Hairpiece: A Film for Nappyheaded People* (Ayoka Chenzira, 1984), *Good Hair, Pretty Hair, Curly Hair* (Andrew Davis, 1991), and *Instant Dread* (Dawn Wilkinson, 1998)—a hilarious film about the political havoc that results from a hair product that produces instant dreadlocks—"crop" up again in Charlene Gilbert's *The Kitchen Blues* (1994) when the dreadlocked Gilbert asks Alanna Small, a girl of about eight with strong opinions, "Do I have good hair?" Alanna hesitates before diplomatically answering, "Yeah, um, you would have good hair if you took your dreads out and straightened it." We get a sense of how memory is continued in the body through the simple act of styling hair, when Alanna says, "I like to do my hair 'cause I, like, always feel how my mother does my hair, and I do that with my dolls and *my* hair."

Like hairstyle, food is an important source of memory in *Daughters of the Dust*. The film devotes a lot of screen time to a lavish celebratory picnic on the beach, in which the camera lingers over platters and baskets of food. Gullah cuisine is something that only survived by word of mouth, or more exactly, by shared practice

73. Frame enlargement from *Daughters of
the Dust.* Courtesy of Kino International.

in the kitchen. The book that Dash, with Toni Cade Bambara and
bell hooks (1992), published in conjunction with the film is full of
recipes, many of which would have been published there for the
first time, in acknowledgment that African American history is a
body of multiple knowledges. In Marlon Riggs's last video, *Black
Is, Black Ain't* (1995), the cumulative, diverse, and often conflicting cultures of Black people in North America are metaphorized in
gumbo, a dish that simmers for a long time as it assimilates its many
ingredients, key to which is okra, a vegetable imported by Africans
during the Middle Passage. Like Dash, Riggs lovingly focuses on the
dish itself and on the many people who critically taste it and offer
their two cents.

Food is central to many cultures, of course. My point is, first, that
in the absence of other records food becomes even more a vehicle of
memory. Second, given that every culture privileges certain sense
modalities as vehicles of knowledge, food is more important within

gustatory epistemologies than it is, for example, within epistemologies based on vision. The centrality of food to African diasporic culture reflects the traditional value of gustatory knowledge in African cultures. Among Hausa speakers of north-central Nigeria, many folk tales and proverbs center around food, tasting, eating, or swallowing (Ritchie 1990, 114–16), in a complex gustatory regime of knowledge. Vision is deceiving; only by eating something, the proverbs suggest, can one really know it. Though it would be inaccurate to assign a gustatory sensorium to all African diasporic peoples on the basis of the Hausa evidence, many African diasporic films and videos place great importance on food, the knowledge entailed in good cooking, and the social rituals around it. For African diasporic people, food is all the more important as a traveling fetish, a reminder of traditional culture that survived the Middle Passage and is embodied anew in every well-cooked gumbo.

Donna James, a Jamaican-born artist living in Nova Scotia, made *Maigre Dog* (1990) to document the piquant proverbs shared by her mother and aunt, in the patois that many Jamaican immigrants assume only when among friends. "New broom sweep clean but old broom know the corners," her aunt says, and the women explain, laughing, "You get a new boyfriend, but the old one, there is something there that you love about him . . . because he knows your ways." Many of these are feisty proverbs about the need to watch your back and to value what is familiar—"Water more than flour: At times things can be really tough with you and you keep quiet and just bear it"; "Sorry for maigre dog, they turn around and bite you. . . . That is so true," James's aunt sighs—useful ideas for immigrants to a new country as well as to women who want to be savvy about love. The women also explain the phrase "The higher the monkey climb, the more him expose" that one of the Handsworth residents mutters ironically when the Home Secretary makes a damage-control visit after the riots, in Black Audio's *Handsworth Songs* (1986). We do not see the women, only hear their rich voices and a calypso song that asks, "Who used to change you diaper. . . ?" James, in her clear Canadian accent, asks about the meaning of the phrases and illustrates them in visual anecdotes, a sweeping broom, a bowl of flour. Like other diasporan artists, she comes to her traditional culture second-hand and must make an effort to learn the language so easily embodied by her foremothers. However, interspersed between the

74. Still from *Maigre Dog*

women's adages, shots in the kitchen dissolve to show more pots and pans piling up, suggesting that in one place the young woman experiences her traditional culture firsthand: through cooking and eating. Similarly, in Selina Williams's *Saar* (1994), talk eases the way into an unfamiliar practice, but eating together is what grounds it. In Vancouver, five Canadian women of African and Caribbean descent gather for a meal and a cleansing ritual called *saar.* Through food and ritual the women invoke a common ancestry that none of them knows firsthand; the stakes of building this community are emphasized by a radio report of the killing of a Somali by a Canadian soldier. And another hybrid-food video, *What's the Difference Between a Yam and a Sweet Potato?* (1992) by Adriene Jenik and J. Evan Dunlap, uses the tubers of the title as metaphors for a cross-cultural lesbian love affair. Paralleling the lovers' fleshy thighs, light and dark, a yam and a sweet potato lie cozily side by side after their long journeys from Africa and South America. A sexy recipe for sweet potato pie with yam jam scrolls down the screen. Eating with one's mothers, sisters, and lovers, all these works suggest, is the beginning of a new embodiment of hybrid culture, which language and visual images can only partially convey.

Dash has stated that she does not intend *Daughters of the Dust* to be an ethnographic film, which would put viewers in the passive position of consumers of knowledge. Instead, the film presents a variety of forms of knowledge and tests them against each other. The

Gullah people of the film, as much as possible given slave owners' prohibition of African languages and religious practices, have continued many of the ways of life of their West African ancestors. While theirs is already a hybrid culture, European, urban, and modern practices are impinging on Gullah life at an accelerating rate. Dash represents this incursion through the characters from the mainland who descend on the island for a family reunion: Yellow Mary, the family relation who was "ruint" in Cuba and returns to visit the family, with the young, light-skinned woman Trula, who appears to be her lover; Aunt Viola, who has embraced Christianity and repudiates all traditional African spirituality; the photographer Mr. Snead, who has been hired to memorialize the family event in frozen, black-and-white images.

The latter two figures especially represent forms of knowledge that will challenge the traditional knowledges of the Gullah people. Many of the dilemmas for characters in the film revolve around choosing which kinds of knowledge will best serve their survival and transformation individually and as a group. In one sequence, the film crosscuts between two scenes: an exchange between Nana Peazant, the matriarch of the clan, and her great-grandson Eli; and some girls dancing on the beach. Nana is urging Eli to keep the family's heritage alive when they move up North. Her voice carries over the shots of the young women dancing in a circle, moving into the middle and out again, sinking down to the sand and rising. Their movement recalls traditional African dance, and African drums and singing echo distantly on the soundtrack. Their dance also resonates with contemporary dances and double-dutch jumprope. Nana urges Eli,

Eli, we carry these memories inside of we. Do you believe that those hundreds and hundreds of Africans dropped here on this other shore would forget everything they once knew? We don't know where these recollections come from. Sometimes we dream 'em. But we carry these memories inside of we. . . . Eli, I'm trying to learn you how to touch your own spirit. I'm trying to give you something to take along with you. Count on those old Africans, Eli. They come to you when you least suspect 'em. They hug you up quick and soft as the warm, sweet wind. Let 'em touch you with the hand of time.

As she speaks, her voice carries over slow-motion shots of the dancers. One dancer turns with her eyes closed, as though looking deep inside; as though her own body remembers her heritage. "We carry these memories inside of we," Nana repeats, and it is clear that the dancing, learned from generation to generation and remembered in the body, is one of the strongest means of holding and transmitting memory.

In another scene, shots of the Peazant women preparing food are intercut with shots of Aunt Viola reading the Bible. The juxtaposition compares the knowledge of oral culture and the intergenerational learning of cooking with hierarchically transmitted, literary knowledge—to say nothing of the sharp cultural difference between Gullah and African traditional ways and Christianity. The women talk easily as they prepare shrimp, okra, chicken, and corn, foods available in West Africa that African diasporic people have adapted to local agronomies. One grandmother, sitting in a circle of children, makes them laugh by giving them little horns, made of the ends of okra, which she sticks to their foreheads. She recounts to them a list of African words, which they repeat, starting with "gumbo"; finally she says, "Now, that all what Grandma remember."

Later, the children's faces are sullen as Aunt Viola reads to them from the Bible with single-minded fervor, describing a "harvest" not of the abundance of the earth but of Christian souls. "When I left this island, I was a sinner and didn't even know it," she tells them. When the children ask her who is on the mainland, she lifts her eyes fervently to the horizon and says, "Jesus Christ, the son of God." Her persona equates living on the mainland with Christianity, and her cold disapproval of the traditional ways on the island make it clear that they are incompatible with the literary learning of the Bible—although later in the film she has an emotional reconciliation. Certainly Christianity has become an integral part of African American oral culture, but Dash points out that it displaced more traditional knowledges. As in Igloolik Isuma's *Nunavut,* Christianity is represented as not only colonizing the spirit but threatening to replace embodied knowledge with disembodied belief.

Sense Knowledge in Diaspora: Translation and Ambivalence

Intercultural cinema seeks to represent sensory experiences that encode cultural memory. Yet it is ambivalent about the possibility, or even the desirability, of representing sense experience in its fullness.

The works I consider here strive to recover sensuous geographies distant in space and time, sense memories faintly present in the body itself, like whiffs of smoke from a distant fire. If they do manage to recover these precious knowledges, they may use screens and ruses to protect them from casual consumption. This ambivalence toward the representation of the homeland is all the more evident in the work of "second-generation" (or more) artists, whose sensuous geographies are a mix of the old culture and the new, whose sensoria are not completely at home in either place.

In part the ambivalence exists because, given cultural differences in the use of the senses, it would be wrong to assume that audiences will be able to reconstruct the sensuous experiences represented in a work. Cinema is capable not only of depicting the process of inscription of sense memories but also of arousing memories in viewers. As Seremetakis argues, material culture requires completion by the viewer: no artifact exists as knowledge unto itself, but only if there is someone to register its meaning at the level of the body (1994, 7). The senses are educated by local objects and experiences, and interaction with a traditional object can awaken these senses. Given cultural differences in the organization of the sensorium, the sensuous geography characteristic of one culture will not be transparent to a viewer from another culture.

Ethnographic representations of one culture for the consumption of another tend to reduce it to what is visible, and hence readily consumable. But within another sensory regime of knowledge, such as gustatory knowledge, cultural memories can be explored while remaining somewhat shielded from the desire of outsiders to comprehend the culture visually. Visual anthropology has been critiqued for forcing the cultures it studies into a regime of the visual, interpreting events in terms of visible evidence, ignoring nonvisual experience, and in general "colonizing" the studied cultures' sensory orders (Howes 1991c, 172). Trying to understand somebody else's sensory organization, I must acknowledge the bluntness of my sensory instruments; I may be visually acute but not attuned to the meanings of smell, weight, proximity, and so forth. The shift in anthropology from visual to discursive approaches does not help matters, for it emphasizes aspects of culture that can be verbalized over those that are embodied (Csordas 1994, 11). If one's sensory organization privileges other senses as well as vision, it will be easier to experience an audiovisual object, like a film, in a multisensory way. If it does not, the object may appear inert because the viewer cannot perceive its multisensory qualities.

Accordingly, the representation of particular sense knowledges will not be transparent to all viewers. To recognize these knowledges requires the same kind of working at the limits of understanding that all intercultural cinema demands. In studying cinema we should attempt to be aware of its multisensory aspects, whether or not they are available to us. Hence the "yielding" brought to the experience of another culture must include an awareness of our own sensory configuration and its limits. When we find there is nothing to see, there may be a lot to feel, or to smell. Cinema may not bring forth these missing senses, but it can certainly evoke them.

Intercultural films and videos often vigorously protect their sense memories. In mainstream cinema, references to the nonaudiovisual senses tend to appear as cinematic excess, an extra treat on top of the richness of audiovisual representation. But for intercultural artists, memories of touch, smell, taste, rhythm are not "extra": they are the very foundation of acts of cultural reclamation and redefinition. This is the difference between recent mainstream movies praised for their "sensuousness"—one might think of the films of Chen Kaige, the later films of Peter Greenaway, Anthony Minghella's *The English Patient* (1996), and any number of other films rich in multisensory allusion—and intercultural works that draw upon the senses. The former approach their subject from a position of wealth: they have all the means of representation at their disposal, and information about taste, for example, merely complements the films' verbal and visual images. The latter are struggling to recreate sensory memories, and to find the diasporan artist's place within his or her sensory tradition. These memories are approached from a position not of wealth of information, sensory and otherwise, but of scarcity.

Recall Hamid Naficy's suggestion that smell, taste, and touch "often provide, more than sight and hearing, poignant reminders of difference and of separation from homeland" (Naficy 1993, 153). Naficy shows that cinema can call upon collective sensory experiences to respond to exiles' longing for their homeland (156). More than someone who has always lived in one place, the exile is acutely aware of his or her sensuous geographies, both of the new land and the one left behind. Aware of the differences between the sensuous geography she grew up with, which informs the way her body inhabits the world, and the one she now inhabits, the exile cannot simply replicate the sensuous wealth of the world she once knew. Of course, this describes more local moves as well, from the farm to the city, for example, or from humid Alabama to gray Boston; sensuous dislocation is a matter of degree. Nevertheless, in large and violent dislocations caused by colonialism and exile, it is especially disingenuous to try to offer up the sensuous experience of the homeland on a plate. Mira Nair might represent a mythical and richly sensuous India in *Kama Sutra* (1996), but the film's kaleidoscope of gleaming bodies, saturated colors, trails of incense, and accented English seems to pander to Western wet dreams rather than appeal to the emigrant's longing for the homeland. Pasolini could represent a mythical and richly sensuous Orient in *Arabian Nights* (1974), but a contemporary Arab filmmaker would be hypocritical to do the same:

We do not go to the West to be indoctrinated by their culture, for the imperialism, hegemony of their culture is nowhere clearer than here in the Third World. But both because it is there that we can be helped in our resistance by all that we do not receive in the Third World: their experimental films and videos, their avant-garde theater, their improvised jazz; and because we can meet people who, unlike those from one's own culture, can look at and genuinely use pre-disaster art and culture without having to resurrect them. . . . When following the devastation of Lebanon, Iraq, and Sudan (and earlier of Palestine), etc., I can have the same close relation with one of the most beautiful books of the Middle East, *A Thousand and One Nights,* as [John] Barth or Pasolini (*Arabian Nights,* 1974) can, then I will know that I am either a hypo-critical Arab writer or already a Western writer. (Toufic 1996, 69–70)

To attempt to recreate a culture lost in the ruins of Beirut, Jalal Toufic writes, would be disingenuous at best, imperialist at worst. Works by Middle Eastern diasporan artists that I have discussed, such as Ra'ad's *Missing Lebanese Wars,* Ra'ad and Salloum's *Talaeen a Junuub,* Haj-Ismail's *I Wet My Hands . . . . ,* Hatoum's *Measures of Distance,* Al-Kassim's *Far From You,* and Toufic's own *Credits Included,* shy away from delivering the sensory richness of their homelands to viewers. To deliver it would be to pretend that the disasters of civil war and exile were only small impediments to the tourist's hungry gaze. It would also be to pretend that these scat-

75 and 76. Stills from *A Box of His Own*

tered artists, living in Rochester, Vancouver, San Francisco, and the internal diaspora of destroyed Beirut, were capable of an immediate sensory connection to a time and place irrevocably lost to them.

The difference between how a diasporan artist would like to re-activate sensory memories of the homeland, and how he actually does, is the subject of Yudi Sewraj's poignant *A Box of His Own* (1997). Sewraj, a Montrealer born in Guyana, returns to his ancestral country for the first time in twenty years. This part of the tape is a video diary, full of bright colors and Sewraj's elated descriptions of food, the humid weather, and the tapping of rain on the tin roof. He revels in this newfound sensuousness, not unlike a tourist enchanted by the unfamiliar smells and tastes of a foreign land. Voiced-over letters to folks back home reveal a growing enchantment with the place, culminating with letters where he breaks up with his white girlfriend and reveals that he is engaged to a Guyanese woman.

When Sewraj returns to Montreal, the tape shifts tone abruptly. The colors give way to gray; the rolling, verdant landscape gives way to the perpendiculars of his sterile apartment. Back home, the artist builds the box of the title: a tiny room with a door, a chair, a video monitor behind the lone viewer's head, and a mirror in which he can gaze at the reflected images of his ancestral land. The "box" is essentially a peep-show booth, where Sewraj positions himself as a voyeur onto the world he briefly and blissfully inhabited, now reduced to a flat and silent image. In Guyana he was surrounded by enthusiastic, long-lost relatives; here the only human contacts are the kindly but distant voices of his worried friends filtered through the answering machine. In this sad scene, the artist reveals his own disavowal: I know that I am a Montrealer and that this cold city has shaped how I perceive the world; but nevertheless I long for the sensuous knowledge that would have been mine (if I hadn't left Guyana). Rather than claim the smells and tastes, the prickle of moisture on his skin and the sound of rain, as his rightful heritage, Sewraj must acknowledge that the longing for those experiences, rather than the experiences themselves, is his heritage. Finally a snappy phone message from the abandoned girlfriend galvanizes a change of heart in Sewraj. The tape concludes in fast rewind, in effect reversing the visit to the homeland and deconstructing the box.

Intercultural movies about food also explore the ambivalent relationship to the sensuous experiences of the homeland. Plenty of documentary and ethnographic films have used images of food and eating to show, as it were, the essence of a culture. Like travel documentaries and commercial pornography, they package sensuous information as yet another commodity. One could call "food porn" a film that reduces cultural rituals around food and eating to a consumable, visual image.[10]

By contrast, intercultural films and videos use food as an entry to memory, troubling any easy access to the memories food represents. Intercultural "food films" and videos point out that the seemingly ahistorical rhythm of cooking and eating food provides an alternative framework for the exploration of cultural memory. The memory of a flavor, as food writer Jeff Weinstein's description in the epigraph to this chapter suggests, traces an elusive course between individual and cultural memory. This memory is not simply that of the exile, longing Proust-like for the memories aroused by the scent of green papaya, pierogies, or salt fish, but the memory that threads between the disparate points in which identities are transformed. For many intercultural filmmakers, their "insiderness" to a traditional culture cannot be assumed. Many of these artists grow up somewhere between their traditional culture and the Western society in which they live. They must struggle to recreate sensory memories, and to use them to "make sense" of the artist's place in a hybrid culture—for example, by learning to cook traditional dishes in a land of hamburgers. In Paul Kwan and Arnold Iger's *Anatomy of a Spring Roll* (1992), the artists compare the social practice of cooking among Vietnamese immigrants and what they see as the solitary, rationalized style of American cooking. To dramatize the difference, Kwan and his mother prepare spring rolls against the background of a Muybridge-style analytic grid, their movements analyzed for efficiency and the resulting product tested on a "crunch-o-meter." His return visit to Saigon serves only to increase his respect for his culture: "The Vietnamese have been colonized and bombed for centuries and they've produced great food. The Americans have been free for 200 years and they've produced the Big Mac."

Given the traditional centrality of cooking to Chinese ritual, medicine, and cosmology (Tuan 1993, 51–53), it is understandable that a sturdy subgenre of Chinese diaspora films and videos deals with food. Some of these works seem to fetishize food, in what seems to be a turning of a colonial gaze on the artists' own traditions. Yet a number of these works show ambivalence toward food and what it traditionally represents. Many Asian video- and filmmakers are presumed to have a rich heritage of food but in fact do not; yet around them non-Asians unproblematically fetishize Asian food and associate Asians' identity with a great meal (Curtis and Pajaczkowska 1994, 208). Thus a sub-subgenre has sprung up, of Chinese diaspora works with a vexed relationship to food and culture. Even in Ang Lee's mainstream hit, *Eat Drink Man Woman,* exquisite dishes remain uneaten as the family sulks around the table. In one scene of Yau Ching's experimental documentary *Flow* (1993), a Chinese-born, New York-based artist cooks up a spattering stir-fry, wearing an elaborate silk robe. Her impractical dress for the kitchen parodies a Western cultural imaginary of Chineseness. In Karen Kew and Ed Sinclair's *Chasing the Dragon* (1993), a voluptuous Asian phone-sex worker named Cherry appeals to a particular Western kink: "How about spicy tofu with black bean sauce?", she croons to a caller. "Is that hot enough for you?" This spoof is the first half of a tape that goes on to explore Western stereotypes of Asian sexuality—"exotic" women, sexually "neutral" men. In a final twist, Cherry turns out to be a man. Food, oral signifier of exoticism, is the locus of displaced Western notions of Asian sensuality; and by extension, of the threat of the foreign. In Shu Lea Cheang's *Fresh Kill* (1994), a wildly hybrid feature with an environmentalist theme, scripted by Jessica Hagedorn, New York yuppies gorge themselves on sushi, the food fetish of the eighties nouveau riche. When the sushi turns out to be made of radioactive fish and the diners notice themselves beginning to phosphoresce, they prudently switch to Tex-Mex. *Fresh Kill* mocks the exoticism and paranoia that surround imported cuisines and, implicitly, the less-manageable immigrants they represent (see Marks 1994b).

Many Asian diaspora works express the struggle to come to terms with hybrid identity in terms of hybrid eating. Just two examples of this thriving genre are *By the Thinnest Root* (1995) by Richard Kim, in which a Korean American youth attempts to please his traditional father by learning to manage chopsticks, and *The Search for Peking Dog* (John Choi, 1995), in which a German housewife, in a misunderstanding characteristic of Western attitudes toward Chinese "omnivorousness," attempts to prepare the delicacy of the title for her Chinese American husband. Filmmaker Laurie Wen, who emigrated to the United States from Hong Kong when she was twelve years old, begins her documentary *The Trained Chinese Tongue* (1994) by describing her childhood ambivalence and resentment toward her culture of origin, especially as it was manifested in cooking. But recently she has begun cooking Chinese meals herself, and she observes that now that she frequents Chinese markets, "I've been wondering about people who live with the same sounds and smells": the old woman wearing six sweaters, the stylish businesswoman, the teenagers trying to learn the names of ingredients. Wen approaches women in the fish market in Boston's Chinatown and asks if they would let her follow them home and watch them cook. The ensuing four encounters demonstrate that commonalities in cultural mem-

77. Frame enlargement from *The Trained Chinese Tongue*

ory are always mediated around differences, and that food provides not only a source of performative, shared cultural memory but also a marker of many kinds of disjunction: of generation, language, class, and place. In the course of these interactions, Wen finds that the ways in which groups share memories of food are highly idiosyncratic. These memories may be the only thing they have in common. Food enters new cultural systems of communication—as with the well-to-do businessmen who use a meal to impress each other in a hybrid of Chinese and middle-class American. These interviews over food seem to be asking: do you taste it the way I taste it? Why not?

In the scene that gives the film its title, the abilities of the tongue to get itself around Chinese words and Chinese food is the subject of most of the conversation. Mr. Bao, a Chinese American businessman whose wife is from Hong Kong, insists that no Asian can pronounce the words "Fort Lauderdale." But, he says, "we Americans" do not have the facility to extract small bones from a piece of chicken inside our mouths; that is only something a "trained Chinese tongue" can do.

This film, like *Daughters of the Dust, Woman from the Lake of Scented Souls, Seeing Is Believing, Measures of Distance,* and many other works I have discussed, shows how sense memories are transformed in the process of diaspora. Cinema can only capture the flavor of home in freeze-dried form: by isolating a moment of cultural plenitude that would henceforth define what the culture is — or was. There is a disingenuousness in the attempt to isolate a typical feature of cultural memory that is only perceived as such in retrospect. *The Trained Chinese Tongue* manages to capture, through the memory of the senses, both the search for a culture of origin and the impossibility of that search from a position of diaspora. And diaspora begins at home; as Jeff Weinstein's lament about the search for the flavor of apple pie reminds us, there is no essential flavor of home:

> My favorite gift this holiday season came from my mother — a stocking stuffer called "Country Baker Apple Pie Scent," by Avon. "Scent the air with the scrumptious aroma of apple pie. Bring back the delicious memories of Mother's kitchen. SHAKE CAN WELL."
>
> It smells precisely like the real thing, if the real thing is that apple pielet wrapped in plastic paper, "flavoring added," sold almost everywhere. This concoction was the first apple pie my neighbor's daughter ever ate. It may have been my first as well. (1988, 129)

Wen's film begins with a memory in which a sensory disjunction expressed a cultural dislocation: when as a girl she practiced the piano at home, the kitchen smells of frying things and black bean sauce "always put a greasy Chinese taint on my Chopin or Beethoven." This early memory relates the ambivalent relationship between the sense knowledges associated with Wen's Chinese birth culture and the American culture she now inhabits. Throughout the film there is an ambivalence between these two kinds of knowledge. Are the cultural knowledges of home, based in the deeply felt senses of smell and taste, more true, and learned Western cultural knowledges false or imposed? — especially when these learned knowledges take the highly disciplined form of Chopin études, which are not only audiovisual but learned by the body of the young musician. Wen's interviews over meals suggest that the relationship between these two kinds of knowledge is ambivalent and complex. The more she pursues other Chinese women to find some point of cultural commonality around food, the more elusive this commonality becomes.

Intercultural cinema is beginning to explore different sensory organizations, and the different orders of knowledge they evoke. Because this work is produced in the flux between cultures, it tends to present sense experience not in freeze-dried form, but in the productive conflict between different ways of knowing. However, audiences will have different degrees of access to the intercultural cinema of the senses, given each of our own cultural backgrounds. Shani Mootoo's magnolia, Marlon Riggs's gumbo, and Steve Reinke's canned peas arouse different sensory associations for me than they did for these artists. The steaming innards of freshly killed animals, which the hunters eagerly devour in *Nunavut,* initially arouse no sensory associations for me, though after a few episodes I find myself salivating at the sight of fresh seal liver. Other images leave me baffled, without any way to embody the experience represented on screen. The bafflement in the face of the representation of unfamiliar sense experiences is an aspect of intercultural relations that is unavoidable and salutary: it provides the ground of respect for cultural differences that must precede intercultural learning.

This bafflement may also compel the viewer of intercultural cinema to confront her own sense envy. As I have noted, popular cinema and television attempt unproblematically to deliver a world of senses to the viewer; travelogues, conventional ethnographic films, art-house imports, and other films present a foreign culture with seeming transparency. Occasionally intercultural films and videos do this as well, in a sort of neocolonialist gaze at their own (or former) culture. Such works, directed to a viewer perfectly comfortable in the dominant culture, represent sense knowledges as commodities, *supplements* to the wealth of the viewer's other resources. Intercultural cinema, in contrast, represents sense knowledges from a position not of wealth but of scarcity, as the precious vessels of memory. These knowledges, difficult to recall and to represent cinematically, will not be available to every viewer. Thus intercultural cinema troubles the ease with which we approach cultures not our own.

Sense envy, the desire of one culture for the sensory knowledge of another, has an enduring history. Like the traveling fetishes I discussed in chapter 2, sense knowledge always undergoes translation in the movement from one culture to another. For example, the use of incense and perfumes, and the resins and animal products on which they are based, have followed a path over the centuries of importation from East to West: musk, cassia, and sandalwood from China to India, frankincense and jasmine from India to Egypt, incense from Egypt to Greece, and all these products thence to Europe (Stoddart 1990, 155, 169–70). At each stop, incense and perfumes took on connotations of an ever more distant, ever more exotic Orient, as well as new connotations, such as the (debated) sanctity of incense in the Catholic Church.[11] All cultures borrow sensory experience from others: this is a factor in cultural change, like the movement of languages. Sacred incense in one culture is taken up as a seductive perfume in another; ordinary soft drinks in one culture are used to commemorate special occasions in another. However, colonial expansion has been especially influenced by sense longing. The spice roads, medieval information highways for sensory knowledge, were founded on the routes cut by the military campaign of the Crusades in the eleventh century. So were the European imports, beginning in the sixteenth century, of tea from China, coffee from Turkey and Arab countries, and chocolate from Mexico (Schivelbusch 1992). All these new sources of sensory stimulation became necessary luxuries to their importers and were the foundations of global movements of conquest, colonizations, and enslavement. Colonized cultures have also made adaptive use of their colonizers' sensory knowledges, and simple trade has also facilitated the travels of new sensory experiences from one culture to another.

As I suggested in my critique of some of the anthropologists of the senses, the contemporary longing in Western countries and urban centers for a soothing "return" to the senses has an undeniable cast of neo-Orientalism. The current interest in smell in postindustrial societies has parallels in the nineteenth-century European fascination with imported scents. Fashions for the scents of the Orient, such as jasmine, sandalwood, and hashish, followed European colonizations of North Africa and India. The Symbolist poets cast down their gazes and instead built languages of smell (Jay 1993a); the Postimpressionist painters drew inspiration from imagined "primitive" cultures, for a world in which knowledge was not at odds with sensuality.

These two waves of interest in smell, and the proximal senses in general, are inextricable from the development of the visual technologies of photography, "pre-cinematic" spectacles, and cinema in the mid- to late nineteenth century, and the proliferation of visual media in the late twentieth. In each case, the appeal to the proximal senses seems to reflect a fear that visual technologies alienate individuals from their bodies. Also in each case, the tendency has been to look to cultures that are perceived as less alienated for sources of nonvisual sensory stimulation. Consequently, at the end of the twentieth century, the interest in smell continues, newly commodified—as in the fashion for aromatherapy, or the appropriation of sweetgrass from Native American rituals by New Age cults.

Yet this rise of multisensory desire does not denote a fundamental reconfiguration of the Western (or more particularly, North American/northern European) sensorium. We cannot simply will ourselves into new forms of sense knowledge. The individual brain may learn quickly, but the acculturated body is slower, and culture is slow to change indeed. Even though eating another culture's food and dancing to its music for long enough gives a little sense of how other people sensuously inhabit their world, we cannot inhabit another culture's sensorium *tout court.* If human existence "is a mode of being that functions in the articulation of thought on what is unthought" (Heidegger, quoted in Foucault 1970, 322), our questioning of the limits of sensory knowledge is a confrontation with an unthought. In other words, much as I might like to, I cannot bootstrap myself into another form of perception. However, we can look for tensions within ocularcentrism that have existed all along, elements that are either within Western culture or have flowed into it from elsewhere. And we can acknowledge the other ways of knowing, including the knowledge of the senses, that will become more widespread as the global movement of diasporic peoples to what we call the West continues. Indeed, one of the ways that "Western" will cease to be be an appropriate adjective to describe the society in which we live is that the organization of our sensoria will increasingly reflect the mixing and merging of cultures.

Intercultural cinema is performing this recombination of sensory experiences. Intercultural filmmakers and videomakers know that it would be false to attempt to reproduce the sensory experience of their culture of origin. Yet they resist the sensory organization of the society in which they find themselves, and they are critical of the cinematic apparatus that tends to reflect this organization. Thus we can look to these works to push the cinematic apparatus in order to represent the memory of home in its multisensory fullness—and when that fails, to represent the emerging sensorium that is a product of both memory and change.

Conclusion:

The portable sensorium

We have reached the end of a long, doubtless taxing, but I hope rewarding journey through the fascinating body of work that is intercultural cinema. I have pursued what I believe are the most interesting and least theorized aspects of these many films and videos, namely the many strategies they use to extract memory from the limitations of the audiovisual moving image. We have moved from memory-images to memory-objects to the memories of touch, smell, and taste. With each chapter the source of memory has seemed to move further from the image proper and closer to the body. With each remove of memory from image to body, it may seem ever more unlikely that cinema would be a rewarding medium through which to try to represent these memories. Yet I have argued that a memory is precious in inverse proportion to its ability to be externalized and expressed. Moreover, for people whose histories are represented in few other ways, it is these valuable and deeply guarded memories of tastes, smells, and caresses that must be coaxed into audiovisual form. Thus it is in intercultural cinema that we find some of the most sincere and most cautious efforts to effect this delicate translation. For intercultural artists it is most valuable to think of the skin of the film not as a screen, but as a membrane that brings its audience into contact with the material forms of memory.

In conclusion, let me ask how cultural sensoria might come to be shaped as global cultures continue to mix and hybridize. Pessimists will argue that commodification and globalization will wipe out cultural differences at the very level of sensuous experience.

However, I see reason for hope that intercultural life will continue to produce new and unmanageable hybrids, given the volatility of sensuous experience. It seems reasonable to worry that as culture becomes globalized, sensuous experience is becoming both universal and placeless. "Non-places," or generic places (malls, airports) are proliferating around the world (Augé 1995) and would seem to bring with them certain sensory organizations. These entail not only an increasingly visual, specifically optical and symbolic, world, but also the abstraction and symbolization of all sense modalities. Although vision is the sense most commonly associated with control and with packaging into signs, any sense can be turned to these uses. Paul Rodaway captures a difference between the rich environment of ambient sound typical of rural life, and the packaged, often electronically reproduced sounds of urban environments, used either as decoration (for example, Muzak) or as warning (sirens, alarm clocks). I find that some urban warning sounds seem to have turned into aural decorations, such as the ubiquitous cycling car alarms that reassuringly signify one's arrival in the city. But all these sounds make for a thin and instrumental auditory relationship to the world, "an auditory geography of hearing rather than listening, of juxtaposition rather than relationship" (Rodaway 1994, 158).

Similarly, since the Middle Ages, smell in Western urban societies has been increasingly purged from its origins as much as possible and re-presented in packaged form. Now scents are sprayed into offices to stimulate workers, bottled at the Body Shop to soothe harried urbanites. The "aroma of the commodity" (Classen, Howes, and Synnott 1994) now floats from the shifting centers of multinational capital to the furthest corners of the market. As smells are synthesized and marketed, their indexical link to a particular place is severed, so that "everyone" can now scent their rooms with mountain pine air freshener whether or not they have ever known a real pine tree (Rodaway 1994, 153). Avon ladies, traveling by canoe when necessary, now ply Crystal Splash cologne to villages in the Amazon (Classen, Howes, and Synnott 1994, 181). (This fact is more ironic in light of the fact that European perfumers travel to the Amazon in search of flowers, woods, and insects on which to base their new formulas.) As commodities, generic smells and tastes replace particular, local ones: fewer people savor the *rodahkinó* than taste the packaged apple pielet, and more people around the world prefer to mask with Eternity the mix of person- and place-smells that is theirs alone. When it is separated from its source and packaged, smell becomes a simulacrum, the scent of nonplace. Interestingly, in John Waters's *Polyester* all the "good" smells, with the dubious exception of a hothouse rose, are synthetic—"new car smell," the flowery air freshener that Divine sprays around her huddled friends at the end, cooing, "Everything's going to be all right. Doesn't that smell better?"—while all the "bad" smells, such as farts and smelly sneakers, are of more or less natural origin. Smell technologies are achieving the work of olfaction in the age of chemical reproduction. Surely there already exists a sensorium of the commodity, in versions both privileged (aromatherapy, Starbucks coffee, cashmere sweaters) and bare-bones (Kraft dinner, Air-wick, America's Top 40 on the radio anywhere in the world). In fact, one might suggest that the uncommodified sensorium has become a luxury of the very rich and the very poor, who can afford not to, or cannot afford to, use the packaged foods and smells and sounds and images that have become necessities to the people in between.

Yet even in this world of increasingly generic senses, particular sense memories are places within nonplaces. Against the tide of the commodification and genericization of sense experience, pools of local sensuous experience are continually created anew. When people move to a new place, even to the sensuous nonplace of a North American suburb, they bring this experience with them. They bring sensory experience in practices like cooking, music, and religious ritual, and around these are created new, small sensuous geographies whose monuments are grocery stores, places of worship, coffee and tea shops, and kitchens. And they bring sensory experience in their very bodies, in the organization of their sensoria, that perceive the new environment in a different light (texture, and smell) than do its older inhabitants. Especially for the hybrid people of the urban metropole, sensuous geographies form a kind of microculture within mass culture. Sometimes this microculture is contained only within the sense memories of a single person.

Also, there is no doubt that the ladies of the Amazon use their Avon products differently than do their North American counterparts. Every sensuous artifact, even the most banal, is uniquely embodied, worked upon, and transformed into a new sensory experience. In Igloolik Isuma's *Nunavut* (1995) the white priest uses packaged biscuits to bribe a boy to come to church. But these biscuits take on a different meaning and a different taste (not to say an odor of sanctity) from what they had in the South, just as surely as the Inuit family transforms the Christmas practices of carol singing and gift giving to a more appropriate local use.

In Los Angeles, where I lived during part of the writing of this book, the farmers' markets taught me that sensuous experience is recombinant. Southern California farmers grow for an international market, which is fairly standardized by requirements of quality, uniformity, and transportability. But they also grow produce for regional populations of recent immigrants and for consumers who for various reasons avoid standardized breeds and farming methods. Vegetables and fruits familiar to Latin American, Caribbean, Chinese, Vietnamese, and other communities in this recombinant city are for sale here; so are organic produce and "boutique" fodder like baby vegetables and frisée lettuce. Many people buy their food at the farmer's market, both long-term Americans in search of new sense experiences and recent arrivals seeking to approximate the sense experiences they remember. Most people end up going home with a basket that represents a world of potential sense experience, and perhaps with some hybrid cooking tips.

As world populations continue to regroup in flows of exile and emigration, sensuous geographies are like islands in the sea of sensory nonplaces. I often used to take the train that crossed the river from Niagara Falls, Ontario, to Niagara Falls, New York. We would wait for an hour as the Canadian staff left the train, the U.S. staff boarded, and U.S. customs officials came through. Invariably, customs interrogated every person of color on the train, as well as confiscating raw fruit and other possible contaminants. Once I was sitting across from an Indian family and envying them their lunch, which despite being neatly packed in plastic containers wafted its aroma across the aisle. The U.S. customs officials suspiciously opened the containers. Although it was obviously cooked and posed no health threat, they confiscated the Indian family's meal (and not, I think, because they wanted to eat it themselves). I am convinced that a less fragrant, less *foreign*-smelling meal would have been safe. Smells do not respect walls or national borders: they drift and infuse and inhabit. The smell of curry must have been an unconscious metonymy for all that the U.S. government, in the persons of its customs agents, fears of unregulated immigration. The Indian (Canadian) family was carrying a sensorium in their Tupperware containers, carving out a sensuous place in the nonplace of the train, and arousing suspicion.

In general, increased regulations on food importation, according to the rules of the European Union and the North American "Free" Trade Agreement, mad cow disease paranoia, and other instances denote not just the fear of infestation but a fear of others' sensuous geographies. For sensuous geographies can be contained in traveling objects—in curries, saris, sweet potatoes, and all the other volatile things I have described in this book. It would seem that cinema is an inert medium that can cross national borders without generating such fear of infection. But as I have argued throughout, cinema has the power to bring those radioactive fossils to life. As it does, it diffuses into the world a strange, new fragrance, which perhaps someday we will know how to smell.

Notes

Preface

1 Cinema studies has dealt with some of the ways cinema represents these
seemingly excessive sensuous experiences, notably in work on melodrama
(see for example Dyer 1985, Thompson 1986). These analyses ultimately
explain excess in terms of a semiotic spillover that resonates on the unconscious level. This argument is valuable but somewhat different from the
embodied response I wish to define. It can be argued that psychoanalytic
explanations ultimately found meaning linguistically, rather than in the
body, thus translating sensuous meaning into verbal meaning. I concentrate
here on the bodily and sensuous responses to cinema that are meaningful as such, since meaning is produced at the very level of our sensuous
perceptions.

Introduction

1 Many of these terms sprang from particular political and/or intellectual
movements and originated in manifestos, legislative initiatives, or germinal
scholarly works. The term "Third World" was adopted at the 1955 Bandung
Conference of nonaligned United Nations members from Africa and Asia
(see Shohat and Stam 1995, 25). "Multicultural" and "antiracist" are both
terms associated with government policy initiatives in Canada (for "multicultural") and Britain (for "antiracist"). A partial list of sources in which
some of these terms have been influentially theorized includes: for *mestizo*
and *mestisaje,* Anzaldúa (1987); for "hybridity," Bhabha (1985); for "imperfect cinema," García Espinosa ([1970] 1997); for "Third Cinema," Solanas
and Getino ([1969] 1983); for "hybrid cinema," Fusco (1991); for "transnational cinema," Zimmermann and Hess (1997); for "interstitial mode of
production," Naficy (1999). It is less relevant to attempt to locate an origin
for the other terms, which are either common usage or burst onto the scene
of intellectual and cultural production so explosively that they cannot be
attributed to an "author."

2 The overwhelming pressure upon academics to produce new scholarship at a faster pace than it can be consumed is doubtless the main reason that so many concepts become stretched beyond recognition and discarded like old socks, "postmodern," "postcolonial," and "hybrid" being some of the most recent casualties.

3 Note that "Black" in the British context includes people of the African and South Asian diasporas; it aligns roughly with the terms "people of color" in the United States and Canada and "visible minorities" in Canada. It is usually capitalized, and I will generally use this form when writing of the British context.

4 I use the term "First Nations" most frequently in this writing, since it signifies these groups' sovereignty with relation to the land. It also connotes the historical indebtedness of eighteenth-century European theorists of the nation to First Nations precedents such as the Iroquois confederacy. The terms "native," indigenous," and "aboriginal" do not connote the existence of these peoples as political entities. However, they are sometimes more appropriate to describe traditionally nomadic people, such as the Inuit, for whom sovereignty does not necessarily (until recently in Canada, with the establishment of the self-governing territory of Nunavut) imply residence in a particular geographic area. "Native American" inscribes the lately arrived European presence into the name of the first inhabitants; and of course "Indian" memorializes European explorers' historic bad navigation skills. Nevertheless, many First Nations people themselves use these latter two terms, for convenience or irony. I use the name of individual nations or tribes wherever possible and appropriate. Still, the search for the "correct" way to name aboriginal groups is doomed to failure, since even tribal names are often European transcriptions and often of the name that the geographically adjacent people had for the group in question. See Durham (1993) for an ironic excursion into this *mise-en-abîme* of naming.

5 These events are well documented in Fusco (1988a), Gilroy (1987), and Mercer (1994a).

6 The exchange between Salman Rushdie (1988) and Stuart Hall (1988c) over *Handsworth Songs*, published in *The Guardian* and reprinted in *Black Film, British Cinema*, shows what is at stake in the double movement of destruction and emergence. Rushdie complained that the film was so busy deconstructing the racist discourse around the Handsworth riots that it never gave voice to the "ghosts of stories" evoked in the film—an oddly positivist complaint from one who so eloquently describes the pain from which new stories arise. In his rejoinder, Hall argued that the film used experimental strategies such as reworked documentary footage and narrative interruption in the struggle, "precisely, to find a new language." Rushdie's desire for full-formed stories, he suggested, was understandable but premature.

1 Réda Bensmaïa (1994) explains this process in a reflection upon one of Deleuze's strange but provocative terms for cinema, the "spiritual automaton." "Cinema as spiritual automaton is that 'machine' that puts thought into contact with an Outside which comes to subvert the nature of the relations of representation that exist, in cinema, between the image and reality" (176; my translation). In a great film, as in any great work of art, there is always something of the open (178): the spiritual automaton is that machine that adds n dimensions to the first and second dimensions of shot-countershot. So whereas for the Lacanian theorists of suture, the pairing of shot with countershot is a way of arresting the fear of the void that waits beyond the edges of the frame, for Deleuze this openness is a source for ever more discoveries, a source of the new. Cinema can choose to seal up those openings or to keep pointing toward them, opening itself to the possibilities of what cannot yet be said.

   I do not argue in writing about the limits of thought, that all representations will become possible in the progress of human culture; for of course over history certain kinds of representation will become impossible as others become possible. Perhaps the desire for representation, the desire to make culture visible and graspable, is itself a historically specific desire, characteristic of a post-Enlightenment will to knowledge. Perhaps we are entering an age that does not place a premium on representation.

2 These "forms of luminosity" have the emergent qualities of Firstness, C. S. Peirce's semiotic category for signs that are pure affect and not yet perceptible. I explore the relationship between Deleuze and Peirce in Marks, in press.

3 I am grateful to John Yemen, a student in my "Hybrid Cinema" class at Carleton University in Spring 1997, for pointing out the powerful effect of this image.

4 Marcel Proust writes that the reconstitution of memories from the bite of tea-soaked madeleine was like "ce jeu où les Japonais s'amusent à tremper dans un bol de porcelaine rempli d'eau, des petits morceaux de papier jusque-là indistincts qui, à peine y sont-ils plongés, s'étirent, se contournent, so colorent, se différencient. . . ." ([1919] 1954, 47). My students compare the process to Sea Monkeys, those little dessicated creatures that can be reconstituted in water.

5 A great number of intercultural films use the body as the medium for some kind of healing ritual. These include, to mention some that I do not discuss elsewhere in these pages, the works of Thomas Allen Harris — *Splash* (1991), *Black Body* (1992), *Heaven, Earth, and Hell* (1994), and *Encounter at the Intergalactic Café* (1997), Barbara McCullough's film *Water Ritual #1: An Urban Site of Purification* (1990), and Pratibha Parmar's *Sari Red* (1988) and *Khush* (1991). Isaac Julien's films *The Attendant* and *Frantz Fanon: White Skin, Black Masks* (1995), use sadomasochism as a way to confront colonial

wounds. Again, the move from overtly activist filmmaking to a contemplation of the body as a site of political expression seems to have taken place a little earlier among British than among North American filmmakers. Numerous other films examine diasporan people's exploration of sexuality outside the fetishizing relations of the white-"other" dyad; for a discussion of some of these see Marks 1993.

2. The Memory of Things

1 For example, Robert Young's *Alambrista* (1978), Luis Valdovino's *Work in Progress* (1990), and Alex Rivera's *Animaquiladora* (1997) all follow the movement of migrant farm workers from Mexico to California (in the satirical solution of *Animaquiladora,* Mexican farm workers can "cyber-commute" to California farms). These workers' misery and political disenfranchisement directly correlate to the U.S. economy's dependence on their exploitability and political invisibility. This reciprocality, the sense that transnationalism is a mutual infection between the United States and Mexico, also informs the the videos and performances of Guillermo Gomez-Peña, for example, *El Naftazteca: Cyber-Aztec TV for 2000 AD* (1995): he addresses an Anglo audience in a hyper-real mixture of Mexican Spanish, English, and the techno-horrific language of the slightly distant future. Amos Gitai's *Bangkok Bahrain* (1985) follows a similar flow of workers between a poor country and a wealthy one; in this case it is Thai men who are employed as manual laborers in Bahrain, while the money that flows into Thailand from outside is mostly from foreign tourists to the sex industry in which many Thai women work. A number of films and videos trace the global commerce of sex work: as well as *Bangkok Bahrain,* there are Dennis O'Rourke's *The Good Woman of Bangkok* (1992); Byun Young Joo's *A Woman Being in Asia* (1993), a documentary on the sex trade between Korean sex workers and Japanese and other male tourists; Kathy High's *Underexposed: The Temple of the Fetus* (1992), a videotape on the traffic in high-tech fertility, which exposes the use of third-world women as incubators for first-world babies; and *The Salt Mines* (1990) by Carlos Aparicio and Susana Aiken, a documentary of the lives of Latinos (all men) living on Manhattan's piers, who live the triply hazardous life of being undocumented, homeless, and sex workers.

2 Of course, since it was facing the sky, the piece of tar paper may have missed a lot too. . . .

3 Indeed Benjamin's distinction between the material history of the object and narrative history is somewhat comparable to Foucault's distinction between seeable and sayable, though to draw in those terms would make this discussion interminable.

4 Eric Michaels describes a similar form of cultural production that is pre-translated for export, namely, acrylic versions of traditional Australian Aboriginal sand paintings, in *Bad Aboriginal Art* (1993).

5 As Gayatri C. Spivak (1990) has pointed out, when the Western intellectual establishment (which includes the art world) includes selected third-
worlders it is doubly silencing others, namely those who do not have access
to elite education and international institutions.

6 In this I am suggesting a life of the object different from what Susan Stewart
posits (1984). Stewart argues that the fetish, or souvenir (at least the "homo-
material object," a term Stewart borrows from Umberto Eco for an object
that existed at the site of the event to be remembered, such as the rib-
bon from a corsage), does not maintain any material relation to an event
but is important precisely because it substitutes for an event: it elicits a
stream of personal narrative that traces the trajectory of desire. In Stewart's
account, any material connection to a primal scene of memory is necessarily effaced in the *narration* of a supposed connection to the remembered
scene: a narration inward, toward the self. By contrast, I argue that the souvenir maintains a thread of *material* connection to the scene it remembers,
and it is precisely in this materiality, not in its willful forgetting, that the
souvenir's significance lies.

7 Scholars have greeted digital imaging technologies as the final severance
between the image and its material referent, as these images may appear to
index reality while being partially or entirely computer-generated (see, for
example, Druckrey 1989, Mitchell 1994). While my argument here would
not apply as strongly to a work shot on digital video, for example, I would
suggest that the difference between digital and analog media is not as radical as many claim. Analog photography, film, and video have been used to
simulate special effects since the inception of each medium; and many artists use digital media as much for their convenience as for their capacity for
electronic alteration. Thus I believe it is more appropriate to talk about indexical and nonindexical *practices* than indexical and nonindexical *media.*

8 It would be interesting to compare this exchange in *Madame l'eau* to the
scenes in Granada TV's *The Kayapo: Out of the Forest* by Michael Beckham (1989), where the Kayapo use traditional organizing and ritual techniques to confront the Brazilian government and the World Bank. The two
water-diverting objects in question (the windmill and the dam) have different sorts of commodity status, in Appadurai's term, and different powers
as recollection-image, in Deleuze's term, and they operate differently as
fetishes produced in the process of intercultural translation, which Pietz
describes.

9 See Appiah (1991) for a humorous yet scathing critique of the mutually sup-
portive appropriation of traditional African art by Western aesthetics and
Western investors.

10 I thank Bill Nichols for mentioning this film to me.

11 Trippi's essay is in the flyer for the exhibition "Trade Routes" at the New
Museum in New York in 1993. The exhibition, described as "an inquiry into
the cultural consequences of the globalization of finance," included works
that explore the patterns of cultural interpenetration, commodification, and

fetishism I have been discussing here. Thanks to Maren Stange for bringing it to my attention.

12 To say that Beharry does something like "give voice" to peasant rituals has the danger of suggesting that, below the apparent exoticism of Hindu culture in general, another, even more exotic/authentic object has been discovered—a sort of fetishism *en abîme*. A number of scholars have alerted us to the danger of fetishizing lower-class "third world" women as the most authentic of them all: these include Chow (1993), 112–14; Trinh (1989), 79–117; Spivak (1990), 59–66; and Kaplan (1997).

13 The cliché of Indian women's sensuality is fascinatingly undone in *Fatima's Letter* (1994) by British artist Alia Syed. The image consists exclusively of shots in Whitechapel Underground Station in east London. They are luminous and often barely recognizable, suggesting the faraway thoughts of the rider who reads the letter of the title. In Urdu and English voice-over, "Fatima" writes of an assassination—of foreign sailors by a group of women—which took place in Pakistan. The women enticed the men, sat them in soft chairs, and offered rich biryanis whose "intoxicating saffron fragrance before you even eat it" assailed the senses of their guests. Then, she writes, the women pressed their breasts against the men's faces, overwhelming them with the scent of jasmine from outside and musk from the pores of their skin. "They got what they deserved"—for the men only realized at the last minute that they were not being seduced but suffocated. The passengers on the underground include a few other South Asian women, one of whom glances at the camera as though in confirmation when Fatima writes that Pakistani immigrant women "recognize each other in reflections but are afraid to look at each other . . . immigrant women are all in disguise." This stunning film offers South Asian women a fantasy of turning their "Oriental sensuality" into a weapon against their former colonizers, and by locating it in the subway uses this fantasy to forge a bond among women.

3. The Memory of Touch

1 These include Jonathan Crary (1990, 1994), Martin Jay (1993), John Tagg (1988), Allan Sekula (1986), and Paul Virilio (1994).

2 Psychoanalytic feminist critiques of visuality include those of Luce Irigaray (1985), Laura Mulvey (1974), Rosalind Krauss (1988), Mieke Bal (1991), Kaja Silverman (1992), Parveen Adams (1993), and many others. A more Foucauldian approach to the critique of visuality characterizes the work of Linda Williams (1989) and Lisa Cartwright (1994), for example.

3 Although these critiques still apply to ethnographic photography and film as it was traditionally practiced and is still practiced in popular variations à la *National Geographic,* it is important to note that anthropologists and ethnographic filmmakers have been among the first to recognize these problems and devise alternatives.

4 For example, one of Peirce's categories of indexical signs, the *rhematic*

indexical sinsign, includes mimetic acts like a spontaneous cry—or, for example, a child's imitation of an airplane with her body—in which the sign directs attention to the object (fear, the airplane) that caused it (Peirce 1950, 115).

5 The words *subject* and *object* are not quite appropriate to the positions I am describing, since *subject* tends to imply both cogito and ego, conceptions of the self that I reject here. Yet it would be awkward, linguistically and epistemologically, to replace *subject* with a bulky term like Heidegger's *Dasein* or *being-in-the-world.* Instead I would like to blur the meanings of these words, as I have indicated.

6 Oddly enough, Caillois is describing mimetic insects in this essay. Insects are similarly laden with meaning (like so much pollen) for Deleuze and Guattari, who describe the mutual mimesis between a wasp and an orchid in *A Thousand Plateaus: Capitalism and Schizophrenia* (1987, 10). At the point where they meet, the wasp and the orchid generate codes from each other on the basis of contact, rather than abstraction. Knowledge of the wasp by the orchid, and the orchid by the wasp, is brought about through a mutual touching rather than the distant coding of vision. Though this is a metaphor for knowledge and language production, it is a resolutely tactile one that consolidates Deleuze and Guattari's antipathy to simple linguistic determination.

7 Merleau-Ponty did revise this view in his later writings, which better acknowledge the degree to which the senses are cultivated.

8 As D. N. Rodowick (1991) points out, our present audiovisual culture produces images that exceed semiotic analysis. Rodowick proposes the term "the figural" for the incommensurable meeting of visible and expressible that defines the electronically circulating image.

9 An exception is Peircean semiotics, which ranges signs along a continuum between embodied and abstract.

10 That this conception of subjectivity is extended to a basis in hearing, for example in Kaja Silverman's *The Acoustic Mirror* (1988), only perpetuates the notion that subjectivity is fundamentally alienated and disembodied.

11 Shaviro's quite particular notion of what it would be to have a tactile experience of film brings to mind Alphonso Lingis's gruesome attempt at an embodied description of orgasm: "a breaking down into a mass of exposed organs, secretions, striated muscles, systems turning into pulp and susceptibility" (1985, 56). These are markedly masculinist notions of embodiment, in which the subject is shattered so violently only because it is so rigidly constituted in the first place. In Leo Bersani's not-entirely-metaphor, if the rectum is a grave, it is one only for a phallic subjectivity that cannot countenance being penetrated itself (Bersani 1988).

12 As Mike Hoolboom puts it in conversation.

13 Thanks to Randi Klebanoff for directing me to Berenson.

14 Thanks to Paolo Cherchi Usai for pointing this out.

15 Auerbach compared these rigid, symbolized figures to those on late-antique

sarcophagi (1953, 116), which are in turn comparable to the figures Riegl identifies in late-Roman metalwork.

16 A thorough taxonomy of modes of tactility in cinema is being researched by Jennifer Barker (in progress).

17 See Marks (1997a) for a discussion of discussion of the deterioration of film and video and its consequences for identification.

18 Gene Youngblood emphasizes that the video image is a physical presence insofar as it is constituted by a barrage of electrons: "On the most fundamental level electronic visualization refers to the video signal itself as a plastic medium, as the 'material' of electronic presence. . . . This isn't visual art or picture-making; it is the thing itself, the visible process of the electronic substance" (1987, 335). I push this assertion as far as possible in Marks (1999).

19 The toy manufacturer Tyco has since manufactured a similar children's video camera.

20 In Levinas's view, the erotic is constituted by the absolute alterity of the other, the fact that we can never come into contact with it. This differs from the phenomenological view that I have adopted, which understands there to be a continuum between the self and the world. See Vasseleu (1998) for a rigorous, if parchingly dry, comparison of the self-other relationship in Irigaray, Levinas, and Merleau-Ponty.

21 I explore the erotic quality of haptic imagery in more detail in Marks (1998).

22 Haptic visuality does have some of the qualities of Gaylyn Studlar's (1988) theory of masochistic identification. Studlar describes a kind of spectatorship in which the film viewer gives himself or herself over to an entire scene, sometimes literally a shimmering surface (as in the Dietrich-von Sternburg spectacles), rather than identifying with characters. Desire in such a space operates differently than in solely optical visuality, since it is not limited to the operations of identification.

4. The Memory of the Senses

1 Smell knowledge is vestigial but persistent, and so are its footnotes. In a footnote, Horkheimer and Adorno refer to a footnote by Wilamowitz-Moellendorff, in turn citing another scholar, which "surprisingly indicates the connection between the concept of snuffling and that of the *noos*, autonomous reason: 'Schwyzer has quite convincingly related *noos* to snorting and snuffling'. . . . Of course Wilamowitz does not claim that the etymological connection helps in elucidating the meaning" (1972, 71n).

2 Recent research suggests that touch is processed partly in the limbic system (Bonda, Petrides, and Evans 1996): this suggests that touch has a similar, but weaker, connection with memory.

3 For more on how art and cinema can represent olfactory experience, see Drobnick (1998) and Marks (1997b).

4 These include Constance Classen, David Howes, and Anthony Synnott

(1994), E. Valentine Daniel (1994), David Howes (1991), Joel C. Kuipers (1994), Vishvajit Pandya (1993), Sylvain Pinard (1990), Ian Ritchie (1990), C. Nadia Seremetakis (1994), Paul Stoller (1989), and Anthony Synnott (1991). Also see Alain Corbin (1986).

5 Science fiction, such as the novels of William Gibson and Pat Cadigan (in whose *Synners* [1991] a stunt actor records herself falling off a cliff) and Kathryn Bigelow's movie *Strange Days* (1995), posits ways that sensory experience can be "reproduced" by recording the sensations of an "actor" and playing them back via direct neural stimulation to the "viewer." What is interesting is how, in order to capture the multisensory effects of these fictitious technologies, these works must resort to verbal descriptions.

6 As my colleague Charles O'Brien tells me.

7 This implied history of the mimetic relationship can be expanded. Both Auerbach and Riegl described the history of representational technologies as histories of the creation of parallel worlds of signs, which needed to shed their mimetic traces of the world before they could be refashioned. This process of increasing abstraction has been extremely partial and uneven: for example, Hebrew mystical scholars recognized a mimetic power in the sacred words themselves, while Greek scribes adapted the Hebrew *aleph-beth* to an abstract and disembodied written alphabet (Abram 1996, 245–55; see also Buck-Morss 1989). Western idealist philosophy, perhaps reaching its apex in Kant's positing that time and space were absolute categories, valued the increasing distance of symbolic systems from the world that bred them. Mimetic thought, and mimetic works that invited a bodily relationship between spectator/reader and object, continued to be produced during the long history of Western idealism, but often in minor traditions. When twentieth-century critics such as Benjamin and Merleau-Ponty sought and found the traces of mimetic relationships in symbolic systems, they identified a mimesis that had been there all along. And when we look to cultures that have nurtured mimetic and sensuous relationships to the world instead of or alongside more abstract representational traditions, we may recognize commonalities with relationships that have, until recently, been deemed insignificant in Western culture.

8 For example, Stan Brakhage's critique of the apparatus pinpointed its cultural bias for a particular kind of embodied perception, that of nineteenth-century Europe, and its naturalization of that bias as the standard of all subsequent filmmaking (1963, n.p.). Fernando Solanas and Octavio Getino sharpened Brakhage's comments on the dictatorial nature of film speeds and stocks, attacking the audiovisual conventions of Hollywood cinema's speed, film gauge, lighting, and conditions of exhibition for representing not only a European but a capitalist point of view (1983, 51). Brakhage's observation that film is gauged for white skin (the "peachy skins" of salon painting) has also been sharpened by the urgency, described by many filmmakers and videomakers, to find the combination of film stock and lighting that can respect the many tonal varieties of darker skins.

9 Erika Muhammad [in progress] examines the work of Jones and other African diasporic artists working in interactive media.

10 I borrow the term from science fiction writer Cadigan (1991), who projects a future in which every channel on the television will play porn—news porn, sports porn, food porn, porn porn, etc. The science fiction here is that, in a future of accelerating visuality, all representation is voyeurism. Cadigan's imagined future epitomizes Marx's argument that, in a society organized around property relations, vision is conceived as possession.

11 Early Christians opposed the use of incense in the church, on the rationale that the "base" senses have no role in spiritual life. The Syrian scholar Arnobius argued that "if the gods are incorporeal, odours and perfumes can have no effect at all on them," since corporeal substances can have no effect on incorporeal beings (Stoddart 1990, 180). Although, as D. Michael Stoddart writes, incense was accepted into Christian ritual in the fourth century C.E. under Emperor Constantine, Christian queasiness about its use continued as Christian philosophers refined their theories of dualism. Thomas Aquinas argued that taste and smell can have no part in beauty and thus cannot appeal to God, Who is beauty itself. "Those senses chiefly regard the beautiful, which are the most cognitive, viz., sight and hearing, as ministering to reason; for we speak of beautiful sights and beautiful sounds. But in reference to the other objects of the senses, we do not use the expression *beautiful,* for we do not speak of beautiful tastes, and beautiful odours" (quoted in Campbell 1996, 168).

Bibliography

Abram, David. 1996. *The Spell of the Sensuous.* New York: Pantheon Books.

Adams, Parveen. 1991. "Per Os(cillation)." In *Psychoanalysis and Cultural Theory: Thresholds,* ed. James Donald. New York: St. Martin's. 68–87.

Ahmad, Aijaz. 1992. *In Theory: Classes, Nations, Literatures.* New York: Verso.

———. 1995. "Postcolonialism: What's in a Name?" In *Late Imperial Culture,* ed. Román de la Campa, E. Ann Kaplan, and Michael Sprinker. London: Verso. 11–32.

Akomfrah, John, and June Givanni. 1993. Discussion at the 38th Robert Flaherty Seminar, Aurora, New York. August 11.

Akomfrah, John, and Kass Banning. 1993. "Feeding off the Dead: Necrophilia and the Black Imaginary." *Border/Lines* 29/30. 28–38.

Alpers, Svetlana. 1983. *The Art of Describing: Dutch Art in the Seventeenth Century.* University of Chicago Press.

Andrade-Watkins, Claire, and Mbye B. Cham, eds. 1988. *Blackframes: Critical Perspectives on Black Independent Cinema.* Cambridge: MIT Press.

Andrew, Dudley. 1997. "A Preface to Disputation." In *The Image in Dispute: Art and Cinema in the Age of Photography,* ed. Dudley Andrew, with Sally Shafto. Austin: University of Texas Press. vii–xiv.

Annett, Judith M., and Julian C. Leslie. 1996. "Effects of Visual and Verbal Interference Tasks on Olfactory Memory: The Role of Complexity." *British Journal of Psychology* 87: 447–60.

Antin, David. 1986. "Video: The Distinctive Characteristics of the Medium." In *Video Culture,* ed. John Hanhardt. Rochester, N.Y.: Visual Studies Workshop. 147–66.

Anzaldúa, Gloria. 1987. *Borderlands/La Frontera.* San Francisco: Spinsters/ Aunt Lute Foundation.

Appadurai, Arjun. 1986. "Commodities and the Politics of Value." In *The Social Life of Things: Commodities in Cultural Perspective,* ed. Appadurai. Cambridge University Press. 3–63.

———. 1996. "Disjuncture and Difference in the Global Cultural Economy." In *Modernity at Large: Cultural Dimensions of Globalization.* Minneapolis: Minnesota University Press. 27–47.

Appiah, Kwame Anthony. 1991. "Is the Post in Postmodern the Post in Post-colonial?" *Critical Inquiry* 17 (Winter): 336–58.

Auerbach, Erich. 1953. *Mimesis*. Princeton: Princeton University Press.

Augé, Marc. 1995. *Non-Places: Introduction to an Anthropology of Super-modernity*. London: Verso.

Auguiste, Reece. 1996. Interview with the author. March 19.

Auguiste, Reece (Black Audio Film Collective). 1989. "Black Independents and Third Cinema: The British Context." In Pines and Willemen, *Questions of Third Cinema*. London: BFI. 212–17.

Bailey, Cameron. 1991. "The State's Witness: Race and Film in the Canadian Context." In Fusco and Colo, *The Hybrid State*. New York: Exit Art.

Bal, Mieke. 1991. *Reading "Rembrandt": Beyond the Word-Image Opposition*. New York: Cambridge University Press.

Balász, Béla. [1923] 1972. *Theory of the Film*. Trans. Edith Bone. New York: Arno.

Bambara, Toni Cade. 1993. "Reading the Signs, Empowering the Eye: *Daughters of the Dust* and the Black American Cinema Movement." In Diawara, *Black American Cinema*. New York: Routledge. 118–44.

Barker, Jennifer. In progress. "The Tactile Eye." Ph.D. diss., University of California, Los Angeles.

Barthes, Roland. [1957] 1972. "The Face of Garbo." *Mythologies*. Trans. Annette Lavers. London: Jonathan Cape. 56–57.

Bauman, Zygmunt. 1990. "Modernity and Ambivalence." In Featherstone, *Global Culture*. London: Sage.

Bazin, André. 1967. "The Ontology of the Photographic Image." In *What Is Cinema?* Vol. 1, ed. and trans. Hugh Gray. Berkeley: University of California Press. 9–16.

Beharry, Shauna. 1996. Interview with the author. August 3.

Belton, John. 1996. "Looking through Video: The Psychology of Video and Film." In *Resolutions: Contemporary Video Practices,* ed. Michael Renov and Erika Suderberg. Minneapolis: University of Minnesota Press. 61–72.

Benjamin, Walter. 1968a. "On Some Motifs in Baudelaire." *Illuminations*. Trans. Harry Zohn. New York: Schocken. 155–200.

———. 1968b. "The Storyteller: Reflections on the Works of Nikolai Leskov." *Illuminations*. Trans. Harry Zohn. New York: Schocken. 83–110.

———. 1968c. "The Work of Art in the Age of Mechanical Reproduction." *Illuminations*. Trans. Harry Zohn. New York: Schocken. 217–52.

———. 1978a. "On the Mimetic Faculty." *Reflections*. Trans. Edmund Jephcott. New York: Harcourt. 333–36.

———. 1978b. "Surrealism: The Last Snapshot of the European Intelligentsia." *Reflections*. Trans. Edmund Jephcott. New York: Harcourt. 177–92.

———. 1986. *Moscow Diary*. Ed. Gary Smith. Trans. Richard Sieburth. Cambridge: Harvard University Press.

Bensmaïa, Réda. 1994. "De l'«automate spirituel» ou le temps dans le cinéma moderne selon Gilles Deleuze." *Cinémas* 5: 1–2 (Fall). 167–86.

Berenson, Bernard. 1896. *The Florentine Painters of the Renaissance.* New York: G.P. Putman's Sons.

Berger, Sally. 1995. "Time Travelers." In "Landscapes," special issue of *Felix* 2:1. 105–12.

Bergson, Henri. [1911]. 1988. *Matter and Memory.* Trans. Nancy Margaret Paul and W. Scott Palmer. New York: Zone.

Bersani, Leo. 1988. "Is the Rectum a Grave?" In *AIDS: Cultural Analysis, Cultural Activism,* ed. Douglas Crimp. Cambridge: MIT Press.

Bettelheim, Bruno. 1960. *The Informed Heart: Autonomy in a Mass Age.* New York: Free Press.

Bhabha, Homi K. 1985. "Signs Taken for Wonders: Questions of Ambivalence and Authority Under a Tree Outside Delhi, May 1817." In " 'Race,' Writing and Difference," special issue of *Critical Inquiry.* Ed. Henry Louis Gates, Jr. Reprint, 1994. *The Location of Culture.* New York: Routledge. 102–22.

———. 1994a. "How Newness Enters the World." In *The Location of Culture.* New York: Routledge. 212–35.

———. 1994b. "The Other Question: The Stereotype and Colonial Discourse." *The Location of Culture.* New York: Routledge. 70–75.

Bonda, Eva, Michael Petrides, and Alan Evans. 1996. "Neural Systems for Tactual Memories." *Journal of Neurophysiology* 75:4 (April): 1730–737.

Bordwell, David, and Kristin Thompson. 1997. *Film Art: An Introduction.* New York: McGraw-Hill.

Bourgeois, Annette. 1997. "Southern Managers Bleeding IBC Dry." *Nuniatsiaq News* (October 24): 5, 21.

Brakhage, Stan. 1963. "The Camera Eye." *Film Culture* 30 (Autumn).

Bray, Anne. 1996. Interview with the author. April 2.

Brisebois, Debbie. 1991. "Whiteout Warning: Courtesy of the Federal Government." In *Video the Changing World.* Ed. Nancy Thede and Alain Ambrosi Montréal: Black Rose. 99–109.

Buck-Morss, Susan. 1989. *The Dialectics of Seeing: Walter Benjamin and the Arcades Project.* Cambridge: MIT Press.

———. 1992. "Aesthetics and Anaesthetics: Walter Benjamin's Artwork Essay Reconsidered." *October* 62 (Fall): 3–41.

Burch, Noël. 1986. "Primitivism and the Avant-Gardes: A Dialectical Approach." In *Narrative, Apparatus, Ideology,* ed. Philip Rosen. New York: Columbia University Press.

Burnett, Ron. 1995. "Video Space/Video Time: The Electronic Image and Portable Video." In Marchessault, *Mirror Machine.* Toronto: YYZ/Center for Research. 142–96.

Cadigan, Pat. 1991. *Synners.* New York: Bantam.

Caillois, Roger. 1984. "Mimicry and Legendary Psychasthenia." Trans. John Shepley. *October* 31 (Winter). 17–32.

Campbell, Neil. 1996. "Aquinas' Reasons for the Aesthetic Irrelevance of Tastes and Smells." *British Journal of Aesthetics* 36:2 (April): 166–76.

Cartwright, Lisa. 1995. *Screening the Body: Tracing Medicine's Visual Culture.* Minneapolis: University of Minnesota Press.

Cavell, Stanley. 1979. *The World Viewed: Reflections on the Ontology of Film,* Cambridge: Harvard University Press.

Cho, Seoungho. 1994. *The Island with Striped Sky* and *Iris. Electronic Arts Intermix Catalogue,* ed. Lori Zippay. New York: Electronic Arts Intermix. N.p.

———. 1997. Interview with the author. December 14.

Chow, Rey. 1993. *Writing Diaspora: Tactics of Intervention in Contemporary Cultural Studies.* Bloomington: Indiana University Press.

———. 1995. *Primitive Passions: Visuality, Sexuality, Ethnography, and Contemporary Chinese Cinema.* New York: Columbia University Press.

Classen, Constance. 1993. *Worlds of Sense: Exploring the Senses in History and Across Cultures.* London: Routledge.

Classen, Constance, David Howes, and Anthony Synnott. 1994. *Aroma: The Cultural History of Smell.* London: Routledge.

Cohn, Norman. 1993. Interview with the author. December 5.

———. 1999. Letter to the editor. *Fuse* 22:1 (Winter): 10.

Connerton, Paul. 1989. *How Societies Remember.* Cambridge: Cambridge University Press.

Corbin, Alain. 1986. *The Foul and the Fragrant: Odor and the French Social Imagination, 18th–19th Centuries.* Trans. M. Kochan, R. Porter, and C. Prendergast. Cambridge: Harvard University Press.

Crary, Jonathan. 1990. *Techniques of the Observer: On Vision and Modernity in the Nineteenth Century.* Cambridge: MIT Press.

———. 1994. "Unbinding Vision." *October* 68 (Spring): 21–44.

Crary, Jonathan, and Sanford Kwinter, eds. 1992. *Incorporations.* New York: Zone.

Crimp, Douglas. 1993. "Right On, Girlfriend!" In *Fear of a Queer Planet,* ed. Michael Warner. Durham, N.C.: Duke University Press.

Csordas, Thomas J., ed. 1994. *Embodiment and Experience: The Existential Ground of Culture and Self.* Cambridge: Cambridge University Press.

Cubitt, Sean. 1998. *Digital Aesthetics.* London: Sage Publications.

Curtis, Barry, and Claire Pajaczkowska. 1994. " 'Getting There': Travel, Time, and Narrative." In *Travellers' Tales: Narratives of Home and Displacement,* ed. George Robertson, Melinda Mash, Lisa Tickner, Jon Bird, Barry Curtis, and Tim Putman. London: Routledge. 199–215.

Daniel, E. Valentine. 1994. "The Pulse as an Icon in Siddha Medicine." In *The Varieties of Sensory Experience,* ed. David Howes. Toronto: University of Toronto Press. 100–110.

Dash, Julie, with Toni Cade Bambara and bell hooks. 1992. *Daughters of the Dust: The Making of an African American Woman's Film.* New York: New Press.

Davies, Paul. 1993. "The Face and the Caress: Levinas's Ethical Alterations of

Sensibility." In Levin, *Modernity and the Hegemony of Vision.* Berkeley: University of California Press. 252–72.

Davis, Zeinabu irene. 1995. "The Future of Black Film: The Debate Continues." In Martin, *Cinemas of the Black Diaspora.* Detroit: Wayne State University Press. 449–54.

Deleuze, Gilles. 1986. *Cinema 1: The Movement-Image.* Trans. Hugh Tomlinson and Barbara Habberjam. Minneapolis: University of Minnesota Press.

———. 1988a. *Bergsonism.* Trans. Hugh Tomlinson and Barbara Habberjam. New York: Zone.

———. 1988b. *Foucault.* Trans. Séan Hand. Minneapolis: University of Minnesota Press.

———. 1989. *Cinema 2: The Time-Image.* Trans. Hugh Tomlinson and Robert Galeta. Minneapolis: University of Minnesota Press.

———. 1992. "Mediators." Trans. Martin Joughin. In Crary and Kwinter, *Incorporations.* New York: Zone.

Deleuze, Gilles, and Félix Guattari. 1983. *Anti-Oedipus.* Trans. Robert Hurley et al. Minneapolis: University of Minnesota Press.

———. 1987. *A Thousand Plateaus: Capitalism and Schizophrenia.* Trans. Brian Massumi. Minneapolis: University of Minnesota Press.

Derrida, Jacques. 1974. *Glas.* Paris: Galilée.

Devereaux, Leslie. 1995. "Experience, Re-Presentation, and Film." In *Fields of Vision: Essays in Film Studies, Visual Anthropology, and Photography,* ed. Leslie Devereaux and Roger Hillman. Berkeley: University of California Press. 56–73.

Diawara, Manthia, ed. 1993. *Black American Cinema.* New York: Routledge.

Doane, Mary Ann. 1987. *The Desire to Desire: The Woman's Film of the 1940s.* Bloomington: Indiana University Press.

Drobnick, Jim. 1998. "Reveries, Assaults, and Evaporating Presences: Olfactory Dimensions in Contemporary Art." *Parachute* 89 (Jan.–March). 10–19.

Durham, Jimmie. 1993. "Cowboys and . . . ." In *A Certain Lack of Coherence: Writings on Art and Cultural Politics,* ed. Jean Fisher. London: Kala. 170–86.

Druckrey, Timothy. 1989. "From Representation to Technology: Photography for the Video Generation." *Afterimage* 17:4 (November): 12–21.

Dyer, Richard. 1985. "Entertainment and Utopia." In *Movies and Methods,* vol. 2, ed. Bill Nichols. Berkeley: University of California Press. 220–32.

———. 1988. "White." In Julien and Mercer, "The Last 'Special Issue' on Race?" *Screen* 29:4. 29–65.

Eisenstein, Sergei. [1947] 1970. "Synchronization of Senses." Trans. Jay Leyda. In *The Film Sense.* New York: Harcourt, Brace, and World. 67–109.

Engen, Trygg. 1991. *Odor Sensation and Memory.* New York: Praeger.

Elbert, Thomas, Christo Pantev, Christian Wienbruch, Brigitte Rockstruh, and Edward Taub. 1995. "Increased Cortical Representation of the Fingers of the Left Hand in String Players." *Science* 270 (13 October): 305–6.

Fabian, Johannes. 1983. *Time and the Other: How Anthropology Makes Its Object.* New York: Columbia University Press.

Featherstone, Mike. 1990. *Global Culture: Nationalism, Globalization and Modernity.* London: Sage.

Ferguson, Russell, et al., eds. 1990. *Out There: Discussions in Contemporary Culture.* Cambridge: MIT Press.

"Festival News." 1995. Brochure, The Eighth Annual Virginia Festival of American Film, Charlottesville, Va.

Finkel, Leif H. 1992. "The Construction of Perception." In Crary and Kwinter, *Incorporations.* New York: Zone. 392–405.

Fisher, Jennifer. 1997. "Relational Sense: Towards a Haptic Aesthetics." *Parachute* 87 (July–September): 4–11.

Foster, Hal, ed. 1988. *Vision and Visuality.* Seattle: Bay Press.

Foucault, Michel. 1970. *The Order of Things: An Archaeology of the Human Sciences.* New York: Vintage.

Freud, Sigmund. 1985. *The Complete Letters of Sigmund Freud to Wilhelm Fleiss, 1887–1904.* Ed. and trans. Jeffrey Moussaieff Masson. Cambridge: Belknap Press of Harvard University Press.

Fung, Richard. 1991. "Looking for My Penis: The Eroticized Asian in Gay Video Porn." In *How Do I Look?: Queer Film and Video,* ed. Bad Object-Choices. Seattle: Bay Press.

Fusco, Coco. 1988a. *Young, British, and Black: The Work of Sankofa and Black Audio Film Collective.* Buffalo, N.Y.: Hallwalls.

———. 1988b. "An Interview with Black Audio Film Collective: John Akomfrah, Reece Auguiste, Lina Gopaul and Avril Johnson." In Fusco, *Young, British, and Black.*

———. 1991. "Stateless Hybrids: An Introduction." In Fusco and Colo, *The Hybrid State.*

Fusco, Coco, and Papo Colo, eds. 1991. *The Hybrid State.* New York: Exit Art.

Gabriel, Teshome H. 1988. "Thoughts on Nomadic Aesthetics and the Black Independent Cinema: Traces of a Journey." In Andrade-Watkins and Cham, *Blackframes.* Cambridge: MIT Press. 62–69.

———. 1989. "Third Cinema as Guardian of Popular Memory: Towards a Third Aesthetics." In Pines and Willemen, *Questions of Third Cinema.* London: BFI. 53–64.

García Espinosa, Julio. [1970] 1997. "For an Imperfect Cinema." Trans. Julianne Burton. In *The New Latin American Cinema,* vol. 1: *Theory, Practices, and Transcontinental Articulations.* Ed. Michael T. Martin. Detroit: Wayne State University Press. 71–82.

Gilroy, Paul. 1987. *There Ain't No Black in the Union Jack: The Cultural Politics of Race and Nation.* London: Hutchinson.

———. 1988. "Nothing But Sweat Inside My Hand: Diaspora Aesthetics and Black Arts in Britain." In *ICA Documents 7: Black Film, British Cinema,* ed. Kobena Mercer. London: Institute of Contemporary Art. 44–46.

Givanni, June. 1995. "Introduction." In *Remote Control: Dilemmas of Black Intervention in British Film and T.V.* London: British Film Institute. 1–11.

Griffin, Ada Gay. 1993. Interview with the author. October 13.

Griffin, Kit. 1990. "Notes on the Moroccan Sensorium." *Anthropologica* 32: 107–11.

Grosz, Elizabeth. 1994. *Volatile Bodies: Toward a Corporeal Feminism.* Bloomington: Indiana University Press.

Gunning, Tom. 1990. "The Cinema of Attractions: Early Cinema, Its Spectator and the Avant-Garde." In *Early Cinema: Space-Frame-Narrative,* ed. Thomas Elsaesser. London: British Film Institute. 56–62.

Hall, Doug, and Sally Jo Fifer, eds. 1990. *Illuminating Video: An Essential Guide to Video Art.* New York: Aperture.

Hall, Edward T. 1969. *The Hidden Dimension.* Garden City, N.Y.: Anchor.

Hall, Stuart. 1986. "Cultural Studies: Two Paradigms." In *Media, Culture and Society,* ed. Richard Collins et al. London: Sage. 33–48.

———. 1988a. "New Ethnicities." In *ICA Documents 7: Black Film, British Cinema,* ed. Kobena Mercer. London: Institute of Contemporary Art. 27–31.

———. 1988b. "Song of Handsworth Praise." In *ICA Documents 7: Black Film, British Cinema,* ed. Kobena Mercer. London: Institute of Contemporary Art. 17.

Hansen, Miriam. 1987. "Benjamin, Cinema and Experience: 'The Blue Flower in the Land of Technology.'" *New German Critique* 40 (Winter). 179–224.

Heller, Morton, and William Schiff, eds. 1991. *The Psychology of Touch.* Hillsdale, N.J.: Lawrence Erlbaum.

Herzogenrath, Wulf. 1977. "Notes on Video as an Artistic Medium." In *The New Television,* ed. Douglas Davis and Allison Simmons. Cambridge: MIT Press. 88–93.

Hildebrand, Adolf. [1893] 1978. *The Problem of Form in Painting and Sculpture.* Trans. Max Meyer and Robert Morris Ogden. New York: Garland Press.

Hines, Pamela J. 1997. "Unconscious Odors." *Science* 278 (3 October): 79.

Hoolboom, Mike. 1997. "Gariné Torossian: Girl From Moush." In *Inside the Pleasure Dome: Fringe Film in Canada.* Toronto: Gutter Press. 148–55.

Horkheimer, Max, and Theodor W. Adorno. 1972. *Dialectic of Enlightenment.* Trans. John Cumming. New York: Herder.

Howes, David, ed. 1991a. *Varieties of Sensory Experience.* Toronto: University of Toronto Press.

———. 1991b. "Introduction: To Summon All the Senses." In Howes, *Varieties of Sensory Experience.* 3–24.

———. 1991c. "Sensorial Anthropology." In Howes, *Varieties of Sensory Experience.* 167–91.

Irigaray, Luce. [1974] 1985. *Speculum of the Other Woman.* Trans. Gillian C. Gill. Ithaca, N.Y.: Cornell University Press.

———. [1984] 1993. *An Ethics of Sexual Difference.* Trans. Carolyn Burke and Gillian C. Gill. Ithaca, N.Y.: Cornell University Press.

Iversen, Margaret. 1993. *Alois Riegl.* Cambridge: MIT Press.

Jafa, Arthur. 1992. "69." In *Black Popular Culture,* ed. Gina Dent. Seattle: Bay Press. 249–54.

Jarman, Derek. 1994. *Chroma.* London: Vintage.

Jay, Martin. 1993a. *Downcast Eyes.* Berkeley: University of California Press.

———. 1993b. "Unsympathetic Magic." Review of *The Nervous System* and *Mimesis and Alterity* by Michael Taussig. *Visual Anthropology Review* 9:2 (Fall). 79–82.

———. 1994. "Martin Jay Replies to Michael Taussig and Paul Stoller." *Visual Anthropology Review* 10:1 (Spring). 163–64.

Johnson, Avril, and Lina Gopaul. 1994. Interview with the author. May 3.

Julien, Isaac, and Kobena Mercer, eds. 1988. "The Last 'Special Issue' on Race?" Special issue of *Screen* 29:4.

Kandinsky, Wassily. [1938] 1968. "Concrete Art." In *Theories of Modern Art,* ed. Herschel B. Chipp. Berkeley: University of California Press. 346–62.

Kaplan, E. Ann. 1997. *Looking for the Other: Feminism, Film, and the Imperial Gaze.* New York: Routledge.

Kopytoff, Igor. 1986. "The Cultural Biography of Things: Commoditization as Process." In *The Social Life of Things: Commodities in Cultural Perspective,* ed. Arjun Appadurai. Cambridge: Cambridge University Press. 64–94.

Krauss, Rosalind. 1991. "Using Language to Do Business as Usual." In *Visual Theory: Painting and Interpretation,* ed. Norman Bryson, Michael Ann Holly, and Keith Moxey. New York: Polity Press/Harper Collins. 79–94.

Kuipers, Joel C. 1994. "Matters of Taste in Wewéya." In Howes, *Varieties of Sensory Experience.* Toronto: University of Toronto Press. 111–27.

Lant, Antonia. 1995. "Haptical Cinema." *October* 75 (Fall): 45–73.

Lastra, James. 1997. "From the Captured Moment to the Cinematic Image: A Transformation in Pictorial Order." In *The Image in Dispute: Art and Cinema in the Age of Photography,* ed. Dudley Andrew, with Sally Shafto. Austin: University of Texas Press. 263–91.

Leder, Drew. 1992. *The Absent Body.* Chicago: University of Chicago Press.

Lejeira, Jacinto. 1996. "Scenario of the Untouchable Body." Trans. Brian Holmes. In "Touch in Contemporary Art," special issue of *Public* 13, ed. David Tomas. 32–47.

Leung, Simon. 1995. "Squatting Through Violence." *Documents* (Spring/Summer): 92–101.

Levin, David Michael, ed. 1993. *Modernity and the Hegemony of Vision.* Berkeley: University of California Press.

Levinas, Emmanuel. 1987. *Collected Philosophical Papers.* Dordrecht: Martinus Nijhoff.

———. 1989. "Time and the Other." Trans. Richard A. Cohen. In *The Levinas Reader,* ed. Séan Hand. Oxford: Blackwell. 37–58.

Lingis, Alphonso. 1985. *Libido: The French Existential Theories.* Bloomington: Indiana University Press.

MacDougall, David. 1994. "Whose Story Is It?" In *Visualizing Theory: Selected Essays from V.A.R., 1990–1994,* ed. Lucien Taylor. New York: Routledge, 1994. 27–36.

Marchessault, Janine, ed. 1995a. *Mirror Machine: Video and Identity.* Toronto: YYZ/Center for Research on Canadian Cultural Industries and Institutions.

———. 1995b. "Amateur Video and the Challenge for Change." In Marchessault, *Mirror Machine.* 13–24.

Marks, Laura U. 1992. "The Language of Terrorism." *Framework* (London), 38/39: 64–73.

———. 1993. "Sexual Hybrids: From Oriental Exotic to Postcolonial Grotesque," *Parachute* 70 (Summer): 22–29.

———. 1994a. "Reconfigured Nationhood: A Partisan History of the Inuit Broadcasting Corporation." *Afterimage* 21:8 (March): 4–7.

———. 1994b. "Fresh Kill." *CineAction* 36: 31–33.

———. 1997a. "Loving a Disappearing Image." In "Cinéma et mélancolie," special issue of *Cinémas,* ed. Denise Pérusse. 1–2 (Autumn): 93–111.

———. 1997b. "The Quays' Institute Benjamenta: An Olfactory View." *Afterimage* 25:2 (September): 11–14.

———. 1998. "Video Haptics and Erotics." *Screen* 39:4 (Winter): 331–48.

———. 1999. "How Electrons Remember." *Millennium Film Journal* 34 (Fall): special issue, "The Digital."

———. In press. "Signs of the Time: Deleuze, Peirce, and the Documentary Image." In *The Brain Is the Screen: Gilles Deleuze and the Philosophy of Cinema,* ed. Gregory Flaxman. Minneapolis: University of Minnesota Press.

Martin, Michael, ed. 1995. *Cinemas of the Black Diaspora: Diversity, Dependence, and Oppositionality.* Detroit: Wayne State University Press.

Marx, Karl. [1844] 1978. "Economic and Philosophical Manuscripts of 1844." Trans. Martin Millisan. In *The Marx-Engels Reader,* 2nd ed., ed. Robert C. Tucker. New York: Norton. 66–125.

Masayesva, Victor, Jr. 1995. "The Emerging Native American Aesthetics in Film and Video." In "Landscapes," special issue of *Felix* 2:1: 156–60.

Maslin, Janet. 1993. "Visions of a Vietnam as Yet Unscarred." *New York Times,* 11 October, C15.

Mauss, Marcel. [1950] 1990. *The Gift: The Form and Reason for Exchange in Archaic Societies.* Trans. W. D. Halls. New York: Norton.

———. [1934] 1992. "Techniques of the Body." In Crary and Kwinter, *Incorporations.* New York: Zone. 454–77.

McFarlane, Scott. 1995. "The Haunt of Race: Canada's Multiculturalism Act, the Politics of Incorporation and Writing through Race." *Fuse* 18:3 (Spring): 18–31.

McLuhan, Marshall. 1962. *The Gutenberg Galaxy: The Making of Typographic Man.* Toronto: University of Toronto Press.

Mercer, Kobena. 1988a. "Diaspora Culture and the Dialogic Imagination." In Andrade-Watkins and Cham, *Blackframes.* Cambridge: MIT Press. 50–61.

———. 1988b. Ed. *ICA Documents 7: Black Film, British Cinema.* London: Institute of Contemporary Arts.

———. 1990. "Black Hair/Style Politics." In Ferguson et al, *Out There.* Cambridge: MIT Press. 247–64.

———. 1994a. "Introduction: Black Britain and the Cultural Politics of Diaspora." *Welcome to the Jungle: New Positions in Black Cultural Studies.* New York: Routledge. 1–31.

———. 1994b. "Recoding Narratives of Race and Nation." *Welcome to the Jungle: New Positions in Black Cultural Studies.* 69–95.

Merleau-Ponty, Maurice. [1945] 1992. *Phenomenology of Perception.* Trans. Colin Smith. London: Routledge.

———. [1947] 1964. "Eye and Mind." Trans. Carleton Dallery. In *The Primacy of Perception, And Other Essays on Phenomenological Psychology, the Philosophy of Art, History, and Politics,* ed. James M. Edie. Evanston: Northwestern University Press, 159–90.

———. [1964] 1968. *The Visible and the Invisible: Followed by Working Notes.* Trans. Alphonso Lingis. Evanston: Northwestern University Press.

———. [1969] 1973. *The Prose of the World.* Trans. John O'Neill, ed. Claude LeFort. Evanston: Northwestern University Press.

Metz, Christian. [1975] 1982. "The Passion for Perceiving." Trans. Ben Brewster. *The Imaginary Signifier: Psychoanalysis and the Cinema.* Bloomington: Indiana University Press. 58–68.

Mitchell, W. J. T. 1986. *Iconology: Images, Text, Ideology.* Chicago: University of Chicago Press.

Mitchell, William J. 1994. *The Reconfigured Eye: Visual Truth in the Post-Photographic Era.* Cambridge: MIT Press.

Montagu, Ashley. 1971. *Touching: The Human Significance of the Skin.* New York: Harper.

Morse, Margaret. 1999. "Home: Smell, Taste, Posture, Gleam." In *Home, Exile, Homeland,* ed. Hamid Naficy. New York and London: Routledge. 63–74.

Muhammad, Erika. In progress. "Inside and Out of the Box: Electronic Culture, the Popular, the Political." Ph.D. diss., New York University.

Mulvey, Laura. 1975. "Visual Pleasure and Narrative Cinema." *Screen* 16:3 (Autumn): 6–18.

Naficy, Hamid. 1993. *The Making of Exile Cultures: Iranian Television in Los Angeles.* Minneapolis: University of Minnesota Press.

———. 1996. "Phobic Spaces and Liminal Panics: Independent Transnational Film Genre." In *Global/Local: Cultural Production and the Transnational Imaginary,* ed. Rob Wilson and Wimal Dissanayake. Durham: Duke University Press. 119–44.

———. 1999. "Between Rocks and Hard Places: The Interstitial Mode of Production in Exilic Cinema." In *Home, Exile, Homeland: Film, Media, and the politic of Place,* ed. Hamid Naficy. New York: Routledge. 125–47.

Naficy, Hamid, and Teshome H. Gabriel, eds. 1991. "Discourse of the Other: Postcoloniality, Positionality, and Subjectivity." Introduction, special issue, *Quarterly Review of Film and Video* 13: 1–3.

Nichols, Bill. 1991. *Representing Reality: Issues and Concepts in Documentary.* Bloomington: Indiana University Press.

Ong, Walter. [1967] 1991. "The Shifting Sensorium." In Howes, *Varieties of Sensory Experience.* Toronto: University of Toronto Press. 25–30.

Ots, Thomas. 1994. "The Silenced Body—The Expressive *Leib:* On the Dialec- **269**
tic of Mind and Life in Chinese Cathartic Healing." In Csordas, *Embodiment
and Experience.* Cambridge: Cambridge University Press. 116–36.

Pandya, Vishvajit. 1990. "Movement and Space: Anadamanese Cartography."
American Ethnologist 17:4: 775–97.

Paz, Octavio. [1961] 1987. "El Mismo Tiempo" ("Identical Time"). In *The Collected Poems of Octavio Paz, 1957–1987,* ed. and trans. Eliot Weinberger.
New York: New Directions. 69–79.

Peck, Raoul. 1992. Discussion at the Robert Flaherty Seminar, Aurora, New
York. August 9.

Pels, Peter. 1995. "The Spirit of Matter, Part 1: Fetishes, Rarities, and Other
Things." Conference paper, "Border Fetishisms." Research Centre Religion
and Society. University of Amsterdam. December 11–13.

Peirce, Charles S. 1950. *The Philosophy of Peirce: Selected Writings,* ed. Justus
Butler. New York: Harcourt Brace and Company.

Pietz, William. 1985. "The Problem of the Fetish, I." *Res* 9 (Spring): 5–17.

———. 1987. "The Problem of the Fetish, II." *Res* 13 (Spring): 23–45.

———. 1988. "The Problem of the Fetish, IIIa. *Res* 16 (Autumn): 105–23.

———. 1993. "Fetishism and Materialism: The Limits of Theory in Marx." In
Fetishism as Cultural Discourse, ed. Emily Apter and William Pietz. Ithaca,
N.Y.: Cornell University Press.

Pinard, Sylvain. 1990. "L'Economie de sens in Inde: Exploration des thèses de
Walter Ong." *Anthropologica* 32. 75–99.

Pines, Jim. 1988. "The Cultural Context of Black British Cinema." In Andrade-
Watkins and Cham, *Blackframes.* Cambridge: MIT Press. 26–36.

Pines, Jim, and Paul Willemen, eds. 1989. *Questions of Third Cinema.* London:
BFI.

Pisters, Patricia. 1998. "From Eye to Brain—Gilles Deleuze: Reconfiguring the
Subject in Film Theory." Ph.D. diss., University of Amsterdam.

Proust, Marcel. [1919] 1954. *À la recherche du temps perdu.* Paris: Gallimard.

Ra'ad, Walid. 1997. "Miraculous Beginnings." In "Entangled Territories: Imagining the Orient," special issue of *Public* 16, ed. Walid Ra'ad and Deborah
Root. 44–52.

Rashid, Ian. 1993. *Beyond Destination: Film, Video and Installations by South
Asian Artists.* Birmingham, England: Ikon Gallery.

Reid-Pfarr, Robert. 1993. "Soul on Ice and Giovanni's Room." Talk at the University of Rochester. December 3.

Renov, Michael, ed. 1993. *Theorizing Documentary.* New York: Routledge.

Riegl, Alöis. [1902] 1995. "Excerpts from *The Dutch Group Portrait.*" Trans.
Benjamin Binstock. *October* 74 (Fall 1995): 3–35.

———. [1927] 1985. *Late Roman Art Industry.* Trans. Rolf Winkes. Rome: Gior-
gio Bretschneider Editore.

Ritchie, Ian. 1990. "Hausa Sensory Symbolism." *Anthropologica* 32. 113–19.

Rodaway, Paul. 1994. *Sensuous Geographies: Body, Sense and Place.* London:
Routledge.

Rodowick, D. N. 1991. "Reading the Figural." *Camera Obscura* 24 (Fall): 13–46.

———. 1997. *Gilles Deleuze's Time Machine.* Durham: Duke University Press.

Rony, Fatimah Tobing. 1996. *The Third Eye: Race, Cinema, and Ethnographic Spectacle.* Durham: Duke University Press.

Ross, Christine. 1995. "The Lamented Moments/Desired Objects of Video Art: Toward an Aesthetics of Discrepancy." In Marchessault, *Mirror Machine.* Toronto: YYZ/Center for Research. 129–41.

Roth, Lorna, and Gail Guthrie Valaskakis. 1989. "Aboriginal Broadcasting in Canada: A Case Study in Democratization." In *Communication For and Against Democracy,* ed. Marc Raboy and Peter A. Bruck. Montreal: Black Rose. 24–36.

Rushdie, Salman. 1988. "*Songs* Doesn't Know the Score." In *ICA Documents 7: Black Film, British Cinema,* ed. Kobena Mercer. London: Institute of Contemporary Art. 16–17.

Said, Edward W. 1979. *Orientalism.* New York: Vintage.

Salloum, Jayce. 1996. *. . . east of here . . . (re)imagining the "orient."* Toronto: YYZ Artists' Outlet.

Scarry, Elaine. 1985. *The Body in Pain: The Making and Unmaking of the World.* New York: Oxford University Press.

Schab, Frank R. 1991. "Odor Memory: Taking Stock." *Psychological Bulletin* 109:2: 242–251.

Schivelbusch, Wolfgang. 1992. *Tastes of Paradise: A Social History of Spices, Stimulants, and Intoxicants.* New York: Pantheon.

Schor, Naomi. 1987. *Reading in Detail: Aesthetics and the Feminine.* New York: Methuen.

Scott, Joan. 1991. "The Evidence of Experience." *Critical Inquiry* 17:4 (Summer): 773–97.

Sekula, Allan. 1989. "The Body and the Archive." In *The Contest of Meaning: Critical Histories of Photography,* ed. Richard Bolton. Cambridge: MIT Press. 343–389.

Seremetakis, C. Nadia. 1994. "The Memory of the Senses, Part I: Marks of the Transitory," and "Implications." In *The Senses Still: Perception and Memory as Material Culture in Modernity,* ed. C. Nadia Seremetakis. Boulder, Co.: Westview. 1–18, 123–40.

Shaviro, Steven. 1993. *The Cinematic Body.* Minneapolis: University of Minnesota Press.

Shohat, Ella. 1992. "Notes on the 'Post-Colonial.'" *Social Text* 31/32: 99–113.

Shohat, Ella, and Robert Stam. 1995. *Unthinking Eurocentrism: Multiculturalism and the Media.* New York: Routledge.

Silverman, Kaja. 1988. *The Acoustic Mirror: The Female Voice in Psychoanalysis and Cinema.* Bloomington: Indiana University Press.

Silverman, Kaja. 1992. *Male Subjectivity at the Margins.* New York: Routledge.

Sobchack, Vivian. 1992. *The Address of the Eye: Phenomenology and Film Experience.* Princeton: Princeton University Press.

Solanas, Fernando, and Octavio Getino. [1969] 1983. "Towards a Third Cinema." In *Movies and Methods,* ed. Bill Nichols. 44–64.

Spivak, Gayatri C. 1990. "Questions of Multi-Culturalism." Interview with Sneja Gunew. In *The Post-Colonial Critic: Interviews, strategies, dialogues,* ed. Sarah Harasym. New York: Routledge. 59–66.

———. 1993. "Marginality in the Teaching Machine." *Outside in the Teaching Machine.* New York: Routledge. 53–76.

Stallybrass, Peter, and Allon White. 1986. *The Politics and Poetics of Transgression.* Ithaca, N.Y.: Cornell University Press.

Stange, Maren. 1994. Remarks of chair on the panel "Documentary Film and Photography: Rethinking Histories," at the conference Visible Evidence 2: New Strategies in Documentary Film and Video, University of Southern California. August 19.

Stein, Barry E., and M. Alex Meredith. 1993. *The Merging of the Senses.* Cambridge: MIT Press.

Steiner, Christopher B. 1995. "The Art of the Trade: On the Creation of Value and Authenticity in the African Art Market." In *The Traffic in Culture: Refiguring Art and Anthropology,* ed. George E. Marcus and Fred R. Myers. Berkeley: University of California Press. 151–65.

Sternburg, Janet. 1994. "Long Exposures: A Poetics of Film and History." *Common Knowledge* 3:1 (Spring): 178–85.

Stewart, Susan. 1984. *On Longing: Narratives of the Miniature, the Gigantic, the Souvenir, the Collection.* Baltimore: Johns Hopkins University Press.

Stoddart, S. Michael. 1990. *The Scented Ape: The Biology and Culture of Human Odour.* Cambridge: Cambridge University Press.

Stoller, Paul. 1989. *The Taste of Ethnographic Things: The Senses in Anthropology.* Philadelphia: University of Pennsylvania Press.

———. 1994. "Double Takes: Stoller on Jay and Taussig." *Visual Anthropology Review* 10:1 (Spring). 155–61.

———. 1995. *Embodying Colonial Memories.* New York: Routledge.

Studlar, Gaylyn. 1988. *In The Realm of Pleasure: Von Sternberg, Dietrich, and the Masochistic Aesthetic.* Urbana, Il.: University of Illinois Press.

Synnott, Anthony. 1991. "Puzzling Over the Senses: From Plato to Marx." In Howes, *Varieties of Sensory Experience.* Toronto: University of Toronto Press. 61–78.

Tagg, John. 1988. *The Burden of Representation: Essays on Photographies and Histories.* Basingstoke, England: Macmillan.

Taussig, Michael. 1993. *Mimesis and Alterity: A Particular History of the Senses.* New York: Routledge.

Taussig, Michael. 1994. "Michael Taussig Replies to Martin Jay." *Visual Anthropology Review* 10:1 (Spring). 154.

Taylor, Lucien, ed. 1994. *Visualizing Theory: Selected Essays from VAR [Visual Anthropology Review], 1990–1994.* New York: Routledge.

Thomas, Nicholas. 1991. *Entangled Objects: Exchange, Material Culture, and Capitalism in the Pacific.* Cambridge: Harvard University Press.

Thompson, Kristin. 1986. "The Concept of Cinematic Excess." In *Narrative, Apparatus, Ideology*, ed. Philip Rosen. New York: Columbia University Press. 130–42.

Torossian, Gariné. 1998. Talk at screening at Canadian Film Institute and SAW Video Co-op, Ottawa. November 28.

Toufic, Jalal. 1996. *Oversensitivity*. Los Angeles: Sun and Moon.

Tran T. Kim-Trang. 1997. Interview with the author. April 20.

———. 1999. Interview with the author. February 10.

Trinh T. Minh-ha. 1989. *Woman, Native, Other: Writing Postcoloniality and Feminism*. Bloomington: Indiana University Press.

———. 1991. *When the Moon Waxes Red: Representation, Gender, and Cultural Politics*. New York: Routledge.

———. 1993. "The Totalizing Quest of Meaning." In Renov, *Theorizing Documentary*. New York: Routledge. 90–107.

Trippi, Laura. 1993. "Trade Routes." Gallery flyer for exhibition, New Museum of Contemporary Art, New York, curated by Laura Trippi, Saskia Sassen, and Gina Dent. September 10–November 7.

Tuan, Yi-Fu. 1993. *Passing Strange and Wonderful: Aesthetics, Nature, and Culture*. Washington, D.C.: Island Press.

Varela, Francisco J., Evan Thompson, and Eleanor Rosch. 1991. *The Embodied Mind: Cognitive Science and Human Experience*. Cambridge: MIT Press.

Vasseleu, Cathryn. 1998. *Textures of Light: Vision and Touch in Irigaray, Levinas, and Merleau-Ponty*. London: Routledge.

Virilio, Paul. 1994. *The Vision Machine*. Trans. Julie Rose. London: British Film Institute; Bloomington: Indiana University Press.

Weiner, Annette. 1992. *Inalienable Possessions: The Paradox of Keeping-While-Giving*. Berkeley: University of California Press.

Weinstein, Jeff. 1988. "Thyme and Word Enough." In *Learning to Eat*. Los Angeles: Sun and Moon. 127–30.

Williams, Linda. 1989. *Hard Core: Power, Pleasure, and the Frenzy of the Visible*. Berkeley: University of California Press.

———. 1995. "Corporeal Observers: Visual Pornographies and the 'Carnal Density of Vision.'" In *Fugitive Images*, ed. Patrice Petro. Bloomington: Indiana University Press. 3–41.

Wilson, Rob, and Wimal Dissanayake, eds. 1996. *Global/Local: Cultural Production and the Transnational Imaginary*. Durham, N.C.: Duke University Press.

Winkler, Cathy (with Kate Winiger). 1996. "Rape Trauma: Contexts of Meaning." In Csordas, *Embodiment and Experience*. Cambridge: Cambridge University Press. 248–68.

Winnicott, D. W. [1951] 1958. "Transitional Objects and Transitional Phenomena." In *Through Paediatrics to Psycho-Analysis: Collected Papers*. London: Tavistock. 229–42.

Wörringer, Wilhelm. [1908] 1948. *Abstraction and Empathy: A Contribution to the Psychology of Style*. Trans. Michael Bullock. New York: Meridian.

———. 1928. *Egyptian Art.* Trans. Bernard Rackham. London: Putnam's.

Young, Iris Marion. 1990. *Throwing Like a Girl and Other Essays in Feminist Philosophy and Social Theory.* Bloomington: Indiana University Press.

Youngblood, Gene. 1970. *Expanded Cinema.* New York: Dutton.

Zimmermann, Patricia R., and John Hess. 1997. "Transnational Documentaries: A Manifesto." *Afterimage* 24:4 (Jan.–Feb.): 10–14.

Zippay, Lori, ed. 1991. *Electronic Arts Intermix: Video.* New York: EAI.

Filmography/Videography

Distributors are listed where known.

Alambrista. Robert Young, U.S., 1978, 110:00, 16mm.

Aletheia. Tran T. Kim-Trang, U.S., 1992, 20:00, video. GIV, VDB, V Tape.

Ananas. Amos Gitai, France, 1984, 76:00, 16mm.

Anatomy of a Spring Roll. Paul Kwan and Arnold Iger, U.S., 1992, 56:00, video. Filmakers Library, ITVS, VO.

And Still I Rise. Ngozi Onwurah, U.K., 1995, 30:00, 16mm. WMM.

. . . And the Word Was God. Ruby Truly, Canada, 1987, 10:00, video. VO.

Animaquiladora. Alex Rivera, U.S., 1997, 10:00, video. VDB.

The Attendant. Isaac Julien, U.K., 1992, 8:00, 35mm. Frameline.

Bangkok Bahrain. Amos Gitai, France, 1985, 78:00, 16mm.

Barrocco. Paul Leduc, Mexico, 1989, 108:00, 16mm. IFC.

The Big Sleep. Seoungho Cho, U.S., 1992, 8:00, video. EAI.

Bitter Strength: Sadistic Response Version. Azian Nurudin, U.S., 1992, 6:00, video. Frameline.

"and they came riding into town on Black and Silver Horses." Lawrence Andrews, U.S., 1992, 30:00, video. VDB.

Black Body. Thomas Allen Harris, U.S., 1992, 5:00, video. EAI, TWN.

Black Is, Black Ain't. Marlon Riggs; co-produced by Nicole Atkinson, co-directed by Christiane Badgley, 1995, 87:00, video. ITVS, Mongrel, NBPC.

Bontoc Eulogy. Marlon Fuentes, U.S., 1995, 70:00, 16mm. California, Cinema Guild, ITVS.

A Box of His Own. Yudi Sewraj, Canada, 1997, 20:00, video. VG, V Tape.

Brasiconoscopio. Mauro Giuntini, Brazil, 1990, 16:00, video.

By the Thinnest Root. Richard Kim, U.S., 1995, 7:00, 16mm.

Calendar. Atom Egoyan, Armenia/Canada, 1993, 75:00, 16mm. Alliance, Zeitgeist.

Cannibal Tours. Dennis O'Rourke, Australia, 1988, 70:00, 16mm. Direct.

Changing Parts. Mona Hatoum, Lebanon, 1985, video, 24:00. VO, V Tape.

Chasing the Dragon. Karen Kew and Ed Sinclair, Canada, 1993, 22:00, video. V Tape.

Chimera. Phil Hoffman, Canada, 1995, 10:00, 16mm. CFMDC.

Chinaman's Peak: Walking the Mountain. Paul Wong, Canada, 1995, 25:00, video. VO.

Chinese Characters. Richard Fung, Canada, 1986, 22:00, video. VDB, V Tape.

Chott el-Djerid (A Portrait in Light and Heat). Bill Viola, U.S., 1979, 28:00, video. EAI.

Chronicle of a Disappearance. Elia Suleiman, Israel/Palestine, 1996, 88:00, 35mm. Aska, IFC, Mongrel.

Converse. Reginald Woolery, U.S., 1992, 6:00, video.

Corps étranger. Mona Hatoum, U.K., 1996, 24:00 loop, video installation. Alexander and Bonin, New York; White Cube, London.

Cowtipping: The Militant Indian Waiter. Randy Redroad, U.S., 1992, 17:00, video. TWN.

Credits Included: A Video in Red and Green. Jalal Toufic, Lebanon/U.S., 1995, 46:00, video. AFD.

Daughters of the Dust. Julie Dash, U.S., 1992, 113:00, 35mm. Kino.

Deluge. Salem Mekuria, U.S., 1995, 60:00, video. TWN.

Diastole. Ines Cardoso, Brazil, 1994, 4:30, video.

Dreaming Rivers. Martine Attile, U.K., 1988, 30:00, 16mm. WMM.

Drive By Shoot. Portia Cobb, U.S., 1994, 12:00, video.

Drowning in Flames. Gariné Torossian, Canada, 1994, 25:00, 16mm. CFMDC.

Ekleipsis. Tran T. Kim-Trang, U.S., 1998, 22:00, video. VDB, V Tape.

El Diablo Nunca Duerme. Lourdes Portillo, U.S./Mexico, 1994, 87:00, 16mm. ITVS, WMM.

El Naftazteca: Cyber-Aztec TV for 2000 AD. Guillermo Gomez-Peña and IEAR Studios, U.S., 1995, 57:00, video. VDB.

Encounter at the Intergalactic Café. Thomas Allen Harris, U.S., 1996, 17:00, video. TWN.

Ex-Voto. Tania Cypriano, U.S., 1990, 7:00, video. GIV, TWN.

Family Viewing. Atom Egoyan, Canada, 1987, 86:00, 35mm.

Far From You. Sami Al-Kassim, Egypt/U.S., 1996, 27:00, 16mm. Sami Al-Kassim, phone: 510-763-4484. Email: *sami@citycom.com.*

Fatima's Letter. Alia Syed, U.K., 1994, 12:00, 16mm. London Film-makers' Co-op, 2–4 Hoxton Sq., London N1 6N0 U.K. Phone: 0171-684-2782. Email: lux@lux.org.uk.

Finagnon. Gary Kibbins, Canada, 1995, 70:00, 16mm. V Tape.

First World Order. Philip Mallory Jones, U.S., 1994, 28:00, video. Also the title of a CD-ROM, in development. EAI, ITVS.

Flow. Yau Ching, U.S., 1993, 38:00, video. EAI, VDB.

Forever Jimmy! Nguyen Tan Hoang, U.S., 1996, 6:00, video.

Frantz Fanon: White Skin, Black Mask. Isaac Julien, U.K. 1996, 52:00, 35mm. California.

Fresh Kill. Shu Lea Cheang, U.S., 1994, 80:00, 35mm. ITVS, WMM.

Girl from Moush. Gariné Torossian, Canada, 1993, 6:00, 16mm. CFMDC.

Good Hair, Pretty Hair, Curly Hair. Andrew Davis, Canada, 1991, 27:00, 16mm. CFMDC.

The Good Woman of Bangkok. Dennis O'Rourke, Australia, 1992, 82:00, 16mm. Direct.

Great Girl. Kim Su Theiler, 1994, U.S., 14:00, 16 mm. WMM.

The Gringo in Mañanaland. Dee Dee Halleck, U.S., 1995, 60:00, video. Idera, VDB.

Hairpiece: A Film for Nappyheaded People. Ayoka Chenzira, U.S., 1984, 10:00, 16mm. TWN.

Handsworth Songs. John Akomfrah/Black Audio Film Collective, U.K., 1986, 58:00, 16mm. Mongrel, NBPC.

He Who Crawls Silently Through the Grass with a Small Bow and One Bad Arrow Hunting for Enough Deer to Feed the Whole Tribe (trailer for *Smoke Signals*). Chris Eyre, U.S., 5:00, 35mm. TWN.

Heaven, Earth, and Hell. Thomas Allen Harris, U.S./Canada, 1994, 26:00, video. EAI, TWN.

Her Sweetness Lingers. Shani Mootoo, Canada, 1994, 12:00, video. VO, V Tape, WMM.

Hiroshima mon amour. Alain Resnais, France, 1959, 88:00, 35mm.

History and Memory: For Akiko and Takashige. Rea Tajiri, U.S., 1991, 30:00, video. EAI, WMM.

Homage by Assassination. Elia Suleiman, Nazareth/U.S., 1992, 28:00, 35mm. IFC.

Hopiit. Victor Masayesva Jr., U.S., 1982, 12:00, video. EAI.

I Blinked Three Times. Seoungho Cho, U.S., 1993, 10:00, video. EAI.

Identical Time. Seoungho Cho, U.S., 1997, 21:00, video. EAI.

Igliniit. Philip Joamie, Canada, 1989–91, television program. IBC.

Imagining Indians. Victor Masayesva Jr., U.S., 1994, 60:00, video. EAI, ITVS.

In and Out of Africa. Lucien Taylor and Ilisa Barbash, U.S., 1992, 69:00, video.

India Hearts Beat. Leila Sujir, Canada, 1988, 13:00, video. VO, Video Pool.

Instant Dread. Dawn Wilkinson, Canada, 1998, 13:00, 35mm.

Instructions for Recovering Forgotten Childhood Memories. Steve Reinke, Canada, 1993, 2:00, video. VG, V Tape.

Island of Flowers. Jorge Furtado, Brazil, 1989, 5:00, 16mm. First run.

The Island with Striped Sky. Seoungho Cho and Sang-Wook Cho, U.S., 1993, 10:00, video. EAI.

Is There Anything Specific You Want Me to Tell You? Yau Ching, U.S., 1991, 12:00, video. EAI, WMM.

Itam Hakim Hopiit. Victor Masayesva Jr., U.S., 1985, 58:00, video. EAI.

I Wet My Hands Etched and Surveyed Vessels Approaching Marks Eyed Inside. Roula Haj-Ismail, Lebanon, 1992, 13:00, video. V Tape.

Jaguar. Jean Rouch, Senegal/France, 1971, 16mm.

Jembe. Philip Mallory Jones, U.S., 1989, 3:00, video. EAI.

Kanehsatake: 270 Years of Resistance. Alanis Obomsawin, Canada, 1993, 119:00, 16mm. NFB.

The Kayapo: Out of the Forest. Michael Beckham, U.K., 1989, 120:00, 16mm.

Khush. Pratibha Parmar, U.K., 1991, 24:00, 16mm. WMM.

Kippinguijauiit. Mosesie Kipanik, Canada, 1986–, television programs. IBC.

The Kitchen Blues. Charlene Gilbert, U.S., 1994, 14:00, video. TWN.

Kore. Tran T. Kim-Trang, U.S., 1994, 17:00, video. VDB, V Tape.

The Last Angel of History. John Akomfrah, U.K., 1995, 45:00, 16mm.

Lebanon: Bits and Pieces. Olga Nakkas, France, 1994, video, 60:00. WMM.

Les maîtres fous. Jean Rouch, Ghana/France, 1955, 35:00, 16mm. Pleiade.

Leylouna notre nuit. Yasmine Khlat, Canada, 1987, 52:00, video. GIV.

Looking for Langston. Isaac Julien/Sankofa, U.K., 1989, 42:00, 16mm. TWN.

Love, Women and Flowers. Marta Rodriguez and Jorge Silva, Colombia, 1988, 58:00, video. WMM.

Lulu. Srinivas Krishna, Canada, 1995, 16mm.

Lumumba: The Death of a Prophet. Raoul Peck, France/Germany/Switzerland, 1992, 69:00, 16mm. California, Idera, Mongrel.

Ma'loul fête sa destruction. Michel Khleifi, Palestine, 40:00, 16mm. AFD.

Madame l'eau. Jean Rouch, France, 1993, 16mm. Pleiade.

Maigre Dog. Donna James, Canada, 1990, 10:00, video. AIM.

Masala. Srinivas Krishna, Canada, 1991, 105:00, 35mm. Alliance.

Measures of Distance. Mona Hatoum, Lebanon/Canada, 1988, 15:25, video. GIV, WMM, VO, V Tape.

Memories from the Department of Amnesia. Janice Tanaka, U.S., 1990, 12:50, video. V Tape, EAI, VDB.

Memory/all echo. Yun-ah Hong, Korea, 1990, 27:00, video. WMM.

Messin' Up God's Glory. Avril Johnson and Afua Namiley-Vlana, U.K., 1993, 10:00, 16mm.

Meta Mayan II. Edin Velez, Guatemala/U.S., 1981, 20:00, video. EAI.

Missing Lebanese Wars. Walid Ra'ad, U.S./Lebanon, 1996, 6:00, video. AFD, VO.

Mississippi Masala. Mira Nair, U.S., 1991, 113:00, 35mm.

Muqaddimah Li-Nihayat Jidal (Introduction to the end of an argument) Speaking for oneself . . . speaking for others. Jayce Salloum and Elia Suleiman, Palestine/U.S./Canada, 1990, 43:00, video. AFD, HE, Idera, VG, VO, V Tape.

My Beautiful Laundrette. Stephen Frears, U.K., 1985, 97:00, 35mm.

My Mother's Place. Richard Fung, Canada, 1990, 49:00, video. Full Frame, VDB.

Mysteries of July. Reece Auguiste, U.K., 1991, 60:00, 16mm. NBPC.

New View/New Eyes. Gitanjali, Canada/India, 1993, 50:00, video. V Tape.

Note to a Stranger. Meena Nanji, U.S., 1992, 6:00, video.

Nunaqpa. Igloolik Isuma Productions, Canada, 1991, 58:00, video. IIP, V Tape.

Nunavut. Igloolik Isuma Productions, Canada, 1995, 13 30:00 episodes, video. IIP, V Tape.

Ocularis: Eye Surrogates. Tran T. Kim-Trang, U.S., 1997, 21:00, video. V Tape, VDB.

Operculum. Tran T. Kim-Trang, U.S., 1993, 14:00, video. V Tape, VDB.

Papapapá. Alex Rivera, U.S., 1996, 28:00, video. VDB.

The Passion of Remembrance. Maureen Blackwood and Isaac Julien/Sankofa, U.K., 1986, 80:00, 16mm. WMM.

People and the Land. Tom Hayes, U.S., 1996, 56:00, video. ITVS.

The Perfumed Nightmare. Kidlat Tahimik, Philippines, 1978, 91:00, 16mm. CFMDC, Flower.

Petit à petit. Jean Rouch, Senegal/France, 1969, 16mm. Pleiade.

Qaggig. Igloolik Isuma Productions, Canada, 1989, 58:00, video. IIP, V Tape.

Quartier Mozart. Jean-Pierre Bekolo, Cameroon, 1992, 80:00, 35mm. Idera, California.

Reassemblage. Trinh T. Minh-ha, Senegal/U.S., 1982, 40:00, 16mm. TWN, WMM.

Remembering Wei Yi-feng, Remembering Myself: An Autobiography. Yvonne Wellbon, U.S., 1995, 29:00, video. TWN, WMM.

Ritual Clowns. Victor Masayesva Jr., U.S., 1988, 18:00, video. EAI.

Saar. Selina Williams, 1994, Canada, 28:00, 16mm. WMM.

Saddam Speaks. Jon Alpert, U.S., 1993, 18:00, video. VO.

The Salt Mines. Susana Aiken and Carlos Aparicio, U.S., 1990, 47:00, video. Frameline.

Sammy and Rosie Get Laid. Stephen Frears, 100:00, U.K., 1986, 35mm.

Sankofa. Haile Gerima, U.S./Germany/Ghana/Burkina Faso, 1993, 125:00, 35mm. Negod Gwad Productions, 48 Q St. NE, Washington, D.C. 20002. Phone: 202-529-0220. Fax: 202-526-6855.

Sans soleil. Chris Marker, France, 1982, 100:00, 16mm. Argos.

Saputi. Igloolik Isuma Productions, Canada, 1994, 30:00, video. IIP, V Tape.

Sari Red. Pratibha Parmar, U.K., 1991, 12:00, video. WMM, V Tape.

The Scent of Green Papaya. Tran Anh Hung, France/Vietnam, 1994, 104:00, 35mm.

The Search for Peking Dog. Jon Choi, U.S., 1995, video.

Secrets in the Open Sea. Walid Ra'ad, U.S., 1997, 6:00, video. AFD, VO.

Seeing Is Believing. Shauna Beharry, Canada, 1991, 7:00, video. GIV.

Seven Songs for Malcolm X. John Akomfrah/Black Audio Film Collective, U.K., 1993, 52:00, 16mm. First, Mongrel, NBPC.

Shoah. Claude Lanzmann, Poland/France, 1985, 273:00 and 290:00, 16mm. Viewfinders.

Shoot for the Contents. Trinh T. Minh-ha, U.S., 1991, 101:00, 16mm. WMM.

Sinar Durjana (Wicked Radiance). Azian Nurudin, U.S., 1992, 5:00, video. Frameline.

Siskyavi: The Place of Chasms. Victor Masayesva Jr., U.S., 1991, 28:00, video. EAI.

Skin Deep. Midi Onodera, Canada, 1995, 85:00, 16mm. WMM.

Slanted Vision. Ming-Yuen S. Ma, Canada/U.S., 1995, 50:00, video. TWN, VO, V Tape.

Slowly, This. Arthur Jafa, U.S., 1995, 30:00, video. TWN.

Smoke Signals. Chris Eyre, U.S., 1998, 88:00, 35mm.

Sniff. Ming-Yuen S. Ma, U.S., 1996, 5:00, video. VO, V Tape.

Some Divine Wind. Roddy Bogawa, U.S., 1991, 72:00, 16mm. TWN.

Species in Danger Ed. Portia Cobb, U.S., 1989, 13:00, video.

Splash. Thomas Allen Harris, U.S., 1991, 10:00, video. EAI, TWN.

Strawberry Fields. Rea Tajiri, U.S., 1997, 86:30, 16mm. Phaedra Cinema, 5455 Wilshire, Ste. 1403, Los Angeles, Calif. 90036. Phone: 213-938-9610. Email: *ghatanaka@aol.com.*

Super Shamou. Barney Pattunguyak, Canada, 1990–94, 3 episodes, television program. Full Frame.

Surname Viet Given Name Nam. Trinh T. Minh-ha, Vietnam/U.S., 1989, 108:00, 16mm. WMM.

Takuginai. Blandina Makkik, Leetia Ineak, Canada, 1987–, television program. IBC.

Talaeen a Junuub (Up From the South). Jayce Salloum, Walid Ra'ad, 1993, 60:00, U.S./Canada, video. AFD, V Tape, VG, TWN.

A Tale of Love. Trinh T. Minh-ha, U.S., 1995, 35mm. WMM.

Testament. John Akomfrah/Black Audio Film Collective, U.K., 1988, 16mm. NBPC.

This Is Not Beirut (There Was and There Was Not). Jayce Salloum, Lebanon/ Canada, 1994, 48:00, video. AFD, V Tape, VG.

Through the Milky Way. Yun-ah Hong, Korea, 1992, 19:00, video. WMM.

Toc Storee. Ming-Yuen S. Ma, U.S., 1993, 21:00, video. TWN, VO, V Tape.

The Trained Chinese Tongue. Laurie Wen, U.S., 1994, 20:00, 16mm. WMM.

Twilight City. Reece Auguiste, U.K., 1989, 60:00, 16mm. NBPC.

Two Lies. Pam Tom, U.S., 1989, 25:00, 16mm. WMM.

Un Chien Délicieux. Ken Feingold, U.S., 1991, video, 18:45. EAI.

Underexposed: The Temple of the Fetus. Kathy High, U.S., 1992, 72:00, video. WMM.

Unsere Afrikareise. Peter Kubelka, Austria, 1961–66, 12:30, 16mm. Canyon.

Video Letters 1–3. Yau Ching, U.S., 1993, 0:38, 3:20, and 5:20, video. EAI.

Videobook. Beverly Singer, U.S., 1995, 5:00, video. EAI.

Vintage: Families of Value. Thomas Allen Harris, U.S., 1995, 72:00, 16mm. TWN.

Visions. Gariné Torossian, Canada, 1992, 4:00, 16mm. CFMDC.

Wassa. Philip Mallory Jones, U.S., 1989, 3:00, video. EAI.

water into fire. Zachery Longboy, Canada, 1993, 10:30, video. V Tape.

The Watermelon Woman. Cheryl Dunyé, U.S., 1996, 90:00, 16mm. First Kino.

Water Ritual #1: An Urban Site of Purification. Barbara McCullough, U.S., 1990, 4:00, 16mm. TWN.

The Way to My Father's Village. Richard Fung, Canada, 1988, 38:00, video. Full Frame, VDB.

What's the Difference Between a Yam and a Sweet Potato? Adriene Jenik and J. Evan Dunlap, U.S., 1992, 5:00, video. EAI.

Who Needs a Heart? John Akomfrah/Black Audio Film Collective, U.K., 1992, 80:00, 16mm.

Who's Gonna Pay For These Donuts Anyway? Janice Tanaka, U.S., 1992, 58:00, video. EAI, VDB, V Tape.

A Woman Being in Asia. Byun Young Joo, Korea, 1993, 60:00, video. Docu Factory VISTA, 4th fl., Koguem Blag, 1535–9, Seocho-3-Dong, Deochu-Gu, Seoul, Korea. Fax: 011-82-2-5975365.

Woman Sesame Oil Maker aka *Women from the Lake of Scented Souls.* Xie Fei, China/Hong Kong/Japan, 1993, 105:00, 35mm.

A Woman Waiting for Her Period. Wei-Ssu Chien, Taiwan/U.S., 1993, 23:00, video. WMM.

Women and Men Are Good Dancers. Arlene Bowman, Canada/U.S., 1995, 40:00, video. TWN, V Tape.

Work in Progress. Luis Valdovino, U.S., 1990, 14:00, video. TWN.

Distributors

AFD   Arab Film Distribution, 2417 10th Ave. E., Seattle, Wash. 98102. Phone: 206-322-0882. Fax: 206-322-4586. Email: *info@arabfilm.com www.arabfilm.com.*

Alliance   Alliance Releasing, 121 Bloor St. E., ste. 1500, Toronto, ON M4W 3M5, Canada. Phone: 416-967-1174. Fax: 416-967-5884.

Argos   Argos Films, 4, rue Edouard-Nortier, Neuilly-sur-Seine 92, France.

Aska   Aska Film Distribution, 1600. De Lorimer, bur. 211, Montréal, PQ H2K 3W5, Canada. Phone: 514-521-0623. Fax: 514-521-6174. Email: *askafilm @login.net.*

California   Resolution Inc./California Newsreel, 149 Ninth St., San Francisco, Calif. 94103. Phone: 415-621-6196.

CFMDC   Canadian Filmmakers Distribution Centre, 37 Hanna St., ste. 220, Toronto, ON M6K 1W8, Canada. Phone: 416-588-0725. Fax: 416-588-7956. Internet: *www.cfmdc.org.*

Cinema Guild   1697 Broadway, New York, N.Y. 10019. Phone: 212-246-5522/800-723-5522. Fax: 212-246-5525.

Direct   Direct Cinema Ltd., POB 10003, Santa Monica, Calif. 90410. Phone: 310-636-8200. Fax: 310-636-8228. Email: *dclvideo@aol.com.*

EAI   Electronic Arts Intermix, 542 W. 22nd St., New York, N.Y. 10011. Phone: 212-337-0680. Fax: 212-337-0697. Internet: *www.eai.org.*

Filmakers Library   124 E. 40th St., New York, N.Y. 10016. Phone: 212-808-4980. Fax: 212-808-4983. Email: *info@filmakers.com.*

First   First Run/Icarus, 153 Waverly Pl., New York, N.Y. 10014. Phone: 800-876-1710. Fax: 212-255-7923. Email: *mail@frif.com*. Internet: *www.frif.com*

Flower   Flower Films, 10341 San Pablo Ave., El Cerrito, Calif. 94530. Phone: 510-525-0942.

Full Frame   Full Frame Film and Video, 517 College St., ste. 325, Toronto, ON M6G 4A2, Canada. Phone: 416-925-9338. Fax: 416-324-8268.

Frameline   346 Ninth St., San Francisco, Calif. 94103. Phone: 415-703-8564. Fax: 415-861-1404. Email: *frameline@aol.com*.

GIV   Groupe Intervention Vidéo, 5505, Boul. St-Laurent, Montréal, PQ H2T 1S6, Canada. Phone: 514-271-5506. Fax: 514-271-6980. Email: *giv@cam.org*.

HE   Heure Exquise, BP 113, Mons en Barouel, France 59370. Phone: 33-20-04-95-74.

Idera   Idera Films, 1037 W. Broadway #400, Vancouver, B.C. V6H 1E3. Phone: 604-738-8815. Fax: 604-738-8400. Email: *idera@web.net*.

IBC   Inuit Broadcasting Corporation, 703-251 Laurier Ave. W., Ottawa, ON K1P 5J6, Canada. Phone: 613-235-1892. Fax: 613-230-8824.

IFC   International Film Circuit/Planet Pictures, P.O. Box 1151, Old Chelsea Stn., New York, N.Y. 10011. Phone: 212-779-0660. Fax: 212-779-9129. Email: *Ifcplanet@aol.com*.

IIP   Igloolik Isuma Productions, P.O. Box 223, Igloolik, Nunavut, X0A 0L0, Canada. Phone: 819-934-8809. Fax: 819-934-8700.

ITVS   Independent Television Service, POB 78008, San Francisco, Calif. 94107. Phone: 415-356-8383. Fax: 415-356-8391. Email: *itvs@itvs.org*. Internet: *www.itvs.org*.

Kino   Kino International, 333 W. 39th St., #503, New York, N.Y. 10018. Phone: 212-629-6880. Fax: 212-714-0871.

Mongrel   Mongrel Media, POB 68547, 360A Bloor St. W., Toronto, ON M5S 3J2, Canada. Phone: 416-516-9775. Fax: 416-516-0651. Outside Canada: Phone: 888-607-FILM. Email: *MongrelMedia@compuserve.com*.

NAATA   National Asian American Television Association, 346 Ninth St., San Francisco, Calif. 94103. Phone: 415-552-9550. Fax: 415-863-7428.

NBPC   National Black Programming Consortium, 761 Oak St., ste. A, Columbus, Ohio 43205. Phone: 614-229-4399. Fax: 614-229-4398.

New Yorker   New Yorker Films, 16 W. 61st St., New York, N.Y. 10023. Phone: 212-247-6110. Fax: 212-307-7855.

NFB   National Film Board of Canada, 3155, rue Côte-de-Liesse, St. Laurent, PQ, Canada H4N 2N4. Phone: 800-267-7710. Internet: *www.nfb.ca*.

Pleiade   Films de la Pleiade [address to be added in proof]

TWN   Third World Newsreel, 335 W. 38th St., New York, N.Y. 10018. Phone: 212-947-9277. Fax: 212-594-6917. Email: *twn@tmn.com*.

VDB   Video Data Bank, School of the Art Institute of Chicago, 112 S. Michigan Ave., Chicago, Il. 60603. Phone: 312-345-3550. Fax: 312-541-8073.

VG   Vidéographe, 460, rue Ste-Catherine ouest #504, Montréal, PQ H3B

1A7, Canada. Phone: 514-866-4720. Fax: 514-866-4725. Email: *signal@cam.org.*

Video Pool   100 Arthur St. #300, Winnipeg, Manitoba R3B 1H3, Canada. Phone: 204-949-9134. Fax: 204-942-1555.

Viewfinders   Box 1555, Evanston, Il. 60204.

VO   Video Out, 1965 Main St., Vancouver, BC V5T 3C1, Canada. Phone: 604-872-8449. Fax: 604-876-1185. Email: *video@portal.ca.*

V Tape   401 Richmond St. W., ste. 452, Toronto, ON M5V 3A8, Canada. Phone: 416-351-1317. Fax: 416-351-1509. Email: *video@astral.magic.ca.* Internet: *www.vtape.org.*

WMM   Women Make Movies, 462 Broadway, ste. 500R, New York, N.Y. 10012. Phone: 212-925-0606. Fax: 212-925-2052. Email: *orders@wmm.com.*

Zeitgeist   Zeitgeist Films, 247 Centre St., 2nd fl., New York, N.Y. 10013. Phone: 212-274-1989. Fax: 212-274-1644. Email: *zeitgeist@aol.com.*

Index

Laura U. Marks is Assistant Professor of Film Studies
at Carleton University.

Library of Congress Cataloging-in-Publication Data

Marks, Laura U.
The skin of the film : intercultural cinema,
embodiment, and the senses / by Laura U. Marks.
p.   cm.
Includes bibliographical references and index.
ISBN 0-8223-2358-3 (cloth : alk. paper). —
ISBN 0-8223-2391-5 (paper : alk. paper)
1. Intercultural communication in motion pictures.
2. Motion pictures—Philosophy.   3. Deleuze,
Gilles—Cinema.   4. Experimental films—History.
5. Video art.
PN1993.5.D44M37   1999
791.43'09172'4—C21   99-26487